On Being Human

A Memoir of
Waking Up, Living Real,
and Listening Hard

JENNIFER PASTILOFF

JOHN
MURRAY
LEARNING

First published in the US in 2019 by Dutton, an imprint of Penguin Random House LLC

This edition published in the UK by John Murray Learning in 2019
An imprint of John Murray Press
A division of Hodder & Stoughton
An Hachette UK company

1

Book design by Katy Riegel

This book is for information or educational purposes only and is not intended to act as a substitute for medical advice or treatment. Any person with a condition requiring medical attention should consult a qualified medical practitioner or suitable therapist.

A CIP catalogue record for this title is available from the British Library

ISBN 978 1 529 35234 4

eBook ISBN 978 1 529 35235 1

Typeset in Arno Pro

Printed and bound in Great Britain by Clays Ltd, Elcograf S.p.A.

John Murray Press policy is to use papers that are natural, renewable and recyclable products and made from wood grown in sustainable forests. The logging and manufacturing processes are expected to conform to the environmental regulations of the country of origin.

John Murray Learning
Carmelite House
50 Victoria Embankment
London EC4Y 0DZ

www.hodder.co.uk

"I devoured *On Being Human* in one sitting—nodding, laughing and connecting from the first word to the last. Jen Pastiloff is a brave and vulnerable leader whose book will help people take a deep breath, recognize themselves, and understand each other. What more can we ask of a book?"
—Glennon Doyle, author of #1 *New York Times* Bestseller
Love Warrior and founder of Together Rising

"*On Being Human* is beautiful and tender, profound and absorbing. I never wanted to put it down. In writing with such clarity and honesty about her jagged path to becoming, Jennifer Pastiloff has told the story of not only herself, but so many of us. I was consoled by this book and also inspired. On every page I felt the presence and the power of Pastiloff's brave and gigantic heart. This is a book friends will tell friends they have to read for years to come. It's an important, enthralling debut."
—Cheryl Strayed, author of #1 *New York Times* Bestseller *Wild*

"With harrowing vulnerability and badass candor, Jen Pastiloff has written a gritty and passionate memoir."
—Elizabeth Gilbert

"This is a memoir at once strong and vulnerable, an absorbing account of Jennifer Pastiloff's inner life, filled with humor and inspiration and sincerity."
—Andrew Solomon, National Book Award-winning author of
Far from the Tree

"Read this f*cking book. Jen is very much part of the light and the balance that is needed in this world right now. I don't even know her but I love her. Read this book."

—P!nk

"Jen Pastiloff is the only human ray of sunshine who could ever make me earnestly consider incorporating unpalatable things like 'manifesting joy' and 'listening' (UGH) into my life. This book is a treasure."
—Samantha Irby, author of *We Are Never Meeting in Real Life* and *Meaty*

"Jen Pastiloff is a rejuvenating supernova! A life force of primal extravagant delight! Frank and funny, she'll boss herself around and change the rest of us in the meantime. I'd want to listen to anything she has to say."

—Naomi Shihab Nye, Pushcart Prize-winning poet and author of *Fuel* and *19 Varieties of Gazelle*

"Forget everything you know about memoir. Of course this is about the comet that is Jen Pastiloff and how she grew up struggling with deafness, depression, and a wrecked body image to go on and crack open the world's heart with yoga/writing retreats, a website named The Manifest-Station, and pure love—but honestly, it's really the memoir of all of us, every single one of us who ever felt I'm not enough, I'm not loved, I'm falling apart, I don't' belong here. I was reading this moving memoir while crying, scribbling down sentences and holding onto them like life lines. I've got you, Jen says, but the true message of this radiant memoir is nothing short that revolutionary love: we've got each other."

—Caroline Leavitt, author of *Pictures of You* and *Is This Tomorrow*

"Jen Pastiloff is the anti-guru. Rarely will you meet anyone more humble, compassionate and ready to learn. She's the kind of leader we need."

—Rene Denfeld, author of *The Child Finder*

"This darkly funny, deeply personal and powerful memoir will speak to anyone who has ever felt outcast: from their bodies, their minds, the world. A must read for human beings."

—Emily Rapp Black, author of *The Still Point of the Turning World* and *Poster Child: A Memoir*

"Listen to me: you're going to think Jen Pastiloff is your BFF after you read this book because when you're done reading it you will feel known. No one is better qualified to write a book called *On Being Human* than this particular human. Having long struggled to accept her own imperfections and struggles, Jen manages to bring these to the page with a humor, heart and generosity that makes room for all of us to be a little kinder to ourselves."

—Elizabeth Crane, author of *Turf* and *The History of Great Things*

"Especially in these dark times for women, there is actually nothing 'simple' about Pastiloff's radical alchemy. Read this book and feel yourself expand."

—Gina Frangello, author of *A Life in Men* and *Every Kind of Wanting*

"This book actually changed my life."

—Lindsay Tucker, *Yoga Journal*

For my father, who left too soon—
and for my son, who came at
exactly the right time

Contents

On Being Human

Foreword

When was the last time someone listened to you?

I mean *really* listened to you. Heard you with their whole body. Can you remember?

Jennifer Pastiloff practices radical listening. She is also mostly deaf, so when I tell you that she listens with her entire body, I promise you, there is nothing else like it. How we first met was she attended a writing workshop of mine in Portland, Oregon. She arrived with a broken foot. She was one of the most beautiful women I'd ever seen. Her eyelashes alone were dazzling. I was mesmerized. Smitten. Immediately and ridiculously. After she left I Googled her late at night like a stalker. The next week she messaged me on Facebook to tell me that my workshop had changed her life. I was so scared to answer her message I disappeared into my own butt (a common introvert tactic akin to sea anemones).

And yet there was something so profoundly attractive about her; something radiating from *inside* of her that literally took my breath away enough that I transcended my idiotic shyness and introversion and eventually answered her. The profoundly attractive thing about Jen Pastiloff is this: her ability to be so fundamentally and authentically present alongside other human beings that you remember who you are, or who you might be, if you could be amazing. And when she sits down to listen to you, your soul comes back to life.

What does it mean, radical listening? Jen Pastiloff embodies a kind of listening that originates in the heart and the gut. Perhaps the fact that she has struggled with hearing loss has given her special sensitivity to what we mean when we claim we are listening to each other. To be honest, I don't know very many good listeners. I seem to meet more and more people who have forgotten that listening is the other side of voice. I am most in love with people who deeply understand voice as being able to tell their story in a way that makes room for other bodies and other stories to coexist. When Jen teaches an On Being Human workshop, a kind of magical hybrid of yoga, story-listening, and storytelling, a whole world opens up where our differences and our similarities are allowed to emerge, reminding us that even as we are individuals we can also make bridges to each other. Honestly, though, you have to take one of her workshops yourself so that you can experience what I mean when I say she listens with her whole body.

The first time I was in one of her workshops and she sat down in front of me to listen to what I'd written, my entire body began to shake. No one had ever looked at me or listened to me or sat with me like that in my entire life (okay, except the times Joan of Arc and Mary Shelley each visited me in a dream, but most people think I'm nuts when I tell them about that). It both scared the crap out of me and simultaneously unearthed a long, partly sad, partly joyous note in my own throat. A truth note. A glimpse of my own heart worth.

I suck at yoga. No really, I do. For one thing, I have scoliosis bad enough to have given me chronic pain since I was thirteen. I have a hip dysplasia that makes sitting, standing, driving, and walking super fun. As a fifty-five-year-old woman, I'm also menopausal, arthritic, and generally stiff and cranky most of the time, even though I was a competitive swimmer for more than twenty years. What I'm saying is, I'm not up for yogi of the year or anything by a long shot. If I get down on the ground I'm not even sure I can get back up by myself. My hips and knees and ankles make noises that sometimes frighten me.

And yet.

What came out of me the first time I participated in one of Jen's On Being Human workshops was something like a wail. A life sorrow buried so deeply within my body I didn't even know I was carrying it. Let me tell you, I know a few things about sorrow. I wrote more than one book about sorrow. But I'd never heard myself make the sounds that came from my own physical and emotional depths that first workshop. *Crying* is not even close. I made a snot sea on my yoga mat. My eyes puffed shut. The word I'd use is *human*. I touched the strength of my own vulnerability. I'd almost forgotten what it felt like to be in a state of fully human, and to have someone see me and hear me all the way to the bone.

Now Jen and I teach workshops together on Writing and the Body. The scared me still exists. I'm just learning how to love her rather than bury her. I learned that from Jen.

When I think about the years that Jen spent waitressing while simultaneously dreaming of being an actress—a story she tells frequently in her workshops—I think about how paradigmatic that story is for all of us. Our life choices surge out of us when the pressure to move gets bigger than the pressure to hold it all in. It's no Cinderella story. Fuck that story. Most of us just bust ass and fail and fall and get up and try again; we buy our own shoes and we get the fancy dresses at discount and we no longer wait for the world to hand us a crown, a glass slipper (who could run away in those?), a gown, or even a decent bra. Almost none of us jump into our dreams without rough beginnings or a damn difficult struggle along the way or giant falls that cause us to have to start the hell over again.

The Jen I know now is an internationally known workshop leader and speaker. How did she shoot the gap between waitress with a dream balloon hovering over her head to international heart-healing rock star?

It may be a very good question. But it's not the only question.

A better question is: How do we recognize beauty and love in the shapes of a life?

When I think about the years Jen has spent mourning the death of her father, or the years she spent struggling with an eating disorder, or the years she spent trying to live with family legacies or dark experiences that torque a life path, or the years she spent helping people build bridges back to their own hearts, I think maybe she is reinventing the word *beautiful*. I think maybe she is asking us what it would be like if we gave beauty back to the world and to each other, instead of striving toward some false fiction that places beauty out of our reach and away from our oh-so-varied bodies.

This book is the story of how Jen invented her life from the inside out, rather than waiting for the world to tell her who she might be. The story travels through doubt and depression, love and loss, grief and death, desire and dream, but more than anything else this story travels through her actual body as she experienced the events of her life. When she began to read lips without realizing her hearing was diminishing as a child, something else was born into her. When she reads your lips, she's not just looking at the words your mouth is making. She's reading your whole body story.

She's giving your beauty and love back to you.

When people come out of her workshops, their faces look different. Suddenly it seems as if beauty and courage and love might emerge from the inside out. What the world may think of us and the stories others project onto us falls away for a while, and we walk back out into the world with something like souls that won't stop singing. Like heart songs that won't shut up. And I gotta be honest . . . between you and me? We could use a little more heart song these days. We could use some fierce joy that won't shut up.

—Lidia Yuknavitch

INTRODUCTION

Beauty Hunting

You Can Have This

WHEN I FINALLY got out the tools to build what I thought I needed to get the life I wanted, I realized that what I needed was within me. But first, I had to rebuild everything. Once I did that, I would be on my way to a different kind of living.

I started with the heart. I took an old phone book, the Yellow Pages, that old relic we used to rely on to find people, and I cracked it against my chest until my old heart came out with a thump. I picked it up off the faux hardwood floor of my living room among toy fire engines and little-boy shoes and placed it on the bookshelf that was just given to me by a woman who lost her baby the day before she was to be induced. I wondered how long before my son tried to climb on the bookshelf, since it resembled a ladder and he loves to climb on anything, including his high chair and things that can (and do) topple over. I thought of the woman's lost baby and my living son and how we never know when we might face things that topple our hearts over and bring us to our knees.

I placed my heart on the highest shelf, between a picture of my father-in-law, *Agha June*, Persian for "Granddad," and a photo of my own father holding me as a baby. My heart, beating and alive, sat isolated on the shelf with the dead fathers. I placed it high enough so that my son couldn't grab it and roll it on the floor yelling *Ball, ball* but not too high that someone couldn't reach out and touch it and feel the weight of it in their palms, or ask it questions like it was a Magic 8 Ball heart.

The questions you could ask my heart: *How did you make it out? Is it scary out here? How are you living unprotected like this?* And like a good Magic 8 Ball, it answered people's questions. *Yes, definitely. As I see it, yes. Without a doubt. Signs point to yes.* And they would place my 8 Ball heart back on the shelf, satisfied with the answers, because it was as if they were being told, *Everything is going to be okay,* and isn't that all anyone ever wants to hear? It's all I ever wanted to hear. My exposed heart gave the askers of these questions comfort to see how they might survive like this, too, and how it would change the way they lived, the way they loved. They would go home and think, *As I see it, yes,* I can be vulnerable, too. *It is decidedly so. Outlook good.*

I would put my 8 Ball heart back in my chest at the end of the day, give my son a bath, kiss my husband, and marvel that I could be two things at once. Wholly unafraid and utterly terrified. Exposed and safe. Deaf and listening. How remarkable that my heart could be out in the world, helping me to listen when my ears failed me, and also be safely nestled inside my body.

And that, in fact, is how this story begins.

Just Say Yes

I want to show you what I mean when I use the phrase *beauty hunting*. But I have to get you to believe me that when you listen to people and when you show up, like *really* show up, there is beauty everywhere. And when you start noticing it, you can't unsee it.

You may ask, *Who are you to show me what beauty is, where it is, and what it can do?* What the hell do I know? I haven't gotten out of my pajamas today, and I drank too much coffee, and I'm just trying to keep my head above the drowning water of all the negative thoughts, so what can I tell you about how people are and about beauty and about the way the world is? I can't. But I can share my journey.

That's all we can do. Right? Isn't that what it means to revel in our humanness? To let ourselves be seen? And when we do that: It's beautiful. Trust me.

Some years ago I connected with Rosie Alma, a reader of my website, The Manifest-Station. She had cystic fibrosis. She'd written a guest-post for the site and followed me on Facebook. In April 2013, she heard I was coming to Atlanta to do a workshop and sent me an e-mail asking me to come visit.

I didn't know how to make this happen during the short time I had in Georgia. I didn't have a car. I was busy. But I told her I would be there. My sister, my nephew Blaise, and I, all went to Emory University Hospital at Wesley Woods. Blaise jumped on the bed and hugged her. She couldn't talk, since she'd just had the double lung transplant. I'm deaf, so I'm used to struggling to hear people speak, so I told her that as long as she moved her lips, all would be right in the world.

I had never been in the presence of such light before. I'm telling you, it was like a corny movie where you hear angels humming in the background. She was so full of life.

And she was dying.

I think of all the bullshit stories that get in our (my) way. If I had not gone to visit her because I couldn't make the time, I would have never met this human before she died. My sister and Blaise went to visit her again one more time after I left Atlanta, and then Rosie suddenly passed away just a week before her twenty-fifth birthday.

I saw the parallel universe. The one where I said, *I wish I could but I can't, I'm busy, I don't have enough time, I don't have a car, I have a workshop to do, I am afraid*, and I saw how many times that parallel universe was the one I lived in and how it was the opposite of beauty hunting. I lived there for a long time. I might have stayed there forever. But I didn't.

I became close with Rosie's family after she died. Rosie never used the term *beauty hunting*, of course, but that girl was the fiercest beauty hunter I ever met. In her yellow nightgown and with all those tubes around her neck and in her arms, she was bow-and-arrowing her way to find the good. There was beauty in that room. And fear. Both existed at once.

You can understand what I mean when I say how one *Yes, I will be there* can change the whole course of a life, and not just one life. Imagine that! One little *Yes, I will come see you at the Wesley Woods hospital* can do that!

So, I will ask you this: How many moments have been missed because you said *No, I can't come to Wesley Woods hospital to see you*?

The exercise in which I ask people in the workshop to write a letter in the voice of someone who loves them is my favorite. The air leaves the room. The way people's hands tremble when they read the letter out loud, and the way their voices shake and tissues get passed around, but all eyes stay on the person reading the letter. This is the way everyone really just wants to be seen and heard. *Don't you, too?*

Becoming the Connector

I can think of all the clichés: *yoga found me; when the student is ready the teacher shall appear; yoga had been in me all along.* And I want to punch them all in the face.

Even though my workshop On Being Human isn't yoga, not in the traditional sense—little about me is traditional in the traditional sense—"yoga" does mean "union" or "connection," and that is what I do in my workshops in my nontraditional way.

Even as a child, my nickname was "The Connector." Also, "The Worrywart." (This sounds like my Yiddish grandmother, my *Bubbe*.) Aside from my workshop being about connection (the thing everyone ends up saying to each other during and after the experience is, "I got you"), yoga was the conduit for my workshop. I have always believed myself to be terrible at most things (typing, cleaning, baking, sewing, math, returning e-mails) except connecting. I excel at connection. And deep listening despite my deafness. I am now able to bring groups of people together because I used some of my street skills and my instincts to craft something that was outside the box and make it my own.

My connector skills were helped along by waiting tables for five hundred years (well, thirteen and a half), so I had what you would call *people skills*, if not serving ones. I was a terrible waitress. I would remember in the middle of the night that Table 32 wanted Cholula sauce or someone asked me for a Grasshopper (mint, wheatgrass, pineapple, ice, blended). I was the worst. If I waited on you during my serving years, I apologize if I messed up your order, brought you the wrong check, double-charged you for your latte, spilled your latte, brought your latte cold, dropped a hair on your plate, made you repeat yourself seven times as I squatted by your table so I could be eye-to-mouth with you and read your lips while I was still in denial that I was deaf. But I'm not sorry if I rested my hand on your shoulder or made you laugh or remembered you from the last time. I was a terrible waitress but a pretty decent human.

On top of my connecting and (forced) listening skills, I'd also studied acting and was a writer (albeit a writer who wasn't writing), so I combined all these things and *voilà*! I created my yoga-not-yoga workshops.

People are always asking me, "But how did you start doing *this*? How did you go from working at The Newsroom as a waitress for almost two decades to being a guest on *Good Morning America* with your Karaoke Yoga and doing your self-designed retreats all over the world? How?"

I get messages like these on a daily basis. People asking me for tips (tips!) on getting started or wanting to know how I went from wanting to die and hating my life and my body and everything about myself to not wanting to die and loving my life a good majority of the time, even when it's difficult. It's worth noting that I did not say, *from wanting to die and hating my life to being happy all the time and loving my perfect life.* I love it, most of the time, but not all the time. My life is not perfect (is anyone's?). An Instagram filter is just a filter that obscures the hard edges of reality.

So when people ask me for advice on how to get started, I wonder: *Started with what? I just woke up and I was leading retreats to Italy and I was writing a book and my son was potty-trained and I was comfortable feeling my feelings instead of thinking that they would kill me.*

What a load of crap. I also wonder what people mean when they ask, *How did you get started?*, because I can't fully explain what I do. The way love and listening alchemize the fear in the room and turn strangers into friends, friends who stay friends and support one another across miles and through countless troubles. The way all the people who try so hard to hide who they are and what they are afraid of and what they want for themselves, until they don't. Until they stop hiding and they let the snot fly and they let themselves truly be seen. In other words, they let themselves become *fall-in-loveable*, a word I made up.

As my workshop started to morph into something more than yoga poses, I began to feel like I was falling in love with everyone in the room who allowed themselves to be vulnerable. And it dawned on me that the part of them I was smitten with was the side they probably tried to hide, just as I had done with my own vulnerability or perceived weaknesses. It wasn't people being strong or snarky or guarded who made me want to know them more, who made me want to wrap my arms around them. It was the ones who had snot dripping from their nose, who whispered, *I am afraid,* who admitted they had no idea what they were doing. It was the ones who let themselves be silly and sing out loud, the ones who told the truth, the ones who shared their stories wholeheartedly. It was when they started to take off their armor and soften that I felt that surge of love, the same one I feel now when my son says *Mommy,* or when he wakes with his hair sticking straight up. It was the feeling I got when someone was utterly themselves without any self-consciousness, when they allowed themselves to be seen. What is more desirable than that?

My workshop is an exercise in allowing yourself to be fall-in-loveable. To make that original connection with yourself. It's also about falling in love. I fall in love every day. (Sorry, Robert, my sweet husband.) I look at people with their quivering lips and their rounded shoulders trying to hide their hearts as they say, "I am afraid I will be alone for the rest of my life," and I fall so totally in love with them that I want to take them home to my one-bedroom apartment and make them coffee and say, *You're not alone, I got you.* I want to say, *Everything is going to be okay.* So I do.

I have spent my whole life trying to hide who I was, trying to hide my clinical depression and my hearing loss and my swallowed grief and the fact that I was a college dropout and that I had no idea what I wanted to do with my life. I also hid that I wanted a big, beautiful life and I wanted to make an impact on other people's lives and make them big and beautiful, too. And then I stopped hiding. When I started to get honest about who I am, people started to . . . *wait for it* . . . respond to me. They started to say things like, *You make me feel less alone. I thought I was the only one. Thank you for being honest.*

I was like, *Um, all I have to do is tell the truth about who I am?* And no one answered, but I took that as a resounding *YES* because people were coming to my workshops and reading my writing and I felt purposeful, full of passion, fueled by equal parts grit and grace. I was afraid that if I told the truth, I would shrivel up and die or get rocks thrown at my head. I was worried that if I let myself feel things, I would explode, and there would be nobody there to pick up the pieces.

I did not shrivel up and die, get rocks thrown at my head, and I certainly did not explode (although I felt like I might at the very end of my pregnancy).

So when people say, *How did you get started?* I want to respond, *Started with what?* I don't know what to call this thing I do, this On Being Human workshop, I don't know what category it falls into, how to label it. It's not a yoga workshop, per se. It's not a writing workshop, not really. It's an experience, yes, but there is no gear involved: no zip lines or fancy equipment.

But it is something. Just because I can't put it into a box doesn't mean it does not deserve to exist or that it doesn't make an impact. I don't want to be in the box, anyway. I call the box "The Just-A Box." Just a yoga teacher. Just a teen. Just a mom. Just a girl. Just a waitress. Just a wife. Just a teacher. I reject that box. Fuck that box. It serves no purpose for me, and it likely doesn't for you, either.

Just because we can't name things does not mean they don't have a place or value in the world. Isn't that part of being human? Not being able to define ourselves in a word? I can't tell anyone how I started this thing, because I don't even know what it is.

The truth is, I am afraid to look back and remember my journey because it's so much easier to be a walking-dead person with no awareness and to just keep moving, all the time moving forward. But that's not really easier. That's your Inner Asshole talking (further referenced as your IA) and it tells you lies. Dirty rotten lies.

It's easier to act like I have always been here so I don't have to revisit any of the darkness. *What if I get stuck there? What if I wake up and want to die again? What if it hurts too much? What if I become the "old me" again?*

So when people say, *How did you get started with this, like, you know, yoga workshop?* I get annoyed—"It's not yoga, okay?" But then I stop and ask my IA to step aside and I peer into my coffee-filled mind and imagine my shock and surprise when I see the truth.

I am still the "old me," and yes, it is yoga.

I teach all these people around the world not to care (so much) about what others think and yet here I am, terrified I will get labeled as a *woo-woo yoga person*, so I don't acknowledge the thing that got me to where I am. Yoga opened the door that said DON'T GO HERE, and I went in. The keeper of that door was my IA, and yours is the gatekeeper of your door, too. When you open the door to the place that says DON'T GO HERE, you find a roomful of people waiting for you, saying, "Ah, there you are. We've got you. We've been waiting."

Yoga unlocked the door and I went in and sat down on the mat and told my Inner Asshole to be quiet, and surprisingly, it did. Then, the next day, it was there again, saying, DON'T GO HERE, so I told it to be quiet. Again. And I did it every day. On my mat.

A few weeks ago, I heard a story on NPR about a priest in Naples, Italy, who is trying to bring together the Mafia and art. Naples is rumored to be filled with Mafiosi and trash. I spend a lot of time in Italy leading my retreats and have been warned not to go there. *They'll con you in Naples,* people say. *They'll take you for a ride, if you know what I mean,* they say. *They will drive you in circles and overcharge you in the taxi. Be careful in Naples.* I've only been once. To the train station, where I took a picture of a magnet that said *Napoli* because I have people who are like family with that last name. The story on NPR talked about a priest who discovered a treasure trove of early Christian art under the cobblestone streets. *Oh, I like this,* I thought as I turned up my hearing aids, which are remote-control operated through the Bluetooth on my iPhone, and thought about my term: *beauty hunting.* NPR said, "Loffredo says crime families often feel trapped by a life they were born into and are eager to find alternatives for their kids. So he put them to work fixing up the seriously neglected catacombs. Mud and dirt covered much of the floor; an old lighting system left much of the artwork in shadows; and a storeroom had been stuffed with waste and old equipment from a nearby hospital. All of it had to go."

Loffredo said, "When we started they were sixteen-year-olds. Now they're in their twenties, and they're paid because they are entrepreneurs. It's not hard to offer alternatives to crime if you're creative and available."

This priest in Napoli is a beauty hunter. He mentioned that crime families often feel trapped by a life they are born into and I thought: *Don't we all.*

We're all crawling and clawing our way to get out from the catacombs of what we think we believe our destiny to be. We are, each of us, beauty hunters, whether we want to be or not. It's part of the human condition. In fact, it's the most beautiful part.

Don Loffredo says this about the mafia: *Don't fight it, cure it, by offering something beautiful in its place.*

THIS IS A BOOK about how I got to where I am. How I crawled and clawed my way out and how, some days, I am back in the catacombs. And how that's okay. I'll tell you how the moments in my life that have haunted me have also made me who I am today. That they have been transformed through the alchemy of togetherness and salvation into moments where strangers come together, as they do, around the world, in rooms with me. This book will take us through some of those rooms, both dark and light, and into rooms yet to be built.

At the end of my life, when I say one final *What have I done?*, let my answer be, *I have done love.* I say that a lot, but my god, don't you want that so desperately that you can taste it and it's like the best thing you've ever tasted and you want it all the time and you know what?

You can.

CHAPTER 1

Rewrite Your Story

Memory: Lost and Found

BEFORE I WAS BORN, I was a memory. A feeling my mother once had, her grandmother Rose holding her in her lap, before Rose had the breast cancer, before it ravaged her body, before her broad shoulders began to slump with the weight of defeat and dying and the wrenching chemotherapy.

Before I was a memory, I was my mother's little head being cradled into her grandmother's chest, after she'd been released from the hospital, after she had run, in her five-year-old body, out into a rural New Jersey road and a car ran over her tiny head.

ROSE LIVED WITH my mother's family at the time. Bubbe Rose was the only one who ever showed my mother any kind of affection or attention, besides my mother's own sister, Ellen. Her mother, my maternal grandmother, Marion, saved money by never turning on the lights. She kept plastic on the sofa for protection. Cockroaches scurried over the dirty floor. She sat in the dark for hours on end.

My mother, at five years old, wanting to die, ran out right in front of a car and that car drove over her.

My mother floated over the houses and imagined landing in one that welcomed her with, *Hello! I am so happy you are here. I am so happy you are alive. I love you. There you are. We got you. We've been waiting for you.*

Isn't it incomprehensible what the imagination is capable of? How deeply we want affection and love? How we are, even at five years old, willing to risk our lives to find it?

There is a scar above my mother's right eye, barely visible. I remember how my mother would always say, *When your time is up, it is up, don't be afraid.* Her time was not up, it would seem, by her reasoning. Bubbe Rose pulling her into her bosom, *Shh, Bubbelah, I love you, it's going to be okay,* and my mother closed her eyes and saw only her own mother saying, *I wish you were never born.*

My mother took her grandmother's love and placed it somewhere inside of her next to the darkness of being unwanted and unloved and I grew from that. An idea as inconceivable as being run over by a two-ton vehicle and surviving with only a tiny scar that has to be pointed out to be noticed at all.

When my mother's grandmother Rose got to the end, my mother held her hand and whispered, *Shh, shhh, it's going to be all right,* reaching inside of herself and away from the darkness to that memory of safety and love, and there she found the idea. The idea was this: *I can give this away, this love, I do not have to keep it here in the dark, I can give it away and create more, even if I don't remember what it feels like to be loved. I can create it.*

All the stories that live inside of me, that I am holding, both sustain and haunt me. The time when my mother was eighteen and had started working in Center City in Philly, at Rohm and Haas, a chemical manufacturer, where she worked in foreign operations marketing and airfreight. She'd bought all new clothes for the job, and came home once to find that her mother had taken a scissors and sliced through all of them in her closet. She sat and wept into half of a skirt, a sleeve, a pant leg, and yet, still, on every Mother's Day, she sent flowers; she tried so hard to reach inside of herself and find a memory besides that of her grandmother Rose that said *I love you*, and when she could not find any, she begged her mother to love her, until she died all those years later when my mother was sixty-three years old. *Please love me, please love me, please love me* and my grandmother sealed her ears to those pleas and sat on her plastic-covered sofa in the dark and did crossword puzzles and complained about the weather.

Before I was born, I was just a memory of love, and thank the gods of coffee and books for that memory, because if my mother did not have her grandmother Rose, if she was left to the machinations of her own mother, she would be forever stuck in that South Philly row house. My grandmother was endlessly picking up men at the nightclub where she was the hatcheck girl. They were dangerous and mean. Sometimes my mother sat in a damp basement with the neighbor my grandmother left her with when she went on dates. I can imagine men pulling my mother to them, her small body a separate planet entirely. How could she have stayed in her body and endured?

Luckily my mother had the memory somewhere inside that body she so often left, a memory of the love she had felt from her grandmother. Before we are molecules, we are memory. Every time my grandmother winced as she looked at my mother, every time she tried to unspeak her into not existing, that's in me.

My mother grew up in a brick row house in South Philadelphia on Reese Street. Her mother's parents, whom she called Bubbe

(Rose) and Zayda (Al), also lived with them. They both died before I was born. It was a dark, narrow space that always smelled like cat pee when I would visit as a child. I rummaged in my grandparents' basement for Barbie doll clothes my great-grandmother Helen, my grandfather's mother, had sewn. My mother's stories have been in me as long as I can remember. Both my mom and my dad treated me like an adult since the time I could talk, so the tales of my grandmother Marion have no origin story for me. I have always known: she was a monster. I remember asking my mom, *Why didn't Grandmom ever say she loved us? Did she hate my sister and me? Why does she sit in the dark all the time? Why is she so mean?*

My grandmother got pregnant with my mom when she was eighteen years old. My grandfather had been a sailor stationed at the Philadelphia Navy Yard and was only home once a year until the time my mom and her sister, Ellen, were teenagers. When I started asking serious questions about why my grandmother was so unkind, it was as if my mother became uncorked and all the years of abuse and neglect and sheer terribleness flowed out of her and into the air. She told me everything.

It was 1983 and I was reading Judy Blume's *Forever*. I was eight years old and my father was still alive and I thought how lucky he was that he had my Bubbe, who was so loving and gentle and grandmotherly, and how unfair it was that my mom had grown up with her monster of a mother. That was my first true moment of realizing that there is no such thing as *fair*. I decided then that *fair* was a made-up word that might as well be in the fairy tale I was reading except I was not reading fairy tales, I was reading about sex and penises named Ralph and any other adult book I could get my grubby paws on.

Marion, my grandmother, worked as a hatcheck girl at Big Bill's, a nightclub in Center City, Philadelphia. She slept every day until three p.m. and they all dreaded the hours from three p.m. until seven thirty, when she finally left for work. *Once she left for work it was calm again*, my mother told me. My grandmother had dates with all those men while my grandfather was away in the navy. My mom said that neither she nor her sister Ellen ever got birthday presents except for when one of the very temporary boyfriends would take them to Lord & Taylor on the Main Line in Philadelphia to pick one out. She said, "She would brag about giving me the present, but it never came from her. It was always from the boyfriends." Clothes from shops along the Main Line, before there were shopping malls. A smoky topaz heart on a gold chain my mother wore all her life. And once, a cocker spaniel named Sandy, whom my grandmother later abandoned in the street.

My mother told me these stories while I sat at our kitchen dinette set in Pennsauken with the yellow vinyl cushions, the backs of my thighs stuck to them, making that noise they make when they peel off, like suction cups, and I watched my mom put flounder in the oven as I wrote stories. I let one leg at a time stick to the vinyl and then pulled it off like a vacuum, thinking it was hilarious because it was something my dad liked to do.

My father had a high-pitched laugh, like a sheep. He'd bray after he asked, "Who did that? Was it you, Jennifer? Rachel?" and then there was laughter and silence and we ate spaghetti and crab, stuffed pork chops, meatballs and gravy, or whatever my mom had made that day. My father never cooked. Never even poured his own cereal, or so the story goes. I recall only my mom doing anything remotely domesticated, like cleaning or cooking, grocery shopping, and making her own salad dressings. My dad's job was to go to work in a men's clothing store, make us laugh, buy us presents, and sing "You Are My Sunshine" to us before bed. Other than that, my mom did it all. Even simple tasks like driving my sister and me to school: my dad often got lost on the three-mile drive.

There were dishes in the sink, patterned plates, long foggy glasses with my father's lip marks. The island in the center of the kitchen had not been built yet. That came after my father died, when my mother used most of his life-insurance money to remodel the kitchen right before we left the house forever.

My mom talked as she made dinner or cleaned the kitchen counter with Clorox. She told me so many stories as if no one had ever listened to her in her entire life, which I came to realize they hadn't. I was the first, and I had to work hard to hear her above my constant tinnitus that I didn't understand or tell anyone about. I assumed this was what everyone heard, how sound existed in everyone's head.

I was fascinated with understanding why we had to go visit my grandmother Marion, why my mother still sent her presents, why my mom didn't hate her. I wanted to know *why why why* and *how how how* as I peeled my sweaty summer leg off the kitchen chair and stuck it back on, again and again, until my mom asked me to stop because the sound was driving her crazy. It felt like an impossible math equation to me and I was awful at math. If my mom had such an odious childhood and such an awful mom, why did we have a relationship with her? It did not make sense.

"That's just the way I am. I forgive," my mother said as she unloaded groceries and put them away; Pepsi for my dad and his Breyers chocolate ice cream. Those are always the groceries of my memories. Coffee, Kools, Breyers.

I never wanted to forgive my grandmother. My mom had told me too many things, things I perhaps already knew, things that lived so far in the marrow of me that I did not even need to hear them spoken aloud in kitchens, yet when I did, I wanted to throw things at walls, and at my mother. I thought about how my mom had been run over by a car when she was five years old. A story I had heard so many times that I wondered if I made it up in my unicorn diary because it felt like it was mine and had always been mine. I touched my eye to see if I had a scar there and sometimes it felt like I did. A tiny ridge under my eyebrow hairs.

My mom said that she had no memory of the faces from the day she was hit, so I made the faces up. She had been on a car ride to New Jersey from Philadelphia with my grandmother and one of the faceless, sometimes kind, sometimes not-so-kind boyfriends. In my mind, he had big hairy hands and brown eyes with eyelashes that pointed straight down. He smelled like cigarettes. My mom had been hit in the head and thrown thirty feet.

"I can't believe I survived and that they saved my eyes," she said every time she talked about it, lifting her thick brown bangs to show me the scar. I touched my own eye and said, "You can barely see it."

"I know," she always said, "but it's there."

We all had thick brown bangs since forever. I was probably born with bangs. It wasn't until I was a teenager that I realized I even had eyebrows. Bangs equal the eighties in my mind.

She had been trying to run away from her mother and the boyfriend while my grandfather was away overseas in the navy. She ran from them and right into the front of a car speeding on a small rural Jersey road. The car handle went through her right eye.

I was curious about my great-grandmother Rose. In my mom's stories, she was always kind and loving, and yet her daughter, my grandmother, was vicious and mean. I thought we were simply extensions of our parents. Whoever they were, *we* were. Or more precisely, would inevitably, and inextricably, become. I wanted to know my mother's Bubbe Rose so I could understand that love was not necessarily inherited, but that it could be created, fashioned from all sorts of things, including pain and car handles going through eyes.

"Tell me about your Bubbe Rose," I said as my mom sat down with her tea. Daddy drank coffee and Mommy had tea. I would come to hate tea.

"My Bubbe got breast cancer when I was fourteen years old. She was fifty-four. I was in ninth grade and they called me into the office to tell me my grandmother had cancer. I didn't even know what cancer was."

Rose begged my mother to give her a whole bottle of pain pills every day. Every day for seven months she asked to be put out of her misery.

"When I look back now, I wish I had given them to her. She suffered so much. The day she died, they called an ambulance, but she wouldn't get into it unless I was with her. I was at the park with my friends but a neighbor came to find me and we went to the hospital in the ambulance. She died in the emergency room. She was completely yellow and she was lying with her mouth open. I was fourteen."

Fourteen was ancient to me at the time. I wondered if I would know anyone who died by the time I was fourteen and I hoped not.

My MOM ARRANGED her grandmother's funeral, down to even the smallest detail. She didn't let her younger sister, Ellen, go to the funeral because she didn't want her to see what death looked like.

"When I saw my Bubbe in the casket she looked beautiful. They waved her thick brown hair and had put lipstick on her. I had never seen her look like that before. I had no idea she would look beautiful lying there with her eyes closed. I was sorry Aunt Honey (my nickname for Ellen) wasn't there," my mom said as she looked into her tea, and I wondered, if I scooted next to her and looked into her chipped mug, would I have seen my own father's impending death and would the leaves tell me that she would not let my sister, Rachel, and I attend his funeral? I doubt it. But I like to imagine I can go back in time and change things, that I would have read tea leaves and understood that I cannot take anything for granted because people die and leave you and that you shouldn't say *I hate you* because what if that is the last thing you ever get to say to someone?

"Did you always want to stay home from school, too?" I asked my mother in the kitchen. I hated the Jewish day school I attended so much. I sucked my thumb in class and looked out the window, pretending I was home. I didn't understand I had hearing loss then, I just knew I wanted to get out of that horrid room, where no one understood me. Where I felt lost, irritated, and bored.

"I can't remember," she said. "I only remember snapshots. Grandmom told me every day that she wished I wasn't born and that nobody liked me. I don't feel like I have any memories other than that."

But of course she did, because I had heard so many of them and they lived in my own memory. I have always had stories I told myself and my mom did, too. Her greatest one was *I can't remember.* It was her battle cry, and it seemed to me, even as a small child, that it was her form of protection, that "not remembering" saved her from remembering.

She could not remember that my grandmother didn't come to her high school graduation, where she won an award from the

National Honor Society, and that she was the only one without parents there. Mom said she couldn't remember her depression; that her brain split and didn't allow it.

"A doctor once told me that I was lucky that I don't remember. He said that I may not have survived my childhood at all if I did," she relayed, but I knew she remembered, at least somewhere in her body, because my body remembers just from hearing some stories. My heart pressed into my throat when my mom told me stories. I swallowed them whole. My little fists dug into my legs as if I could kill my grandmother with my own pain.

Love: Found and Lost

My mom was seventeen when she met my twenty-year-old father on the 5th Street trolley car on the way to work in Center City. It was 1966 and they all took trolleys or buses back then, no one drove to work.

"I thought Daddy was cute and tall with long legs," my mom said. (I inherited many things from my father, like the marks between the eyebrows known as the "11" and a love of coffee and a good sense of humor, but long legs were not bequeathed to me.)

"Grandmom never let anyone come over because the house was always so messy so I never had a friend over. Not until Daddy."

Mom told me how my father didn't care if her house was messy, and somehow he made it past the barrier of my grandmother, or else he only visited while Marion was asleep or at Big Bill's, checking hats, which may have been my mom's euphemism for sex. My mom spent most of her time before she married my father at my dad's house, where he lived with his parents, Reba and Jacob.

"Daddy and I got married when I was twenty," my mom said as she ran her fingers over her chin, a habit she continues, as if she is feeling for invisible chin hairs, or, as she claims, *visible* chin hairs. It's her nervous habit.

"Right after we got married, Daddy had to go into the hospital for back surgery. I was living with Daddy and his parents at the time, but I called Grandmom and said I wanted to come home and stay with her while he was in the hospital. She said no."

I looked at my mother in disbelief. Who had parents that purposefully made them feel so unwanted? My own parents made me feel so safe that I never wanted to leave my house. I wanted to stay home all day and watch *All My Children* with my mom and wait for my dad to walk in with chocolate-covered marshmallows or bootlegged VHS tapes.

Move Toward the Light

One of the things I ask in my workshops is, "In order to be where you want to be, what do you need to let go of?" The question was inspired by Wayne Dyer repeating *Don't die with your music still inside of you,* over and over on my post-waitressing-shift, speed-walking sessions by the ocean, where I half ran, half walked with him in my earbuds. *I promise, Wayne. I promise, Daddy,* I would say aloud as I walked in the park overlooking the Pacific Ocean. I vowed I would not die with my music in me, as my father had done. I just didn't know how I would do it.

I've had (and I have) so many bullshit stories. It's all part of this being human thing. The way out? Recognizing them and eradicating them so they don't rearrange your DNA and live in your body as truth. How do I know? Because that is what happened with my bullshit stories. The biggest story I let live inside of me for almost thirty years? The gargantuan belief that played as a mantra: *I am a bad person.*

Only a bad person would kill her father. Only a bad person would make him feel sick and then say, *I hate you.* A terrible no-good bad person. It would take me until I was thirty-three years old to stop chanting that phrase to myself all day. It would take going on antidepressants and quieting my IA so I could do things, like: fall in love, allow myself to be loved in return, take a yoga teacher training. It would take until I was thirty-five, when I started facilitating my workshops, to begin to see myself in others. I was able to finally have compassion for the eight-year-old me by listening to the people in my workshops. The people weeping onto their journals about how bad they were, how if anyone got to know the "real them," they would not be loved. I looked at them and I realized if they were so off base about who they really were, maybe I was as well? If I could have empathy for the women in front of me, why not for myself?

I wish I had remained in therapy, but I never stayed long enough to open up. I saw therapists sporadically throughout my life, never consistently. In sixth grade, my mother found another child psychologist for me and I would only go if he let me bring a friend into the session and bought us candy like gummy colas and let us play board games on the floor. I never spoke about my feelings. It was through the community I built that I realized the mantra I had structured my life around, *I am a bad person,* was a big fat lie.

So, as people write down their lists, all the things they want to

let go of, after I have gotten them sweaty after *vinyasa* so their de-
fenses are down (at least that's my hope), I ask them to add some of
their bullshit stories to the list.

Some people cock their heads and look at me like they don't understand what I am asking. So I give examples. *Here are some of
mine*, I say, *I am a bad person, I am not a real writer, I am broke, I am
unlovable.* The heads straighten, they get it. We all have them. I continue, *I am going to be just like my grandmother. I am my mother. I
can't remember anything.*

I have them write the stories down but I ask that they rewrite at
least one of them. How is it that we forget that our IA lies to us?
How is it that we often forget that just because we think something,
or someone has told us something, that it is true? How is it that we
forget we have agency and that we can change our minds? Rewriting your story isn't easy, because each day you have to wake up and
kick the old bullshit story out of bed until it gets the message and
stops trying to crawl in bed with you. Sometimes rewriting the
bullshit story feels corny, like some fairy tale, but that's only because it feels so foreign. It can feel like a lie. Rewriting your bullshit
story might feel like an untruth, like you are just pulling a card
from one of those inspirational card decks that you don't quite believe, even though you really *really* want to. Rewriting it can also
feel oddly uncomfortable because we are programmed to care
about what people may think. *Who am I to think I am loveable or
smart or beautiful? People will think I am full of myself. I am much
more palatable when I am self-deprecating.*

To help understand why telling ourselves stories can feel corny, I
posted on Facebook and asked what people thought. My friend Angela Giles, who helps me run The Manifest-Station and who has attended many of my workshops, said something brilliant: "It feels

weird for a couple of reasons. The stories we tell ourselves are interior, they are this fucked-up monologue that we repeat over and over to no one but ourselves. To try to reframe it by putting it on paper makes it exterior, the words exist outside of the body, away from the mind, and in a space where they can't be taken back or unseen. Then to try to tell yourself that the bullshit story is false by saying pretty much the opposite really feels forced and stupid. Like it is *that* moment we are a fraud, not the gazillion other moments that we told ourselves a lie."

And this is another thing I learned about yoga: to acknowledge the truth about where you are. "The truth is, corny or not, learning to regard ourselves as deserving, as valuable, and as capable doesn't mean just hollow pep talks. It means having an honest, openhearted way of evaluating our capabilities, noting our flaws along with our strengths," my friend Betsy Graziani Fasbinder wrote.

I also often ask the room, "Does it feel corny if I ask you to call yourself garbage or fat or to list the things you don't like about yourself?" Why is accepting ourselves so much harder? I can say *I hate you* to myself easily. When I say *I love you* to myself, it makes me roll my eyes sometimes. If I can't snap out of my eye-rolling state of mind, I try a mantra like, *I am enough* or *I am here. I am here* is a powerful one for me because my self-hate was so strong it could have easily killed me. One of the most important parts of rewiring is spending time with people who don't allow me to get away with my bullshit stories. People who remind me who I really am, since so many of our bullshit stories seem to be based in forgetting that. Someone's bullshit story might be, *I am ugly.* What if they rewrote it to be: *I am enough.* Or, *I am beautiful.* It might feel awkward and cheesy, but eventually, when we change our mantras, and our behaviors, the bullshit stories fall away. I am not a bad person. I am enough. I am here. I am love. That is how I rewrote mine. And I seek out that version of myself every day. Every single day. I remind myself of *that* rather than the bullshit story. Spoiler alert: It's not easy. But it's possible.

One of the biggest bullshit stories I hear (and I use myself) is, *It isn't the right time.*

There is no perfect time for anything, is what I have learned. Which is why I ask the people in my workshops, *What are you waiting for?*

Even as a child I understood that the stories we tell ourselves can become real. I wanted to understand my family so badly as I listened to my mom's roach-filled childhood, yet I was so afraid that within them were the roots of my destiny that would someday bloom into some horrifying tree bearing rotten fruit. I wanted to go back in time and give my mom the childhood she deserved. Why do some people get such a crappy draw? Was everything inherited, including trauma and abuse and a proclivity toward coffee or tea, or crossword puzzles? Was all the armor we built over the years to protect us already there, long before our parents took us home in the back of taxicabs? I wanted to know so I could write my way out of it, so I could create a different ending for myself. I stayed away from crossword puzzles for the rest of my life. And cigarettes.

HOW DO WE FIND love and happiness when we think and have been told that we do not deserve it? How do we allow ourselves to be seen and be vulnerable, even if we've never experienced care and tenderness?

Another way to ask: *How do we find light when we think we belong to darkness?*

I'VE ALWAYS BEEN fascinated with the way light falls across spaces and objects—staircases, people's faces, picture frames on the shelf, babies' heads, pregnant bellies, kitchen floors. In 1980, when we lived in Pennsauken, after we'd moved from South Philly, there was a den down a set of stairs from the dining room. The den was dark, the shelves were brown wood. It felt like you were in a bunker below ground, so as we watched VHS tapes of *E.T.* and *Annie*, it felt like being in a dark movie theater. It was then that I noticed how light made me feel. How I craved and abhorred it at the same time. How much I wanted to be up and out in the light-filled world, but how I kept running down the stairs to the den to be with my father in his cutoff jeans, to be near him, to be hidden from the world. I associated darkness with feeling safe.

CHAPTER 2

The Art of Unknowing

You're Not Alone

MY FATHER WAS MY WORLD.

I remember going with him to Dunkin' Donuts one day, just him and me. The two of us sliding across the floor in our sneakers toward the case that held all the doughnuts. He got a coffee with more cream in it than coffee and I had a Munchkin and a cinnamon glazed doughnut and he let me sip his coffee, like he had let me take a puff of his pipe, simply because I begged to try it. We sat in his brown Chevy, both in the front seat, laughing and Pastiloffing (spilling crumbs and coffee on ourselves as well as the car upholstery).

It always felt like my dad and me against the world. Or at least against my mom. They had gotten married young and were ill-suited for each other. My mother, so long abused, was constantly seeking love and validation; my father, a good Jewish boy whose mother would not leave the house until he awoke so she could make him breakfast, even into his twenties, had always expected attention. My father thought the world owed him something and wanted to be waited on by my mother in the same way my Bubbe had waited on him, waiting in her best dress. So my mom did just that, even when it was against her nature.

And in the way fate works, the cruel and funny asshole that it can be, my father withheld love from my mom and my mom did whatever she could to get it, a replica of the environment she had growing up. Daddy seemed to sense that he could take out his anger on my mother, his anger at what he felt were the injustices of the world: namely, that he had to get up and drive to Philadelphia to manage a men's clothing store instead of being a stand-up comedian. The thing is, he could have gone and done whatever he wanted. He was charming and hilarious and good-looking. But he was afraid. He took speed all day long—prescription diet pills, cocaine—and then downers at night, valium, barbiturates.

He smoked eighty cigarettes a day. The *could haves* never got past the fear or the drugs or the doubt. My father had the original bullshit stories. I would be an adult before I realized that you don't have to kill yourself to change. The will to grow must outweigh the need to feel safe. You have to want it badly enough. My father didn't want it. To this day, people tell me that Melvin Pastiloff was the funniest person they have ever known. He died in 1983, so those people have met scores of people by now. And still he remains the funniest.

MY FATHER WASN'T always the way he was when he died. He was a prince to my mom before they were married. Before my parents were married, when my father was in the army, he wrote my mom the loveliest letters full of *I miss you*s and *I love you*s and *I promise*s. Maybe the army turned my father, a city kid from Philadelphia, into a scared little boy. Or maybe he, too, learned cruelty from his mother.

My mom said that the first time my father brought her home to meet his parents, they walked in and my Bubbe was standing in the kitchen reading the paper. My dad said, "Look, Mom, this is Barb. Isn't she beautiful?" And my Bubbe apparently took a few minutes before lifting her eyes from the Yiddish paper to look at my mom. "She's okay," she replied with an indiscernible shrug before looking back down to finish the paper.

I never wanted to be just *okay*. I wanted to be a world to some-one. *I will never settle for "okay,"* I remember thinking when my mom relayed the story. And yet I would go on to settle. And I would beg to be loved, as much as I promised I would never be like my mother.

In Pennsauken, each night our dad marched my sister and me up the stairs saying *hut two three four, hut two three four*. He must've gotten that from those long marches during the short time he was in the army. He ended another one of his letters to my mom by say-ing, *I just can't take this army shit. You know, the running, the march-ing, the exercises, the cleaning. I'm just not cut out for it.*

That was true, he wasn't. He never had to lift a finger (and he re-ally didn't until the day he died), so it must have been the shock of his life to be forced to follow orders. Maybe this is why he was so frustrated that he didn't achieve what he wanted to in life. He wanted to set his own path, but he never quite figured out what that was, what it looked like, or how he might carve it. Instead, my par-ents did what so many other couples did at that time—followed a normative road that led them to the suburbs.

Following their best friends, they left Philadelphia and moved to the suburbs of New Jersey. My parents bought the house in Pennsauken for a whopping $38,000. It was the house next door to

"Uncle John and Aunt Gwen's house," their best friends. My memories of those years are some of my happiest. I knew I was loved.

UNLIKE WHAT MY FATHER provided for our mother, he was able to give my sister and me unconditional love because we worshipped him. I idolized him until the very end. My mom waited on him hand and foot but she did not glorify him like we did, like everyone who knew him did. Behind closed doors he was abusive to my mom, but on the street, at the block parties, at work, holidays, he was the life of the party. Of course in the beginning of their relationship she was drawn to his humor. And to his long legs and blue eyes. Mostly, she wanted to belong to someone. In the beginning the relationship felt safe. Until it wasn't.

THEIR BEDROOM ALWAYS smelled like Ralph Lauren Polo cologne. My father worked in a men's clothing store in Center City, Philly, where he sold Ralph Lauren Polo products to the men who came in, to the men who cheated on their wives, to that one guy from Hall and Oates, to the cops who looked the other way, to the businessmen, to the men who worked on Jewelers Row, to the men who did drugs with him.

The room also smelled like leather. It had his gold-chain smell, the Jewish star of David on the end, hair peeking through where his Polo button-down opened below that small indentation below the throat. The room smelled like a father.

It was always me and my dad up in my parents' bedroom, giggling, the television show *M*A*S*H* on in the background. He treated me like a confidante, a pal, a mentee. He treated me like a daughter, too, but in my mind, first and foremost, we were buds and my mom was the enemy. That's how he framed it. *You and me, kiddo. You and me.* That was our narrative, Bonnie and Clyde, two peas in a pod, birds of a feather. We had secret codes to communicate. We'd press a finger into one nostril and say, "You know what I mean?" in a nasally Smurf kind of voice. I thought my father was God.

I also believed that I belonged to Daddy and Rachel belonged to Mommy, as if it was an unspoken understanding. After he died, my mom would say, "I know you wish I died instead of your dad," and I would stay silent. I would come to understand that she didn't know any better, that she was doing the best she could, and that her lack of self-worth prevented her from standing up to my dad. It stopped her from saying, "Go make your own damn coffee. Tie your own fucking tie. Stop telling Jennifer I am the bad guy." Instead, my father made us into teams and she just held my sister on her hip as she cooked dinner and poured his Pepsi. My sister was only five when he died; she doesn't remember much but she is envious I got more time with our father. We talk on the phone now and try to remember his voice and we make up versions of what we think happened. Neither of us gets it right.

No one ever gets it exactly right when it comes to memories and personal histories.

Escape versus love

Just before he died, my father had an affair with a woman who wore a lot of eye shadow. They met at the store in Center City, Philadelphia, where he sold the expensive Polo suits and cologne with charm and humor. My mom told me about his affair one afternoon while I was sitting on the sofa in the den watching *Knight Rider*. *Your father had an affair with (redacted) and I am leaving*. I floated away, imagining I was driving KITT, the car from *Knight Rider*, and yet, how could I make that sentence go away? The knowing that my father betrayed us for a skinny woman who wore a lot of eye shadow and had dyed blond hair, who looked nothing like us: me, my sister, my mom. I knew who the woman was; we'd met her when we went into Philly to visit him and she was always nice to my sister Rachel and me. We knew all the employees in the store. Mel was beloved and everyone wanted to meet his kids and show off for them.

I wondered if this was what all husbands did to their wives. I wondered if my father would leave us for Eye-shadow Lady. I wondered if he didn't think we were as beautiful as she was, and that's why he strayed.

One day, I found letters that Eye-shadow Lady had sent my father during their affair. Somehow they'd survived inside a box with photographs, through various moves and deaths. I discovered them all the way in California. He'd been dead two years, but the anger I felt was as big as a person standing on the carpet next to me, looming above me. The rage filled my throat until I couldn't breathe. I wanted to go to Philly and tell her husband. I wanted to destroy *her* life. Instead I ruined the letters.

I wish I hadn't.

I would look at them now as a scientist would. I would search for evidence of who my father was, of what his love looked like. I don't know if they were really in love with each other, but as an adult I recognize how escape can feel like love, so I think if I had the letters I would recognize myself.

But as a child I was afraid that he would stop loving me, that it would no longer be me and him, but just me, and I did not want to be alone. That was my greatest fear (isn't it everybody's?): being alone in the world. My parents battled for my attention and I only wanted my dad. If they were going to divorce, I would 100 percent, without a doubt, choose my dad. As my mother pretended to forget the sad parts of her childhood, I would fail to remember my father's transgressions. I began my apprenticeship to the art of unknowing, a skill that would then take all my life to unravel.

And so escape and love became intertwined, and from this grew a sense of not knowing, ignoring, pretending not to know. This unknowing became a theme. My hearing loss, for example. It was progressively getting worse over my childhood and then adulthood, and yet I avoided it. I pretended to not know it was happening to me, inside my own body. It wasn't severe when I was a child, only the tinnitus was, and yet, I ignored it all. I talked to no one about it. Anything I felt—grief, depression, shock, anger—I simply starved it away or exercised or drank too much wine or slept. I simply would not know. It was something I learned as a child that had somehow carried me into adulthood. Until it would no longer carry me. Until I learned to look deep into the face of whatever it was, and what I found was this: it didn't kill me. *I see you*, I would say to my sadness, *I hear you*, I said to my deafness, the irony not lost on me. And I began to do something about it. I stopped pretending that I couldn't feel anything. I started talking about my story to anyone who would listen, in blogs, online, in essays, in my workshops. I started asking others to share what they had thought would kill them. They did. And there were so many things—deaths of children, of parents, deaths of partners, miscarriages, homes lost in floods, depression, shame, anorexia—and yet, there they were. Alive. I wish I could do a workshop with my father. I wish I could understand the demons he was chasing and how they were not so dissimilar to my own. How he so badly wanted to escape his body, wanted everyone to love him, wanted the world to exist on his own terms. How afraid he was. I would ask him to make the workshop laugh with his jokes. Maybe we'd host an event and prove that inherited trauma is a real thing but that we could indeed rewrite our stories because *look at us, still alive, father and daughter, conquering the world, together. Come take our workshop and battle your demons as a family!*

In my workshops, I encourage us to face things. Head-on. But we hold hands doing it because it's scary and hard and it's through connection that we can bear to know. Ram Dass says, "After all, we're just walking each other home." It's the embodiment of saying *I got you.*

The Lucky House

What will always live in my body: the way the kitchen smelled when I walked in, and all the people staring at me with their blank faces: Gwen, John, Aunt Honey, Carmel, and Anthony from next door, Blanche and her blind dog Pepper from across the street, Bonny and Joe from two houses down, the Loves, who lived on the other side of us. I knew what the faces were trying to say, what they were trying to convey to my eight-year-old self without breaking me.

Your father died.

Instead, they said,

"Sit down, Jennifer."

I did not. I kept standing. I was wearing the *Annie* T-shirt painted by my friend's mom that I wore every day. Above Annie's orange hair it stated J E N N I F E R L O V E S in matching orange paint. Annie had big empty eyes with no pupils, eyelashes, or eyebrows. My pockets were filled with paper covered in my scribbled stories. I wore sneakers that Velcroed across the top. I bent down, undid the Velcro, fastened it again.

"We have something to tell you."

I did the Velcro. I undid the Velcro.

"Here, have a doughnut," one of the mouths might have said.

My mother never let us have doughnuts. We had wheat germ (yuck) sprinkled on our no-sugar cereal from the local health food store that has since been replaced with a Whole Foods. My father drank Pepsi in tall chilled glasses and ate waffles with chocolate ice cream every night before bed, but the rest of us ate whole-wheat bread and brown wheat germ and other cardboard crap. My mom never bought doughnuts, so when I went into the kitchen that morning, I knew. To see the kitchen decorated with doughnut boxes was like walking into a morgue.

In that moment, the smell of sugar thick in the air, all the faces telling me to sit down, I learned in an instant how to shut down and keep going.

In order to shut down my feelings, my senses kicked into over-drive. The kitchen smelled yeasty, and all the people stared at me with their blank seasick faces, the linoleum lifting up below my sneakers as I grabbed counter corners to steady the kitchen sea. Right before my heart fell out and rolled onto the kitchen seafloor, as their lips moved in soundless circles, I heard ringing. I heard church bells and crying cats. I heard the ringing that was my name-less companion I was ashamed to tell anyone about until I was in my late twenties and I learned what it was called and what it was. Tinnitus. I tasted metal, blood, my own fingers rushing to my mouth. I saw my life ending in a Jersey kitchen with ugly blinds and 1980s linoleum, surrounded by outstretched hands claiming to offer doughnuts but instead grabbing at me, reaching inside of me and taking my heart away. My father's own heart had killed him. I would abandon mine. How could I bear to walk through the world, heartless and alone, with only the dial tones hissing and whooshing in my ears? How would I know where to go? What to do? How could I possibly find a safe place?

THERE WERE SIX BOXES of Dunkin' Donuts, including Munchkins, the little doughnut holes, which were my favorite. I eyed them and imagined throwing doughnuts at every person in the kitchen, and although I can't remember how many people were in the room, it felt like one million.

"Jennifer, it's your father," the jelly doughnut said.

"Sweetie, he's in a better place," the apple cider whispered.

"Honey, everything's going to be okay," a glazed cruller lied.

I know already. He died.

One million people stopped eating their feelings at that moment to look at me playing with my sneakers. I wouldn't look back at them. I said it again this time aloud,

"I know. He died."

I said it again and again, "I know. I know. I know."

My parents' best friends, whom we called *Aunt* and *Uncle,* leaned into me. Aunt Gwen said, "Jennifer, come here."

I shook my head and didn't take a step.

I heard noises that sounded like muffled versions of *It's going to be okay he's going to be in your heart forever he's in a better place now I am so sorry we are so sorry do you want a doughnut here have a doughnut have a Munchkin you love Munchkins your father loved you very much here have a doughnut.*

Lying faces and chewing mouths. Why couldn't anyone tell the truth? It would not be okay. It would never be okay again.

I knew walking into that kitchen on July 15, 1983. I could tell from the way I was sinking that my lifeline was lying dead in a hospital bed, having suffered coronary atherosclerotic disease. I wanted to die, too.

His two left descending arteries, which bring blood to the heart, were 85 and 90 percent blocked. His heart no longer had a source.

I decided, then and there in the kitchen, that I would never eat again for the rest of my life. I would never breathe again for the rest of my life. I swore I would not let myself feel, because if I ever had to feel *this* again, my skin would come off and I would disintegrate. Yet in this moment this is just what I wanted.

I wanted my father, I wanted life the way it was last year, I wanted to tell someone that I had what sounded like an ocean in my head. Most of all I wanted a time machine. To return to the day before.

"You're just upset," another doughnut said, but I don't remember which.

"I am not upset. I'm fine. I don't care." I turned and walked out of the kitchen and into the living room. I dug the corner of the glass coffee table into my knee. In my head, a chant that I used as my mantra for years after was loud and clear:

Be strong. Be strong. Be strong. Don't cry. Be strong. Be strong. Don't cry.

I returned to the kitchen and said, "I'm going to Jessica's house." I walked through the front door and around the block. I don't remember actually going into the Litwins' house, but I walked around the block again and again as sweat made hair stick to my forehead. Every time I passed the Litwins' house, I said to myself, *Lucky*. Lucky there is a mother and a father and two brothers. Lucky they are whole. Lucky house. *I am not lucky*, I said to myself. *What have I done? I am bad and unlucky. I am bad and unlucky.* Jessica's mom, Susan, who painted my *Annie* sweatshirt, would die of ovarian cancer years later, when I was a nineteen-year-old sophomore at NYU. "Luck" rhymes with "fuck," which is the truth; it's more accurate because there is no such thing as luck. There is only, *You better enjoy your luck in this moment because there are no guarantees, no lucky houses, no one person who can remain untouched by loss.* We never know how fate will play out with cancer, hearts that stop, rare genetic diseases, life. *Luck* is a fantasy word, but I didn't know that then.

I walked past the Lucky House twenty-seven times. I wondered why pastries were supposed to make people forget that someone died. I wondered if I should be dead, too. I wondered why God hated me. I wondered where pain went if you didn't let yourself feel it. Did it vanish into air, like dust? Could I vanish? Could the noises in my head devour me from the inside out?

Be strong. Be strong. Be strong. Don't cry. Be strong. Be strong. Don't cry.

My father was my best friend. My parents were going to get a divorce and he was going to take me with him. He had said, "You take Rachel. I'll take Jennifer," during an argument we'd overheard.

My sister's whole life has been an echo of that sentiment. *Why am I not wanted?* I don't remember overhearing that conversation, but isn't that how memory works? Were you really there or have you just told the tale so many times that you think you were? My sister used to constantly ask us *why daddy didn't want me,* so that conversation was part of the fabric of our nascent personalities, part of what we knew to be true. We had no idea it was a bullshit story. My mom would explain that he did not mean it, that I was older and he thought it would just be easier to care for an eight-year-old than a five-year-old.

I have a duplicitous relationship with being wanted. I need everyone to want me and yet I don't believe them when they say they do, because how could they? After all, I was a bad person. My IA never let that mantra quiet down. I want to believe my father didn't say that, or at the very least, my dear sister did not hear that, but it's part of our fabric, this narrative of choosing.

The night before he died, my dad was propped up in bed, leaning against the yellow-flowered pillowcases. He'd been searching for his cigarettes, his hands feeling around the nightstand, knocking over his ashtray and his Pepsi.

"Jennifer, have you seen my Kools?"

"No," I lied.

Then I started laughing, because I couldn't lie to my best friend. I told the truth: "I flushed them down the toilet."

"You're being bad and making me not feel good," he said.

"But you promised. You promised you would stop smoking."

"Go across the street and ask Kirk for a hard pack of Kools. Stop playing around."

In 1983, you could go across the street to the store on the corner, Kirk's Newsroom, and put stuff on your "tab." A pound of American cheese, thinly sliced; a hard pack of Kools; Tastykakes. There were three video game machines in the back, too. The only one I liked was Pac-Man. The irony that I ended up waiting tables for almost fourteen years at a place called "The Newsroom" is not lost on me. At Kirk's we entered through the back door, which faced our house. On Christmas, Kirk left us eggnog on our doorstep even though we were Jewish.

"You promised you would quit," I told my dad. "We just learned in school how bad smoking is and you smoke four whole packs a day! You promised you would stop. You always break your promises. I hate you."

I hate you. I hate you. I hate you. Hate. Hate. Hate. Words that would resonate in my muscles for the rest of my life. *I hate you. I hate me.*

Be strong. Be strong. Be strong. Don't cry. Don't let yourself feel.

As I walked past the Litwin Lucky House, where none of their parents were dead, I imagined that the night before had gone differently.

I pictured my father's arm reaching across the yellow sheets toward the nightstand. In my fantasy scene, he finds his cigarettes. I jump on the bed just to hear him laugh and watch *M*A*S*H* with him. My mom brings us waffles and ice cream and we eat them and I fall asleep in their bed and I wake up to a house full of lucky people—a mom, a dad, and two daughters.

AFTER WALKING AWAY from the Lucky House, I still did not cry. I went back to my own house on Drexel Avenue. After walking around the block for hours, with blisters on my feet and sweat on my upper lip, I opened the screen door and walked upstairs and into my room and curled myself into the space between the headboard of my bed and the wall. I used to press my ear to the wall and listen to my mom and dad fight, or my dad laugh. The sound of his laugh would travel up the vent into my ears and all would be well in the world. His laugh was one of the only sounds that canceled out the noise I always heard inside my head. There was my mom and there was my dad and I could hear their voices, and if I stayed put, nothing would change, ever. This was my wish: an unchanging world, an immovable life, sameness all the time.

But as I sat there that day, or night, or whatever time it was because time stopped existing when the Dunkin' Donuts boxes showed up, I heard only muffled voices. People were still in the house. *A thirty-four-year-old woman with two little girls, eight and five. Can you imagine? It's just so sad.* Voices whispering those words and other *can you imagines?*

Back then my ears worked. They weren't fully broken yet. Only my heart was.

Your Heart Is Your Gift: Offer It

So many people I meet in my workshops come with a broken heart. They come up to me and offer their hearts in their shaking hands saying, *Look. Here is my heart. I don't know how I will go on without this. I can't put it back.*

I have them do something that most of them hate, at first. I ask them to get a partner and gaze into that person's eyes without looking away for three minutes, without speaking. Some fidget, some laugh, some cry, some talk. Until they settle in to just being with the other person. The intimacy is astounding, and as much as they kick and scream, afterward they feel connected to that person. I remember the writer Emily Rapp Black rolled her eyes so hard when I asked her to do this when we were in Vermont, and yet, the woman whose eyes she looked into that day is now one of her best friends, as she is one of mine: Angela Giles. Last summer in France, a seventy-year-old woman who was there with her daughter, who was there on scholarship because she had lost her own fourteen-year-old daughter, looked into someone's eyes. I had each person place a hand on the other person's heart. It was like a lady church. Or synagogue. Or whatever you'd call it. It was holy and sacred and the woman who had lost her granddaughter was sobbing. She said, "It's like her body disappeared and I was just holding a soul. I was just left holding a soul."

That's what happens when we begin to shed our armor—the essence of who we really are gets exposed. You can call it a *soul* if you like, call it what you will, but whatever you name it, it is *not* your Inner Asshole. I'd believed for too long that my body was the entirety of me, my worth determined by virtue of my body. I knew it wasn't a magic trick that under the armor, or the façade, and even under the body, lay the deepest truth that we could ever know. What is that deepest truth? That we are love. We are not our bullshit stories, we are not the size of our thighs, we are not things we spoke as a child, we are not our depression, we are not our disabilities, we are not the lies other people have told us about ourselves. We are love. That is what she meant when she said she was left holding a soul. She felt it as if it was as palpable as stone. It was no trick. Your heart, held out to another, will always be the greatest gift you can offer.

Building the Armor: Perfecting the Art of Unknowing

After my father died and we moved to Southern California "to start our lives over," as our mom explained, my sister and I started squinting a lot. In all the photos, our hands shield our eyes from the sun; we weren't used to the relentless brightness.

Our front window in Santa Monica faced north onto Idaho

Avenue. There was a tiny balcony. Frank, my mom's boyfriend who had picked her up while we were sitting on the beach during our *Daddy died, let's take a vacation* vacation, slept over most nights. My mother started speaking more softly, making her own pizza, eating sushi, watching the sun set. No one watched sunsets in the eighties in New Jersey. Frank liked sunsets. He ran on the beach barefoot and watched the bruise of a sun go down, every single night.

I would open the sliding-glass door and stick my head out to take a breath, hold it, and then come back inside. Like I was saving the oxygen. Except sometimes I think I would forget to let it back out and it would stay stuck inside of me. I tried not to breathe a lot back then.

I chose the bottom bunk in the room I shared with my sister so I could feel like I was in a cave. My dark little cocoon: what I came to think of was my natural habitat. We played 45 records on our shared stereo. "Caribbean Queen" by Billy Ocean. "Like a Virgin" by Madonna. "Against All Odds" by Phil Collins. "Cruel Summer" by Bananarama. I closed the door when I wanted to write my stories. My sister came in anyway and I yelled at her. I hated sharing a room. We fought nonstop. She copied everything I did and I couldn't stand it. *Let me live my life!* I yelled at her all the time. I felt alone in the world, my only accomplice lying in a Jewish cemetery in Pennsauken, New Jersey.

I walk by that old Santa Monica apartment sometimes. It's only a few blocks from where I live now. I can almost see myself, my sister, Frank, my mom. I see us sitting on the black chenille sofa, the curtains my mom made, swung wide open, light pouring into the living room. I often stop and wish I still had that apartment because of that big window. That light.

I wanted our Jersey den back, even though I did not want to go back to New Jersey ever again. I was afraid if I returned to that state I would not be able to deal with my guilt and grief and I would explode. I wanted my den back and my father back, but there I was, living with my mother's new boyfriend and his Doberman pinscher, Gondor, watching black-and-white *Twilight Zone* episodes. I'd go into Frank's backyard, where he had a cactus collection and antique bathtubs buried in the yard with real fish swimming in them. My sister and I sat among the cacti and stared up at the sun. We named the fish. Mel the Jew was one fish. We named the sun. The sun was named *Daddy*.

I thought I understood what was happening. I thought I understood and simply didn't care, whereas my sister cried all the time. She'd weep and say, *I want a daddy. I want a daddy.* I was strong, I told myself. I didn't need anyone.

WE DID NOT go to Daddy's funeral. My mother wouldn't let us, because someone, or many someones, had told her it would fuck us up, in so many words. I wish we had gone. I wish I had heard all the stories everyone told about how funny he was, how he lit up a room as much as he lit up his cigarettes, one after the other. My mother regrets now not letting us go, but what did she know then? She was thirty-four years old and suddenly a single mom. *What does anyone ever know?* I would come to wonder for the rest of my life.

The first time we went to the cemetery, I was eight years old. I wouldn't look at the headstone, designed by my mother. I turned and stared directly into the sun instead—half hoping I would go blind. We moved to California a few days after that. I was angry at my dad and I also couldn't handle the idea of him being in the ground, so I thought if I pretended that he wasn't dead or in the ground, if I pretended everything was normal, if I forced myself to be strong, then I could survive. Strength would save me, or at least *pretending* to be strong would save me. Eventually the hardness would have to become real. The armor would grow to become part of my skin. *It has to or I won't make it,* I thought.

When we visited the grave, which wasn't often because of distance (we moved three thousand miles away) and because I couldn't bear the way my chest caved in and I couldn't speak when I was there, we put rocks on the grave. I acted like someone who was grieving even though I couldn't feel a thing. I used to pathetically pick up stones off other graves like a thief so I would look sad. *Look at me over here, mourning. Look at me, feeling feelings.*

A FEW NIGHTS EARLIER, months after my father had passed away, we were sitting at the kitchen table. My Aunt Honey was there, and there was an empty seat where my father belonged. I looked up from my plate and asked, "Where is my father?"

I kept asking until I pushed my chair from the table and climbed into the hamper in the hallway. That night my mom decided she would move us to California. To start over. I had been seeing a therapist in Philadelphia but I told everyone I felt fine and everyone believed me so everyone was a fucking idiot.

Before we left, we had to go see my dad in the cemetery for the unveiling of the tombstone, nine months after his death. I held my breath the whole time, rocks in my hands I wished were knives instead. I turned my back so I was no longer facing the headstone and listened to the ocean in my ears, knowing that soon enough it would be the real ocean and dumb New Jersey would be three thousand miles away with my father's dead body.

AS MUCH AS I pretended to forget my father, he permeated everything and everyone. He was everywhere: in the sunshine, the sunsets, the sea air, the fish in the bathtubs, the shining cars, the flip-flopped beachgoers, the sand and the surf and the birds and the spindly palm trees swaying on the pier. He was unstoppable and everywhere.

As the years have passed, I've looked for remains of him in the most bizarre of places you wouldn't even believe (Uluwatu in Bali in a little lap pool; a cemetery in Lewisburg, parts of Pennsylvania that I used to jog through; old books with crumbling pages; the faces of dogs).

But to the outside world, I built armor around myself, thick and impenetrable. To keep him out. I would not make the mistake of being soft ever again. I would stunt myself in that moment in time, forever reliving a pain I would not let myself feel when it happened. Instead placing it in the deepest parts of myself and then burying it under layers of rock so it could not get out, nor could anyone get in. Nothing could touch me.

And so good-bye to New Jersey and death and dying and cold winters, and hello to Southern California. The three of us arrived in a station wagon—my mother, my sister, and I—and it was a simple case of "Should we turn left or right?" Which, I've come to realize, is the way most of life works.

Door number one: you stay in college, wear turtlenecks, work in a university. Door number two: you drop out of college, run for three hours a day, wait tables.

Turn right: he does drugs "one last time" and dies. Turn left: and there he is on the sofa in his frayed cutoffs and we never have to make the trek to California.

So a *should we turn left or right* happens and we choose left instead of right and end up in Santa Monica, where we live next to a man, his two daughters, and their beagle, Darwin, whom they keep locked up in a cage.

CHAPTER 3

I'm Right Here

Please Come Back

I DIDN'T KNOW it then, we never know in the moment, but it was the move to California that changed everything. I made friends. My first friend was Loren, who stood by me when I got married twenty-six years later. Our moms had met in a store that sold VCRs, where my mom had been working selling electronics. They made a playdate for us after talking and discovering their daughters were the same age. We had just moved and I had exactly zero friends. Luckily I had a Matchmaker Mom; she was and is a Connector as well.

I started writing even more in California. I made a droning sound when I wrote—my own emergency broadcast system alert. For hours at a time, I made that sound as if alerting the world to some imminent catastrophe. I didn't know what tinnitus was, and making that sound was my way of mimicking the sound inside my brain. People made fun of me for it, so I forced the sound back into my body and locked it inside of my head, right next to the responsibility for my father's death. There is a room in all of us where we lock our shame. I vowed to never unlock mine.

"Jen, that sound you make is so annoying."

"You have the most nasal voice."

"You have to stop making that noise in public."

"What is that? Can't you not make that noise when you concentrate? It drives me crazy."

At some point I stopped making the noise out loud, but I never stopped hearing it. I heard sound when no external sound was present and I often wondered what else I heard that wasn't really there. It did not occur to me that I had hearing loss, or tinnitus. I didn't know that word back then, but if I did I would have spelled it for you. I was a master speller. I was proud of that, if nothing else. That and the books I read.

I don't remember not being able to hear, only that my teachers were always saying that I didn't pay attention. I felt like I was paying attention, but I always had to sit in the front row and I learned the best when I read something rather than the teacher speaking it.

"Jennifer, pay attention."

These words became a refrain in my own head, another mantra. *I have to pay attention. I have to pay attention.*

I tried so hard, but the ringing got in the way of the voices, so I would doodle on my notebook or write a story as the teacher was talking. I never finished my stories. I had hundreds of beginnings, a few middles, and no endings.

"Jennifer, where are you right now?" my sixth grade teacher, Mrs. Gimenez, asked me.

"I'm right here," I said.

"You need to pay attention and to listen better."

"I'm listening," I said, and I thought I was. When I was in sixth grade, my hearing was not something I thought about. I assumed that the teachers were right and that I wasn't paying attention. I thought I was a space cadet, as they called me. I never told anyone about the ringing in my head. I got so used to hearing it all the time that it felt like a private companion. I grew to have a tolerance and high threshold for pain.

We can get used to so many things.

"I'm right here," I would say, looking up at whichever teacher was asking me where I was.

IN SOUTH DAKOTA, Chicago, New York, Philadelphia, wherever I happen to be leading a workshop, I offer this as a mantra to anyone who might be drifting away: *Come back*. Maybe their eyes are darting around the room, or they are looking at their phone. I spent so much of my life drifting out of my body that I use it as my mind tattoo when I need to. *Jen, come back*. I tell the rooms—whether I am in London or Tampa or Dallas, whichever city my workshop is being held, it doesn't matter—I say, "You can borrow this mantra. We all need it sometimes. *Come back*." It's a gentle urging to return to your body. *Oh, here I am*. It's not a bossing around from the IA, it's a hand patting the empty seat next to your own, saying, *Here, sit here. You're safe with me*. It's a way of being able to say, "I'm right here," that refrain I found myself saying to every teacher as a child in school. *Come back*.

Pretending to Be Present

I didn't understand that reading lips was helping me make it through each day, that without it I would be only half hearing what someone was saying. I did not want to face anything, not my father's death, not the fact that anything was wrong with my ears or whatever was causing that godforsaken sound in my head, not the fact that I felt sad all the time. I was strong and tough and I could just keep going. As long as my voice kept saying, "I am right here," people would believe me, even if I wasn't really there, even if I wasn't really hearing them, even if I wasn't feeling a damn thing, which proves that most people will believe the bullshit stories we put forth. How careful we should be with what we convince people of about ourselves.

I was constantly sick and missing school (which I loved, because I hated school), so I was always behind with schoolwork. I had chronic ear infections and a host of other medical problems related to adenoids, sinuses, ears, tonsils. At the time, hearing loss wasn't on the table. Even if it was there, I did not want to acknowledge it. There it was again: the willful unknowing. The doctors warned my mother that at some point I might develop hearing loss, but I ignored that because I didn't imagine I would live to see a future. I figured thirty-eight was the age of death, if I lived that long. I began to perfect the art of avoiding.

The first time I cried for my father was three years after he died, three thousand miles away, in an improv class at the Santa Monica Playhouse. I was eleven. The improv teachers were always asking, *What's your objective?* You always had to have an objective for every scene and you had to want that thing more than anything. To get understanding, to break up with someone, to get an apology—these were objectives. We were in the room above the theater at the Santa Monica Playhouse. I was sitting on a chair with a green velvet back and my body collapsed into itself. I was in the *Hot Seat*, as they called it, where you just sit there and people say things to you. I don't even remember what was said, if it was kind or awful, but I started to cry and I couldn't stop. The whole idea behind improvisation was being in the moment and that was something I had stopped doing. I let my-self experience what was happening in my body, in that room, and the dam opened up. I cried for ten minutes. Afterward, we jumped up and down and answered as a group, "Energy and Enthusiasm!" when asked, "What are the two things you need for acting?" I was afraid to ever feel that unmoored again. My main note in acting was always "You think too much, Jennifer. You are too in your head." My sole objective was to not feel anything, so I was never a good actor. Though it would take me twenty years to realize that fact.

Gaining Ground, and Then Losing It

In 1988, I was a guest star on *Punky Brewster*, a popular television show. It was about a spunky little girl named Penelope, "Punky," who ends up getting adopted by an older man named Henry Warn-imont after she is abandoned by her mother in a supermarket. Weekly, in thirty-minute capsules broken up by commercials for Burger King, Prell Shampoo, Hamburger Helper, Rice-A-Roni, the show chronicled all their wacky adventures, as well as Punky's mis-matched socks and funky outfits and squad of friends and her ador-able golden retriever, Brandon. I was obsessed with the show. Coincidentally, when I was that age, I looked a lot like the show's star, Soleil Moon Frye, and people used to ask me for my autograph when I was at the mall. The writer of a play that was showing at the Santa Monica Playhouse, where I took all my acting and improv classes and performed in plays, was also a writer and producer on *Punky* and he called me in when they needed some bit players for a day role. I played a girl named Traci who was one of the Fireflys (think Girl Scouts). There was a deaf girl named Maria in the

Fireflys and we were making fun of her. The rest of the kids in the group, myself included, were laughing and pointing and giggling at her because she was deaf and spoke differently than we did and because she used sign language. The episode was called "What's Your Sign?" and I generally don't believe in signs, but this one is kind of in your face. How was I to know, at thirteen, that one day I would be like that Firefly who couldn't hear, who had to read lips and felt lost and alone and like everyone was laughing at me?

But back then I just loved acting. Especially being in live plays: the thrill of being onstage, of hiding in plain sight, the rush of nerves as the lights came up, and how I didn't know if I would remember my lines or not. Each time I was onstage, it felt like I might actually die of fright. I loved that electric shock of aliveness right before the possible death-by-fear took place. The not knowing jerked me into an awakeness I hadn't felt since my dad had died.

I wanted to matter as much as I had to my father when he brought home presents for me every night. I wanted to be a world to someone. I loved pretending the body I was in was no longer mine. I could avoid anything I felt by being someone else. It was the perfect escape route.

I FELT LIKE I was making progress, coming into my own. And so after we'd been in California for four years and two months, when my mother told me we were moving back to New Jersey, I thought she was kidding. We were living eight blocks from the beach in Santa Monica. The average daily temperature was 75 degrees. All. The. Time. My ghosts didn't live in sunny So Cal. They lived in South Jersey near the Shop N Bag grocery store off Route 38 in Pennsauken.

I had just finished seventh grade at Lincoln Middle School in Santa Monica, and I believed my acting career was taking off. I tried to get my mom to let me stay in California and live with friends. I was thirteen and she wouldn't let me. I hated her almost more than I hated myself. I believed she was "ruining my life" on top of letting my dad die. She was just a placeholder until I could find a true way to express my self-loathing. I needed someone to hate, someone to blame. My mom was the unlucky recipient of my vitriol, namely because of sheer proximity. She was the closest. I could reach out and touch her, even though I never did. I was mirroring my father's behavior toward her. I would withhold affection, I would direct all my anger toward her, I would blame her for everything. I was continuing his legacy.

Mom wanted to move back to New Jersey to be closer to her family. It seemed like the biggest lie I had ever heard and I had heard many by this point. She and Frank had broken up because he couldn't stop doing drugs, and on a visit home she'd reconnected with Brian, her high school boyfriend before my father. That was the real reason we were leaving.

We moved back for a man, although she would later explain that it was more complicated than that. It would take me until my late thirties to find compassion for my mother about this choice and so many other ones. I would have to see my own nuanced life, so much more than being able to be described in one word; I would have to see all the women who came to my workshops, and how nothing was ever just one way. I would have to realize that the Just-A Box was a place I tried to put not only myself, but everyone around me. How you could be abused and still miss your family. How you could have kids and not make every decision be about them. How you could feel grief and also relief. Maybe my mother moved back for all the reasons, but at the time, my thirteen-year-old mind could only judge.

Despite my pleading and my rants, we moved back to New Jersey, and that began my phase of being at war with myself in an entirely new and focused way.

CHAPTER 4

The Disappearing Act

I STARTED THE EIGHTH GRADE in Cherry Hill, New Jersey, at John A. Carusi Middle School. I was so depressed that I would sleep with a pillow over my head in case I was lucky enough to have it suffocate me in my sleep. I longed to be back in California with my *ex-stepdad*, Frank. In California, I hated him for the sheer fact that he was not my father, but by the time we had been dragged back to the pit of the earth (New Jersey), I would have happily lived with Frank for the rest of my life. Frank, who knew every single question on *Jeopardy!*. Frank, who took us to El Matador Beach in Malibu and showed us how to body surf and to not care about getting sand in our avocado and sprout sandwiches. We didn't eat avocados in Jersey in the eighties.

We moved into our own place in Erlton, an older part of Cherry Hill. It was a hundred-year-old house with a porch swing and blue steps and a church across the street. We didn't have any furniture. It was being shipped out from California and hadn't arrived yet, so we slept in sleeping bags on the living room floor in front of the TV. I read books while my mom and my sister fell asleep to whatever show was playing, *Murder, She Wrote; Unsolved Mysteries; Growing Pains; 227; The Golden Girls.*

I continued to be absent more days than I attended school. I blocked out the memory of those infections, but what I couldn't block out was loneliness and fear and that every other girl had the name Jennifer, so I changed mine to Jenni, then Jenna then Jenny then Jen. I didn't know what was going on with my ears, but the descent continued. And it would finally, fully deteriorate during my pregnancy with my son. To this day, no one knows exactly why I have hearing loss or tinnitus, but from the moment I was born, I had issues with my ears, as does my sister and my father's sister. Chronic ear infections, ringing, distorted hearing. My hearing loss has been progressive, from bad to worse to nearly absolute. I didn't understand that a lot of the loneliness I felt as a kid was because I wasn't hearing well, if at all. It was not something that I acknowledged, along with my grief, or anger.

I would rather stay home from school every day than struggle with the ringing in my head that I never talked about, let alone thought about. Like most things, I pretended it wasn't there. I didn't know that at some point it would resurface and I would have to look at it, address it. *Oh hello, pain. Hello, grief. Hello, ears. Hello, things whose existence I have denied.* I always pressed the phone into my head, hard, and I assumed that I did not pay attention, like all my teachers told me, so it would have never dawned on me that pressing the phone into my ears was a way to get myself closer to sound. The things we get used to. I have no idea how much I missed.

THAT YEAR I was stuck between worlds. All I did was try and get through the day without crying or going to the nurse's office, and then I'd come home and talk to my friends back in California until it was time to go to bed. I had my own line, which was a big deal. My mom was trying to get on my good side, seeing how depressed I was being back on the East Coast, so I also had call waiting.

I missed the acting I had been doing in Santa Monica because it had allowed me to express myself in ways I hadn't been able to, but I was not interested in what I thought would be silly regional Jersey theater camp. What a depressed elitist.

Eighth grade was a dark and moody nine months. I resented my mother for moving us back, I hated the weather and the way people spoke, I hated the way the girls wore their hair even though I wanted mine to look the same. I hated the *idea* of New Jersey more than I hated New Jersey. No one talked to me during those first few months on the bus, even after we moved into our own house and out of Aunt Gwen and Uncle John's. This was way before cell phones or iPads, so there was nothing to distract you from the *nobody likes me and I have no one to talk to so I will just sit and stare out the window or read.* I read a lot.

One day in the middle of eighth grade, my friend Jen called from California to tell me that my mom's soon-to-be ex-husband Frank (whom I had grown to finally think fondly of as my stepfather) had killed someone. Someone we knew, in self-defense.

The earth split in half and I fell in.

It can't be possible, I thought. Someone I knew and had begrudgingly loved had taken a gun and shot someone in a doorjamb. Someone we had just been living with had murdered someone? *This can't be,* I whimpered, swimming in mud and roots down in the rabbit hole.

I came out of the rabbit hole with braces (clear on top, metal on bottom) and, much to my amazement, started to like (maybe even love, just a little bit) New Jersey. The *I did it in self-defense* second husband of my mother really did do it in self-defense and eventually got out of prison on good behavior. (I wondered if my mother's first husband, my father, could also say *I did it in self-defense*. About all of it: the drugs, the cheating, his death. But how would my father justify what he did?)

THINGS KEPT GETTING better in ninth grade when I started being paid attention to by the older guys, and I felt validated because boys wanted me. I began to see my worth as being exactly equal to what I looked like, and I wondered if I could stay desirable, maybe no one would leave. I got tan. I fried my pale freckly skin with baby oil until I got sun poisoning and the red burn faded into a tan, and I was considered pretty. My breasts were big, I let my hideous bangs grow out and I started wearing eyeliner and lipstick. I wore textured Mexican Baja striped ponchos that were all the rage in 1990, Girbaud jeans and Doc Martens.

My insides were rotten, I knew that, but if I could make my outsides look good, I could fool the world. Or at least men. I wanted them all to want me, all the time. Once I got a taste of being wanted, I felt like I mattered. I was absolutely lost within myself, so I spent my time looking at the sea of faces of boys, wondering if I could somehow find my worth inside their desire of me.

Not to spoil the ending, but the answer was no.

IN MY WORKSHOPS, I meet so many women with body issues. It's like all of us have collectively swallowed a pill that made us believe our worth was equivalent to our appearances. *I am not enough* is the most common refrain, or mantra, I hear. No matter which city I am in. No matter what age group I'm in. Sometimes, even when I am teaching my GPower workshops for young people (G stands for "Girl" and for "Gender nonconforming"), girls as young as eight will share with me that they feel *fat, ugly, not enough.* They use those words.

They feel disgusting and ashamed. Broken. Old. Wrinkled. Fat. Crippled. Whatever it may be, and yet, we all talk about it and share our own stories of feeling the same shame and we find that we are living a lie. That our fuckability or hotness or weight means nothing, and when we hear each other, when we refuse to look away, we see ourselves. We see our perfectly imperfect selves in each other. We see how at one point or another we've all experienced searching for our value through someone else's validation. We understand what a shared world means. A shared world is a bearable world. And it's the only one we've got.

CHAPTER 5

Where Are You in Your Body Right Now?

I USED TO WORK in a supermarket in Margate, New Jersey, "down the shore."

Most of that summer is a blur of sunburns and beer and wanting to find someone to have sex with so I would no longer be the only virgin out of my girlfriends. I vividly remember the sound of items scanned into the register and how the ring-cling-beep sound became a kind of meditation. I had no other way to make it through the day of bagging and dragging Lucky Charms over the belt unless I lost myself in the sound of the beeps. $1.49. *Beep.* $7.98. *Beep.* 97 cents. *Beep.* (This was the early nineties, so you could still get something for under a dollar.)

I ate bagels and I drank bottles of beer at night. I was sixteen. I wanted to have sex because it seemed I was the last person on earth who hadn't, so I was always on the lookout for a potential guy to do it with. I finally found one. His name was Ethan and he wrestled. He was renting a shore house with a bunch of other guys from the Main Line area of Philadelphia. They were older, and I remember thinking none of them had faces. But they had bodies.

So I found the one with more of a face than the others and took him in the bedroom he shared with someone else, or his girlfriend for all I knew, and we attempted to have sex. I don't think we really did it, but I was sixteen and had no idea. I asked him, *Are we doing it?* It was humiliating, but I felt like I could sort of say I was no longer a virgin. I walked out of the house and never saw Ethan again. *Love me love me love me* was what I felt, but I hated myself, so it was hard to find someone who would counter this opinion.

I wish I could remember more about my time working at Casel's Supermarket, but all I remember is the sex that wasn't the sex, the feeling of *love me love me love me,* and I remember it was the last summer I ate bagels. It was the last summer before I started to starve the life out of myself. The last summer before I began, in earnest, to try to lose my body.

I was not quite seventeen years old, so I had my learner's permit but not my driver's license yet. My mother, never one to follow rules, and in an attempt to keep me happy, let me take the Isuzu Trooper out to go pick up Adam, my new boyfriend who lived a few miles away. She is also the most impulsive human on the planet (see: move to California then move back to New Jersey) and she probably said yes on a whim.

Adam was shy and quiet, and Jewish. I was going to go pick him up in the Trooper and bring him back to our house on Madison Avenue in Cherry Hill, New Jersey. Our house, at that time, was a revolving door.

My mother slept at her divorced boyfriend's house every other weekend, so I'd have these parties where we drank beer and did very dumb things and made very large messes. My house was the *cool house.* The family had the reputation of: *Let's go to Jen's, her mom lets us do whatever we want. Her mom doesn't care. Her mom is cool.*

The cool house never locked its door. Literally, my mom never locked *any* of our doors, which sends chills down my spine now (and did then as well). I was always getting up in the middle of the night to lock the front door, the back door, the basement door. So many doors. Everyone knew you could just walk into the cool house without knocking. *Jen's mom doesn't care.* I loved that she had that reputation of being the cool mom, and I would never have admitted this then, but I fantasized that she was strict, that she made me do my homework at night, that we had some sort of boundaries.

I played the part. *Yeah, we have no rules and it's the best!* Being the cool mom meant she left us alone on the weekends. She knew we had parties, and although she said she wasn't thrilled about it, she never stopped them. She kept leaving us alone and I kept having people over. I'd call my friend Randy and tell him I was "having people over" and he'd spread the word. It was me who threw the parties but my sister was always home. I usually banished her to her bedroom, but sometimes I would catch her drinking beer with the guys who went up to tease her or smoke cigarettes with her.

We got to stay home from school whenever we wanted and we didn't have curfews. My sister sneaked out a lot at night, smoked cigarettes, wore baggy jeans three sizes too big for her, and hung out with skaters. We did whatever we wanted.

It was chaos.

I picked up my almost-boyfriend Adam and we went up to my room. We made our way onto my bed and started kissing. I was filled with adrenaline because I had driven (illegally) to go get him on the other side of Cherry Hill. I was shaking. *I was a race car driver, I was a soccer mom, I was driving a convertible. I was behind the wheel. I was running the show.*

We turned the lights off and crawled into my twin bed and started making out with the duvet cover over our heads. At the time, my mother made curtains for people. She would wait to sew them until the night before, which is why she allowed me to go get Adam in the first place with only my learner's permit. She was down in the basement, pins in her mouth, some weird criminal show on TV (if there is one thing I can count on, it is my mom's love of cold case murder shows), a cold cup of tea next to the sewing machine, and yards and yards of fabric with which she had to make a Roman shade by nine a.m. the following day.

I was behind the wheel! I had a boy in my bed! I was running the show. I was an adult.

I took off my Champion sweatshirt. My heart was beating as his chest pressed into mine and I thought about how funny life was. How this boy with whom I'd gone to the Yeshiva school when I was five years old now lay next to and on top of me, under my glow-in-the-dark stars. At the Yeshiva school, we learned Hebrew all morning and only after lunch were we allowed to speak English. I didn't remember Adam from all those years back, it was the B.D.D. era (Before Dad Died), but still, how like life to do that. So many fortuitous occurrences, so many lightning cracks of chance that have to be examined with awe, because truthfully, how else can you explain ending up back in New Jersey after leaving P.D.D. era (Post Dad Died)?

He was on top of me. We still had our jeans on, bare chests pressing into each other. He wore Z Cavaricci jeans, smelled like Drakkar Noir, and had thick curly hair. So much hair. I felt a rush of heat between my legs, the ache of wanting to be filled that I would later transfer to my stomach.

This is a body. This is a body. This is a heart. This is a heart.

My own heart thumped so loudly it actually drowned out the thump of the feet stomping up the stairs. As they got to the top of the stairs my heart stopped beating. It was too late. I heard a gaggle of boys outside my door. *The cool house! Never locked! Go right in! Jen's mom doesn't care!*

The mafia of boys flicked the light on and jumped into my bed, thinking it was just me in there. Once they realized I wasn't alone, that there were two bodies in my little twin bed, they had a field day.

They flung my down comforter to the floor. My buddies: a group of rambunctious and horny teenage boys. I had girlfriends, too, but because we had the *cool house* reputation all the guys always came to hang out at our house, where they knew they could be obnoxious. They could drink beer and wine coolers and light their farts on fire on our front porch swing.

And there I was.

I have never wanted to disappear as much as I did in that moment.

Hysterical, I grabbed my now inside-out sweatshirt and covered my chest. They laughed and patted Adam on the back. The incident had sealed it for us. The humiliation bonded us. He'd become my "official" boyfriend in a breath, in a moment, as fast as a light switch flicking on. Although I am not sure how humiliated he actually was. He might have been sort of proud. My guy friends were the "popular" kids at school. There were ten of them and they had all seen me topless.

After they left, I swore I could never leave my house again. I could never show my face anywhere. I was too upset to drive so I made my mom drive my new boyfriend home and put her curtain making on hold, although I can't remember because like most of our great personal tragedies, they get murky with time.

Naturally, I blamed it on my mother. *Why can't you ever lock the doors?*

Instead of her being the cool mom, I wanted her to *force* me to do things and feel things. I wanted her to have made me deal with my grief over my dad's death instead of believing me when I said, "I'm fine." With everything left up to my own will, since a young age, I chose poorly. I wanted her to force me back into therapy and to have made me stick with it until I was an adult. Forever, even. I wanted her to make me do things for the rest of my life or else do them for me.

She didn't lock the doors, yet I locked everything in and everyone out.

I needed someone to blame for my humiliation. I blamed it on myself. I blamed it on my luck. I blamed it on my dad. I blamed it on my breasts. (*If they weren't so big, this wouldn't have been such a big deal*, I lamented.) I cried to my mom down in the basement as I lay next to the washing machine and all the dirty towels. I said that I could never go back to school, that my life was over. It felt mortifying to have my body seen by the guys. I got so much attention for the size of my breasts, so I was always trying to hide them under baggy sweatshirts. I felt exposed and vulnerable and insanely ashamed.

As much as I acted like I loved having the *cool house*, I knew that no one respected my home or my mom the way they did other people's houses and parents. My house was a no-consequence zone and everyone knew it. The walls were peeling in our kitchen and people would write their names with Sharpies next to the wall phone by the fridge when they opened it to get a drink or to see what food was there. In other homes, prison might have been the result of such behavior.

My friend Randy made me a mix tape to apologize—full of Morrissey and The Smiths, New Order and Steel Pulse, and all the bands we listened to on our way to house parties. I forgave the boys, and my mortification eventually turned into a funny story we would tell years later. *Remember when we walked in on you and Adam and scared you guys on your little bed? How upset you were? The look on your face! Remember when you guys slept in the wrong house down the shore, in a stranger's waterbed?*

I was months away from losing my breasts almost completely due to extreme weight loss from anorexia. The incident on the stairs (I visualize those boys as elephants stomping up the stairs) happened before a piece of me broke off. The piece of me that allowed myself small pleasures like cheesesteaks and hoagies and lying around on the sofa all weekend. That night the elephants walked in on Adam and me, I was still curvy and large-breasted. I wasn't exercising to the point of fainting on the StairMaster in my mom's bedroom. I was a beautiful teenage girl making out with her about-to-be boyfriend.

The boys seeing me topless was a precursor to my descent, or maybe it was the beginning of the breaking. I'd had self-loathing for a long time, but it was not as fine-tuned as when I moved deeply into anorexia months later. The self-hate was amorphous when I was sixteen, floating around, looking for something to latch on to. Self-hatred floating around the room like dust particles, more noticeable in the light. Switch the light on, *ah, there it is.*

I can pinpoint the actual moment my self-hate began to solidify into an eating disorder. I'd told a doctor that I wanted a breast reduction. He said, *You're crazy. You want smaller breasts? Lose five pounds.*

I lost five and ten and then twenty and finally twenty-five. I would not stop losing weight. I'd found a way to stop feeling. I only felt hunger. Eventually I learned to eat my own hunger. I'd press in the area between my ribs until I felt nauseous, and that would override it. The hunger would fade. The feeling of being hungry was something I became addicted to. The more depressed I felt, or sad, or upset, the hungrier I would let myself get. Adam had no idea what bad shape I was in, only that my body quickly morphed into a frail skeleton.

I got so much attention for my weight loss—perpetual scrutiny, constant critique, whispers behind my back and to my face. Jealousy from other girls who also believed their worth was equivalent to how small they could get, worry that I was dying, relentless comments on my body. I felt like I mattered more once I got skinny. What a bullshit story.

If I'd had smaller breasts, the night my friends saw my boobs would not have been any less mortifying, but I used to imagine it that way. As if I'd perhaps had tiny taut breasts, I would have been proud that they saw my perfect little body, instead of ashamed. An alternate ending like in those *Choose Your Own Adventure* books that I loved so much as a kid. I wanted to imagine a way out of my feelings.

Shame is a terrible, wondrous, and powerful thing. It can make us into ninety-pound sexless things. It can make us into shadows of who we were, of that person who once was behind the wheel.

That night in bed with Adam was the beginning of my recognition of self-hate. *I hate my body. I hate my body. I hate my body.*

But shame is fleeting. It will latch on to different things as needed.

How many things have been filed under *Shame* that could have been filed under *This Is What Young People Do, It's Not as Bad as You Think, You Have Nothing to Be Ashamed of, You Are Beautiful.*

I thought that if I could perfect my outside, no one would see how bad I was on the inside.

A Letter to Yourself

To this day I hold shame in my stomach, and also in my hands. But I also hold joy in my hands. I speak with my hands like my Yiddish Bubbe or the South Philly Italians I grew up with in Jersey—large, broad gestures, as if I need to be a mime artist for people to understand me. As if I need bodily accompaniment for my words. I touch a lot. I show that I am listening with my hands. But I also have great shame in my hands. I hate my fingers. My wrinkly fat fingers for which finding rings that fit is a challenge. The size of my hands, like a chubby little doll's instead of a grown woman's. I want to sit on my hands and hide them from people. But I also use them to love, to write, to pick up my son. How can so many things be two things at once? I focus on this a lot in my workshops, the duality of everything. How we can be two, or many, things at once.

MY BELLY HAS never been flat, except for about a year when I was fading away from anorexia, but even then, it was protruded, like a starving child's might be. I, like many women, fight the urge to believe that my self-worth is equivalent to my physical appearance. *I am thin and good. I take up less space and therefore I am valuable. I am pretty, so I am worth something.* These are all bullshit stories.

When I see people, I want to hide, as if they will notice my stomach has a bulge, or I have gained weight, and they will think I am terrible. I feel my stomach gurgle, and my hands, the cohorts in shame, rush to my middle and rub it, as if to make it disappear. The disappearing act, the one tried for so many years, by depriving my-self of food, and love.

Sometimes when I feel shame, it's loud, as if my IA has a mega-phone for my deaf ears and I feel it there, in my gut. I feel a million eyes staring at me, which is a real joke, because no one is looking; we are all too busy worrying about ourselves. A million eyes and fingers grabbing at the rolls on my stomach. I think about food. I think about wine. I think about how tomorrow I will deny myself all sorts of things so I can go back to taking up less space. My hands cover my stomach, the place I had a baby die, the place I grew a baby.

I am far from perfect now, but as I go through these moments of self-doubt or when my IA is especially loud, I share it instead of act-ing like I have all the answers. I sit and get quiet and connect to being in my body in a way I was literally never able to do until my thirties. I listen for clues, for answers, for questions. I listen to any-thing my body has to say because it always has something to say. Lidia Yuknavitch likes to say, *Your body has a point of view*. In our workshops, I ask participants to write from where they feel most connected in their body at that moment.

They write letters from their back or their shoulders or their hearts or whatever body part (including their head if they feel stuck there), and from there, I ask them to find a mantra, or mind tattoo, that opens them up as opposed to shutting them down. Say someone writes from the shoulders something like, "I'm tired. I feel like I am holding up a world. I need a break." A mantra they might plant in their mind to replace their Inner Asshole's mantra or their bullshit story might be: *Let go*. Or maybe, *I deserve a break*. Or maybe, *I don't need to carry so much*. Or maybe, *This isn't mine*. The choice is theirs, but when they drop in and listen from a place of being in their body, it's immediately obvious what is needed. I ask the room, *If your body*

could tell you something instead of shutting down, what would it tell you?
I never listened to my own body because my IA was a megaphone in my head, a broken record repeating itself a thousand times a day: *Do Not Feel. It Is Not Safe to Feel. You Are a Bad Person. You Do Not Deserve Anything.*

I encourage other people to take up space, which is a relatively new thing for me. I spent so long wanting to disappear that the idea of taking up space in the world feels like a crime.

It isn't.

Your emotions are always holding something for you until you are ready to tell the story that will change your life. With my deaf ears I have learned to listen to the telling, unlike as a young adult when I starved it away and pushed my sadness back into my body as I cried in my sleep from hunger.

CHAPTER 6

Sisters, Stepfathers, "Friends"

SENIOR YEAR OF HIGH SCHOOL I took a pill called Diet Pep and hid in the library at lunch so no one would get on my case about not eating. If I did eat, I would eat two apples and force myself to drink a gallon of water. I was always peeing and also shaking from the diet pills. I would make sure anything I put in my mouth had zero fat and I swore off wheat, dairy, eggs, oil, and meat. Adam and I were still together, and he and my mom often conspired to get me to eat. My mom would cry and say that I looked like a boy. "Your ribs stick out! You are going to die," she'd wail. I knew I had a problem, but I didn't think it would affect my future or if I would be able to have kids or not or any of the nonsense she was throwing at me because I had a theory that I would not be around for any of that. She threated to send me away to an eating disorder recovery center, to therapy, to a hospital. But she never did and I held it against her along with a million other transgressions.

We acted like sisters who bickered, more than like mother and daughter most of the time, whereas by this point in my teenage years, my sister hated me because I ignored her. She is erased from my teen memories, only to pop back in when I was twenty-one and we began to grow close. My mom was like my sister and my real sister was smoking cigarettes and sneaking out of the house. She fought with my mom all the time. It was like she was trying to live out her role as "problem child." My sister's hatred was validation of my hatred of myself. She always felt like I was favored, first by my father and then my mother, and when I was fading away from an eating disorder, I got even more attention.

A year after I graduated high school, she would inform my mother that she was dropping out of high school and going to live in Philadelphia where she would get her GED and work in a health food store. I would already be gone and my mom, disciplinarian she was not, let her. I was furious with my mother.

"She needs discipline," I yelled into the phone. "She needs a mom, not a sister!"

Despite this insight, I kept abusing myself. I would pour baby oil on my skin and get sun poisoning because I hated how pale I was. I ran for two hours a day and did the StairMaster in my mom's bedroom for another hour and then I went into the basement and lifted weights next to the washing machine and the dirty clothes. Adam never knew what to do or say. When we first started dating, I was a healthy teenage girl. By the time I was graduating from high school, I looked like a Boy Scout. No hips, no chest, tiny legs, bony knees. People called me a lollipop because my head looked too big for my body, and I told them to stop teasing me but inside I was shouting, *More, more, more.*

Sick equaled thin and thin got me noticed. Being noticed made me feel loved. That was my objective, and I wasn't acting at all.

What Is a Body?

A couple of weeks before I graduated high school, I got a call that made the world shake again. I was sitting on the sofa in our den reading *The Bluest Eye* by Toni Morrison when the phone rang.

"Hi, Jen? It's Christine." Christine was Frank's sister-in-law, although she had never been married to Frank's brother, but they had two kids together and I didn't know how else to describe her so I called her my aunt. Another *not-aunt* aunt.

"Where's your mom?" my *not-really-aunt* Aunt Christine asked.

"She's down the shore installing a drapery."

"Tell her to call me as soon as she can," she cried into the phone.

"Christine. What is it? What's wrong?"

She paused for so long that I thought she hung up. "Hello?" I asked.

"Frank died," she said, and I have no memory of the rest. I left my body and floated up to the ceiling where I looked down and saw a skeletal girl with a book on her lap and a phone by her ear, pulling her eyebrows out. I hung up the phone and ran for three hours straight around Cooper River Park in Pennsauken, where we had lived before my dad died. I hooked my Walkman to my waistband and stared off into space as I ran and tried to enter the space ahead but I could never catch it.

Frank had died in his sleep. He was thirty-nine years old. My dad had been thirty-eight. All three of us flew out to California to help sort his things and go to his funeral—me, my mother, and Rachel. I was one week away from graduating high school and it had been almost ten years to the day since my father had died. We went to the beach in Malibu for Frank's service, where his brother Tom paddled out on a surfboard and scattered his ashes. I was freezing even though it was June and warm. I had no body fat at all and the adrenaline from the funeral made me shake even harder. My mom was constantly sneaking olive oil and her beloved ghee into things she made for me—black beans and stews we lovingly called "mush," with eggplant, lentils, mushrooms, anything in the fridge—hoping to make me gain weight. If I caught her I would cry and refuse to eat. I was in control. At least I felt like I was. Nothing could have been further from the truth. I was spiraling. *You can't make me do anything,* I would yell, even though I always secretly wished my mother would force me to get help.

I was supposed to read a poem I had just written for Frank after I found out he'd passed but I couldn't. I had started to cry and then something broke in me and I could not stop crying. I could not get up and read the poem because I was sobbing and shaking so hard. Ten years of tears came out of me on that beach. I had not cried for my father except once in that acting class in Santa Monica years earlier, but there I was, crying for both of these dead fathers, stomach growling, my fingernails purple, some stranger's sweater I would forget to return holding me together like wool glue. I was afraid that if I took the sweater off, I would crumple into the sand, so I pulled it tighter around my bony shoulders as I chanted *JB* to myself. *JB. Just breathe, Jen.* But I couldn't. I had held in ten years' worth of tears. I couldn't breathe, and yet, from my waterless body came a whole ocean. I drowned in my own salt water.

I wanted to go back in my fantasy time machine, the only thing I ever wanted in life, and re-meet Frank. I would like him this time. I would not resist his affections or resent him for not being my dad. I would tell him how I loved his bathtub fish and his habits of colleting cacti and running barefoot. I would tell him I was sorry for being a jerk in the beginning. *I was just sad,* I would say. I couldn't have said it all those years ago but I would say it now, *Frank, I was just really sad and I missed my daddy. I didn't hate you.*

We threw roses into the ocean and the waves took them out to sea. I still couldn't breathe, so someone else read the poem I wrote. In hindsight I wish I had gotten up and read it because then that memory of me, up there in the burning sun, in front of all those people, would be buried somewhere in my body.

I was glad we weren't burying Frank, that, instead, we were sprinkling his ashes in his beloved Pacific Ocean. I wished we had done that for my dad. I took another rose and pretended it was my father's body and I walked down to the edge of the water and said, *Here,* and *I am sorry.*

I spent the summer in California, hanging out with my friends I'd left behind before New York University started in the fall. I'd stay at Christine's. I spent most days lying out on her driveway in my little blue-and-white bikini from Marshalls, baby oil slathered on my body, and then I'd exercise four hours a day in the bright sunshine. Most of my friends had summer jobs or were doing something productive, whereas I was just trying to fry and run the stairs.

I would walk to the Santa Monica Stairs, a set of steps that leads down into the Santa Monica Canyon, which have been converted (despite the neighbors' chagrin and protesting) into an outdoor gym. Every day, with my Walkman hooked onto my spandex shorts, I'd speed-walk past the park on the corner of Lincoln Boulevard and California Avenue and a bunch of men playing basketball. One day as I walked by, one of the men, whom I recognized as an actor I had just seen in a movie, asked me out. He asked his friend to hold the ball and walked over to me as I did my little walk on by. I'd be lying if I said I hadn't noticed him every single day. I timed my walks so they would be the same time as his pickup games with his boys. He wore a bandana and had long hair.

He came to pick me up that night in his big car with a beer can in between his legs. That should have told me everything I needed to know about the dude. His thighs squeezed a can of Michelob in place as he drove. We went to see *In the Line of Fire* and he asked me to sit on his lap during the movie. As embarrassed as I was, I did it. All ninety pounds of me sat on an older drunk man's lap in a movie theater with a mixture of excitement and disgust. I didn't want to, but I thought that maybe it was what adults did on dates? And was I just being a prude and overly self-conscious to say no? After the movie, which I remember none of, we went to the Circle Bar on Main Street in Venice, where I proceeded to get wasted because I weighed nothing and I ate nothing and five vodka and cranberries were just too much on all that nothingness. We ended up back at his place with him on top of me and inside of me until I yelled, *Stop, wait. Get a condom*, which thankfully, he did. When he came back, I told him I had changed my mind and didn't want to have sex. He was angry, I apologized. We got dressed and he drove me to Christine's.

I barfed red chunks all over his Cadillac and he kissed me and my red chunk mouth before I apologized again for what I thought of as ruining the night. *Why apologize when you've simply said no?* one might wonder. Why apologize when you've done nothing wrong except be an eighteen-year-old girl who'd made a couple of really dumb choices? Why apologize for having a body, which is, essentially, what all the starvation was about?

I felt ruined after that night. Another thing I needed to feel guilty for because I was still dating Adam and I was convinced I had gotten AIDS from Bandana Dude. It was the height of AIDS paranoia, and all anyone talked about was the fear of catching AIDS.

I was a ruined person and had been for a long time. Ruin ruin ruin. *You ruin everything, Jen.*

That summer, all I could think about was my body. I went on a cross-country camping road trip with my mom and Brian, the man we left California for, and his two children. I thought I was such a martyr because I opted to go on the trip instead of staying home and exercising for four hours a day, which is all I wanted to do. Exercise and writing down what I had taken bites of that day. *One bite of pasta. One bite of a potato. Three bites of tuna. Rice cakes. Couple of dried peaches. Two pretzels.*

CHAPTER 7

Fear and Loathing in New York

GROSS.

Gross was the word I used the most when I thought about myself. I felt gross all the time. My mantra, the mind tattoo I had on repeat, was, *I am so gross.* I decided that I would start a cleanse before NYU started in the fall, so I cut out all wheat, yeast, flour, dairy, meat. No sugar. During the cross-country trip with my mom and her boyfriend and his kids, I got anxious and wanted nothing more than to get out of the minivan. I wanted to go home, I hated the way I looked, I hated the way I felt in my body. *Gross.* Sitting in the car for so long, I was positive I gained at least ten pounds. I obsessed about what I ate, what I didn't eat, how much I had exercised, how much I would deprive myself the next day. Rules, rules, rules: all impossible to follow. And it was always about the next day. Tomorrow I will start not eating. Tomorrow I will stop being bad. Tomorrow I will be good. Today I will feel guilty for not starting until tomorrow.

Tomorrow I was going to college. Which seemed impossible, because I had barely made it through high school, but I was so ready to get out of Cherry Hill, New Jersey. I applied early decision to

NYU General Studies Program, which was a two-year program within NYU that allowed you to transfer to any other school within NYU after two years. I did terribly on my SATs, I missed more school days than I attended, not because I was sick but because I simply didn't feel like going and my mom didn't make me. My ear infections had ended as I hit puberty but my disdain for school and rules had not. I didn't do any extracurricular activities. I took my little Volkswagen and drove home most days after third period. There was no way I could get into any other school within NYU besides GSP with my track record. I was ashamed that it was "just" the General Studies Program, so I never mentioned that part to people. (*That damn Just-A Box again.*) I didn't know that it would be the best thing that ever happened to me, the highlight of all my college years, the most intimate classes I had ever had, the most caring and attentive teachers. I just felt dumb and gross, but I was happy to be escaping New Jersey even if it meant I would be paying back college loans for the rest of my life on a degree I never finished.

I felt riddled with guilt over having had *sort of sex* with Bandana Dude while I was still with Adam. As usual, I wanted to go back in time and redo the past, a feeling that consumed me. *If only I could go back and change it,* I thought at least once a minute. I would not have killed my father with my words *I hate you,* I would not have cheated on Adam. I replayed things that occurred in irreversible succession and imagined that time wasn't real and I could move moments around like chess pieces, that the events of our lives, specifically my life, were not irreversible at all. That instead of being immovable and fixed in some space-time continuum, I could adjust the things that happened at will. I wrote in my journal: *I probably have AIDS, I am a bad person, I'm sorry, I need a tan.* Over and over.

My college roommate Stephanie and I were both from New

Jersey, which surprised me because I had never met anyone like her before, especially not in New Jersey. Her creativity was disarming. I knew she would be famous one day (and she is except she goes by Stephonik now). She looked like a model with her long red hair and she sang like Björk and she painted and wrote and took photographs. I felt short and talentless next to her, but she thought I was a poetic genius. She was the most curious person I had ever met, always asking me questions that sparked new ideas and new poems.

We moved our dorm room desks next to each other so it looked like one long wooden desk, and we sat up all night on our Apple computers and wrote poems, about our bodies, our families, the boys we thought about. We lived in a suite on the seventeenth floor of Hayden Hall, on the west-side corner of Washington Square Park, smack-dab in the middle of Greenwich Village. I mastered the art of fooling people when it was time to eat. If I knew I was going out to eat, I would starve myself for a whole day so I could eat at a restaurant. I wanted to fool everyone, so I acted as if I ate whatever I wanted, with abandon, and my teeny-tiny frame was just my bone structure. Everyone saw through me, of course. Also, once I allowed myself food, I usually couldn't stop. I would overorder and overeat and the rush of adrenaline from the excitement of food was better than an orgasm until I got home and hated myself.

I ate rice cakes with creamed honey, or dried peaches that my mom sent me from Trader Joe's in care packages, hoping to convince me to eat something. Or else I just sucked on puffed corn cereal so I wouldn't faint in classes. I took Super Dieter's Tea and Diet Pep, a diet pill made from ephedra that made me feel suicidal and more depressed, but I thought it made me look skinny. I eventually stopped taking Diet Pep after they pulled it from shelves. Most days I didn't eat all day and then found myself awake, sitting on the kitchen floor of our suite eating cold rice from a Chinese take-out container, or a stale muffin from the trash. I didn't sleepwalk. I sleepate. I wouldn't even remember until I saw wrappers by my bed the next morning.

IT FELT LIKE our life in that dorm would last forever. I thought I would live in that building for the rest of my life. Time was dead to me, a thing other people experienced but I only had a vague idea of. I would nod and pretend I was like a normal person with normal notions of time, but it felt impossible for me to talk about what I would be doing the following summer, let alone in five years, or what I wanted to do with my life. My life? My life was right there on that seventeenth floor, paintbrush in my hand, stomach growling, which only ever made me feel powerful, like I could handle anything. *Fuck you, hunger,* I thought. *I am strong. I am stronger than you. Fuck you. You can't touch me.*

I could not imagine a future, so the idea that one day in June of 1994 we would leave the dorm room and move on was not even a morsel of a thought in my head. If I started to think about even two months into the future, I would have panic attacks. I would pace and call Adam, who was at college in Boston, and ask, "What are we going to do this summer? You aren't going to break up with me, right? We'll always be together? Right? Right?" I needed a guarantee all the time that he wouldn't leave me. *It's going to be okay, right?*

After our conversations, which were always pretty much the same—me begging for a promise that he would never leave, him saying he wouldn't—I paced and paced and then when I couldn't stand it anymore, I'd go into the bathroom and pick my face, trying to fix myself. I dug so deep into my skin that I bled. Of course I went for my face; I needed something to attack. And it was right there.

When I exhausted the landscape of my face, I turned my attention to my favorite obsession. I pushed on my stomach, my diaphragm, and made sure it felt empty. In my imagination I could push my arm all the way through to the other side. *I am empty! I am strong!*

I wrote poems about being jealous of a tree because it could live on air. I wrote about branches, and loss, and hanging on. I wrote poems every moment that I was awake, and while I was asleep, too. I lived poetry—felt the cadence of words on my tongue and the end of a line in my bones.

As busy as I was writing my poems, being jealous of trees, thinking about my skin, trying to push my arm through my stomach, I was also starting to realize that other things were happening. That other people suffered.

Halfway through freshman year, a kid in one of the rooms below us jumped to his death. Fifteen floors. We heard the sound of his body hitting the pavement below and then the frantic cries of the people who had seen it. I'll never forget that thud. The sound of a body that couldn't take it anymore. A body who couldn't stand himself in the mirror. That sound haunted me as I tried to write poems about my father and my stepfather and my own body. *Thump.* I hated myself, but at the time I thought this act took courage, and I would never have the courage to jump from the sixteenth floor onto a dumpster. And besides, if I jumped out of a window, I would ruin my mom and Rachel's lives, and I had already ruined enough.

A few weeks after my NYU neighbor died, my mom called to tell me that Susan Litwin was dying. Susan was Jessica Litwin's mother, the woman who had painted me the *Annie* sweatshirt that I wore all the time before my dad died. Maybe their house wasn't so lucky after all. Maybe the idea that everyone besides me was lucky was a bullshit story? This was my first insight that began to unravel the lies I had told myself since my father died. In my workshops now, I ask people to go deep and look at what bullshit stories may be governing the pages of their own lives. *Everyone besides me has a good life; everyone else is lucky; it's easy for everyone else; God hates me; I'm fat; I'm a terrible person; I'm doing it all wrong; things will never get better; I will never change; I'm too tired; I'm a failure.*

CHAPTER 8

Doing and Undoing Pain

MY MOM SAID she'd gone to see Susan at her home, where she was in hospice, and Susan told my mom that she was going to go be with Mel, my father. "Mel came to see me last night," she said. "I'm going where he is." She knew she was about to die that night. My mom relayed this to me as I wrapped and unwrapped the phone cord around my finger.

When she died, I didn't go to her funeral. I didn't want someone else's funeral to take the place of the funeral I hadn't gotten to go to. If I hadn't been able to say good-bye to my father, I didn't want to say good-bye to a neighbor. Later, I would come to understand that my mom hadn't known what to do with two girls, five and eight. She'd wanted to make the right decision. Someone had advised her that being at our father's funeral would be the wrong decision, that it would damage us, and she had listened, and instead it was the not going that had caused the damage. But we listen to people when we're not sure if we should go right or left.

I COULDN'T BEAR to think of Jessica not having a mother anymore, so I picked my face.

I ate dried fruit and pushed on my stomach. Every night, I checked to make sure I could feel all my ribs, the sharp angle of my hipbones. Checking my body was the only thing that made me feel safe, and I asked everyone, all the time: *Is it going to be okay? It's going to be okay, right? Right?*

No matter the truth; I simply wanted to be told: *Yes, yes, it is all going to be okay.*

I've always been afraid of disappearing, so I used to look in the mirror compulsively to check to see if I was still there.

But I've also been just as afraid of being here.

The Shame Wall

Shame comes up all the time in my workshops. Recently someone asked me why I used to feel so much shame at being hard of hearing. She looked confused, as if she could not comprehend the feeling. I explained that I wasn't sure why, that shame wasn't logical, it often made no sense and was derivative of something else. I felt like I was broken and that was the biggest source of my shame. She nodded and started to cry.

"I feel broken, too," she said, as she explained to me how her father had just died and she was going through a divorce in a small town and felt like a failure for her marriage not working.

Once, after seeing their show at The Groundlings Theatre in West Hollywood, I took this intimate workshop with two women who created something called *Taboo Tales*. I read their tag line and felt like it was speaking right to me: *The more we talk about how fucked up we are, the more normal we all feel.* I was pregnant at the time of the workshop and weaning down on my antidepressants (which I wound up staying on after all, just at a lower dose). They had us do this exercise where we wrote about something that caused us shame but that we wouldn't want anyone to know.

I share mostly everything, so this was hard for me. But I came up with the time I stole in high school; the one time I hitched a ride with a stranger in a parking lot of the Cherry Hill Mall because security had been after me. It was not my finest moment.

They then asked us to write down words that we thought people might say about us, if they only knew. I wrote words like *thief, fraud, liar, bad, horrible person*. Other people wrote words like *whore, cheat, bad person, bad mom, deformed*. It was horrifying looking at all the words. But what we realized in that moment was that those words were the reasons we don't share our stories.

In other words, those words were in the voice of our Inner Assholes. I loved the exercise so much I brought a variation of it to my workshop. I had everyone put their words all over the wall and I dubbed it "the Shame Wall." I tell the people in the room that we are going to dismantle the Shame Wall. That the work of our lives was dismantling the Shame Walls we've built on our bodies, literally as armor.

Sometimes I have people pick words off the wall and burn them or destroy them in some symbolic way that demonstrates action being taken toward disrupting the shame that we have living inside of us. Sometimes people stand in front of the Shame Wall and weep, recognizing words that others wrote that they also carry. *Pig, fat cow, monster, liar, slut, crazy.*

THAT WHOLE FIRST YEAR at NYU, I rode the Peter Pan bus to visit Adam at the University of Massachusetts in Amherst as I listened to "Tiny Dancer" and "Levon" by Elton John on my Walkman until the battery ran out. I wrote poems on the bus under the dim overhead light from my seat.

Adam had no idea that I was struggling with the *sort of sex* I had in California. He knew I had fooled around with an older man (I told him) but didn't know I had convinced myself I had contracted AIDS. We'd hit a rough patch a few months before, when he'd broken up with me because the more he thought about me being with someone else, the more he couldn't bear it. After a few weeks of being broken up and listening to The Cranberries and Counting Crows CDs on repeat, we got back together and I felt like I could breathe again. I told myself I would not survive if we didn't get back together. Losing Adam felt similar to the loss of my father. *This is my fault,* I wrote on little sticky notes to myself.

I no longer could find the mantra of *I am strong. I will not cry.* I stopped being able to function. I just wanted my mom. I couldn't stop crying. I felt like I was forgetting to breathe, so I would write *JB* on my wrist to remind myself *Just Breathe Just Breathe Just Breathe.* *JB. JB. JB.*

But then we got back together and I felt a smidge of safety again in the world, like there was a raft I could cling to that wouldn't disappear. Every other Thursday, I took the bus to Massachusetts. Every Sunday night I cried all the way home. I talked to the people sitting next to me and extracted secrets from strangers. A woman's bony shoulder pressed into mine while she told me that she was scared of planes, but that her son and his wife lived in California and she would like to get out there someday. She drank bourbon from a brown bag, her yellow teeth stuck to dry lips. I thought about how we're all scared of something.

After we had been going out for four years, two of those years long-distance Massachusetts/New York, Adam broke up with me over the phone. By then, I was living in a graduate housing dorm on 25th Street between Second and Third Avenues. Junior year I hadn't paid in time and NYU had run out of room in the regular dorms, so I got housed in a hotel called South Gate Towers off Seventh Avenue.

Adam came to the hotel on his weekends to visit me in New York and we loved the fact that we were in a real hotel room (with a kitchen!) instead of a dorm room. In New York City. Second semester of junior year I moved to a recently erected building full of grad students and me. Again I had my own place. I got dirty looks every day, especially from the grad students who had roommates.

I called Adam to see if he'd decided if he wanted to sublet an apartment over the summer with me. It was February, and my big idea was to get him to commit to an apartment with me even though the idea of summer seemed like ten years away. I never made plans for the future, but this was an exception. This was survival.

"I can't do this anymore," he said, barely above a whisper.

"What?" I said, the ground dropping out beneath me, the noise on 25th Street fading away like I was in a sound vacuum.

"I think we should take a break," he said as I heard voices in the background. I heard a girl's voice.

"Why are you talking so softly?" I asked.

"I'm sorry, Jenny."

"No," I said. Just no.

"Jen, I'm telling you. I think we should do our own thing this summer."

"Don't you love me anymore?" I cried, walking back and forth, as far as the phone cord would let me travel.

"I do, but I think we need to take some time."

"No. You don't get to do this over the phone after four years—"

"Jen, come on."

"No, you come on," I yelled. "How dare you pull this bullshit. You don't even have the courage to look at me!"

"I'm sorry. I'll call you tomorrow," he said, and hung up.

He'd transferred from UMass to Boston University and was living in downtown Boston. Naturally I got on the Peter Pan bus, a teary-eyed, skinny, and freezing mess, schlepping all the way to Boston in the snow so he could break up with me to my face.

I spent the weekend in his apartment in downtown Boston, curled in a ball, listening to Sarah McLachlan's *Fumbling Towards Ecstasy* album and sobbing. And when he put my spaghetti-limp body on the bus back to New York City, he hugged me for three solid minutes. I felt his familiar body against my skeletal frame, and again I had hope: *Maybe he won't let go.* Eventually he did and that was the last time I saw him for years.

After I went back to school, I left my body completely. I have no memory of those last few months from February to May, when the semester ended.

I couldn't pay attention. I couldn't eat. I couldn't sleep. I started getting further and further behind in my classes until I was completely lost. I was incoherent with hunger and heartbreak and also, looking back, I couldn't hear. The damage was nowhere as severe as it would later become, but the ringing was there and some hearing loss, despite the fact that I would not face it. By the time I was twenty-two, I accepted my hearing was going because I was taking acting classes and I couldn't hear a thing unless I sat in the front row and read lips. I had gotten so used to being disconnected from what was happening with my body that I ignored my progressive deafness until I was forty years old and completely deaf without the help of hearing aids.

Virginia Woolf, Walter Pater, Thomas Hardy, the anthology of American literature, it all blended in and I was too hungry to read. I asked my professors if I could take incompletes and turn in my papers later, as well as taking my finals late. I had done so well the first three years of school, I was always sitting at the front of the class and staying after and asking questions.

I promise it'll only be a few months, I said to my teachers. Famous last words.

Something had opened up inside of me that I couldn't close. I took the purple NYU trolley to my classes, since I didn't have the energy to walk. I got off at my stop and climbed the four flights to my room. By the time I made it up the stairs, I wanted to faint. I lay flat on the kitchen floor, waiting for my laxative tea to brew, fantasizing about my time machine. I ate nothing except dried seaweed and alfalfa sprouts, like a little sandwich, with fat-free honey mustard dressing on it. I allowed myself three of them but I would dream of hamburgers and oatmeal. The way the oatmeal might fall on my tongue and how it might feel like my face when it hit the ground, pavement in my mouth. I was losing consciousness at night on my dirty kitchen floor.

I lost all sense of where I was in time and space. Something ripped apart and I wanted my father back. *I am not strong. Why did you leave me?*

One night, I heard C. K. Williams read his work, along with a bunch of other well-known poets. I sat in the front, as usual. The poem "The Question" was the one that did it—I looked up from my notes and stared right through C.K., right to the center of the

world, and was only brought back when he finished the poem, those
last few lines

> *No, last summer in Cleveland I didn't have a lover, I have never*
>   *been to Cleveland, I love you.*
> *There is no Cleveland, I adore you, and, as you'll remember,*
>   *there was no last summer:*
> *The world last summer didn't exist yet, last summer still was*
>   *universal darkness, chaos, pain.*

Ah, I thought. He is undoing pain. Would you look at that? He is
unmaking what he has carefully, or not so carefully, made.

Ah, I remember thinking with my twenty-one-year-old brain, *I
can go back and reconfigure.*

Watch what I can do.

"I WOULD NEVER dance in public."

"I would never sing in front of strangers."

"I can't cry in front of people."

"I can't feel things."

All the things that people say they can't do when they walk into
my workshops, I tell them to remember them all. I tell them to
memorize the energy of the room during opening circle, or in the
first few minutes of a workshop, and to remember that moment,
when fear has alchemized into love. When shame has begun to
evaporate a little. All the things we think we can't do. I am reminded
of my twenty-one-year-old self during these moments, how I used
to think, *Watch what I can do.* How so many of us can do what we
thought was impossible. We can start over. We can heal. We can

feel. We can live with heartbreak. We can sing a goddamned off-key tune in front of others.

It's one of my favorite moments in a workshop, when someone has a breakthrough, a moment of utter surprise or delight at themselves. "Wow, I did not think I would cry." "I did not think I would have so much fun dancing like a big old dork." And that opening up happened because of this sentiment, the one I've come to live by: *I got you.* Those words mean something. They mean everything.

What Words Can Do

I started molding with language, building places I could revisit, even if I never visited them the first time. I began to tear down my own Clevelands as if they never existed, and, for all I knew, maybe they hadn't. I was starting to understand that something could be two things at once—that something could be there and also not be there.

I thought about my bus rides through the snowy northeastern winters to see Adam in Massachusetts. I started to look for signs of duplicity. Here is love and here it is gone. Just like that. *Existing and not existing*, I thought, after that last time I rode the bus to see him, for good. I began to erase my Cleveland before it swallowed me whole and left me on the floor by a cheap futon bed on Boylston Street, staring out the window at the take-out Thai place with its broken flashing neon sign. *I deserve more than a phone call. I deserve more than this,* I said to the snow falling from the window that wouldn't close all the way. *I deserve more than this,* I said to the claw-legged tub that only ran cold water.

I loved C.K. because his poetry ran on—it seemed to have no

horizon, no ending point. I felt like he was talking to only me (isn't that what all good writing does?), singling me out in a room full of shoelace-faced students. I felt like he was whispering into my freezing ears. *This is what poetry can look like,* he said. *This is what words can do.* As he conversed with me through his poems, he taught me what was possible. If it weren't for him (and a few other poets who crawled into my slowly-going-deaf ears), right at that particular moment in time, I might still be riding the C train without the knowledge that words could change the world. I didn't quite realize the capacity they had until these poets (Rita Dove, Donna Masini, Louise Glück, Naomi Shihab Nye, Lucille Clifton, Joy Harjo, C. K. Williams, Derek Walcott, Seamus Heaney, Sharon Olds, Stanley Kunitz) quietly, without so much as a word of warning, showed up. They marched in and planted their word-flags, and even when they left, their flags kept waving for me so that no matter where I went, I had a place that felt like home. These words were the only thing keeping me tethered.

My father, Frank, now Adam. All gone. I read André Breton's poem "Free Union." This line: *My wife ... Whose waist is the waist of an otter caught in the teeth of a tiger,* and I couldn't go on. It was a poem about how much he loved his wife. I didn't want to see any evidence in the world that there were people who stayed in love, of men who didn't leave.

Every night I lay flat on the floor of my apartment and wondered if I was having a nervous breakdown. Was I too young for a nervous breakdown? I looked like a little boy, with my narrow hips, and I thought if I kept getting smaller and smaller I would eventually be back in my eight-year-old body and everything could be rearranged. Or else I would just eventually disappear.

I was so disconnected from my body that I didn't think I could do or be or accomplish anything that mattered, and so I dropped out of college. At the time I said, "Just for a semester," but it ended up being forever. I became a waitress near my mother's work, in California, at a restaurant that needed a hostess. I had never told the truth to myself, so telling myself I would go back to NYU in the fall was a comfortable lie, it fell easily from my lips, just as others had. *I don't care that he died. I ate today. Just a semester.* I figured I could be a hostess because I was good with people, even though I had never worked in a restaurant. How hard could it be? And anyway, it was just going to be for a summer. (Lie. Bullshit story.)

I was back in this place full of light, but it would take me a long time to find it.

CHAPTER 9

The Just-A Box

You Are Never "Just" an Anything

AFTER MY MOM moved back to California for the second time in our lives, she rented a big studio off Robertson Boulevard in West Hollywood, where she sewed curtains, made draperies, and ran her business. She called it "King's Road Ltd," because it was her dream to go to King's Road in London one day. She started to rent a studio out to actors and photographers and acting teachers. King's Road Ltd became "Back Alley Studios." I took acting classes with two of the teachers as a trade to knock off some of their rent. They were both terrible. Or else I was. Or maybe both.

My mom met a man named Robert who was making a short film and renting the studio. Mom said she wanted me to meet Robert, that he was a writer and so was I and I can't remember what else she said except that he was British and sweet. So we went to this restaurant near my mom's studio called The Newsroom. I was twenty-one and weighed eighty-nine pounds. My hair was long and dark and hung to my waist.

Those were my severe anorexia days, but I could still find things at The Newsroom like a fruit plate or a salad called "It's Alive! It's

Alive!" that was all vegan and raw with a piece of sprouted wheat-free bread on the side. The food was delicious and the menu was huge, so the three of us went for lunch.

The Newsroom was supposed to be a riff on an actual newsroom. The servers' shirts said *All the food . . . that's fit to eat* and there was a newsstand in front with hundreds of magazines and newspapers. There was a juice bar and a regular bar and a patio where people could smoke.

We sat at a round table by the computer system where the servers put their orders in. My mom and I ordered iced tea. Robert drank water. I took forever to order, as is usually the case with people who are obsessed with food, either abstaining from it or consuming it or cooking it or throwing it up. I ordered a fruit plate and a side of wheat-free bread and a side of ketchup (fat-free). I was obsessed with fat-free in the nineties. Wasn't everyone? Every few years the "free" changes. Fat-free, sugar-free, carb-free, gluten-free, grain-free. My mother got the mushroom ravioli, which I ogled. I denied myself the things I really wanted, but if someone else got them I would take bites because if it wasn't in front of me, it wasn't mine. I pulled the mushrooms out of the dough filling of the ravioli and left that part on my mom's plate. Robert laughed at us.

"We're a pair, huh?" I said.

He laughed as he chewed and swallowed a bite of his turkey sandwich.

"When are you going back to New York?" he asked.

"The end of August," I said. "School starts in September. I might take a semester off, though. . . . I'm debating it."

His soft brown eyes lit up. "Oh?"

"Yeah, I went through a bad breakup. Maybe I'll stay out here in

L.A. with my mom and recharge and then go back for the spring semester and graduate six months late. I work in the admin office at
school and the dean says I'll lose an IQ point for every year I am in
California."

Robert laughed. "I've been here for a few years and I think that
is definitely true." He had beautiful brown eyes with long lashes
that our baby would later inherit. The kind of eyes that don't dart
around the room. But in that moment, I was infatuated with a guy
who couldn't look me in the face or sit still. A guy who had a motorcycle. Any punishing guy.

Robert put down his fork when we were speaking. He stood up
if I stood up. He was the most polite guy I had ever met. I was bored
and confused why my mom had arranged this meeting. Of course
she was trying to set us up, even though she wouldn't admit it. She
just wanted me to get over Adam and she saw this sweet guy as a
possibility. She only finally admitted that she was trying to get us
together back then, when she took credit for it at my wedding. *You
can thank yo Momma,* she singsonged.

I can't, for the life of me, recall what my mom said while Robert
and I were chatting. What I would come to find out later was that
he was born in Tehran and went to International School there for
the first fifteen years of his life. I remember getting up and leaving
the table to check out the magazines at the front of the café. Nicolas
Cage was on the cover of *Vanity Fair.* I grabbed it and handed it to
my mom and told her to tell the waiter to add it to our bill (which
Robert ended up paying for since he is the most well-mannered human on earth), and which I am sure she forgot because she stuck the
magazine in her bag. That was the first of many, many stolen magazines at The Newsroom.

As we left the restaurant, I stopped by the host stand on a whim and asked if they needed any help for the summer. *No, I have never worked in a restaurant before,* I said truthfully, when they asked. *Yes, I can be a hostess.*

Easy summer gig. Just a few months. Famous last words.

Busting Out of the Just-A Box

I was in Philly doing a workshop in 2011, and when I started to talk about the Just-A Box, a few women in the front row started to cry immediately. I said that I wanted us all to bust out of the Just-A Box. I asked the question I always ask, *Who would you be if nobody told you who you were?* Because no one is *just a mom, just a waitress, just a girl, just a yoga teacher.* This is the Just-A Box. The voice that minimizes us and tells us we are just the one thing that life has decided we are. A group of mothers had all come together to my workshop and they nodded furiously when I said the line about being "just a mom." I had them do something I call the "Hi-Ya flow"—I usually play "Lose Yourself" by Eminem while they kick and yell *Hi-Ya*. I encourage them to dork it out and make noise and take up space, which, for some people, feels impossible. Until they start to really feel it in their body, as it took me years and years to do, that feeling of *That's right, I am not just an anything. I will not be put into a box any longer. I do not have to be just one thing.* It's liberating. It took me until I started sharing my story to really understand this concept. Then, the next thing I ask them to consider is this, *May I have the courage to be who I say I am.*

That was the hardest part for me, because my IA didn't want to be ignored. Sometimes it was the only voice I could hear. *You're just a waitress. You're just a college dropout, you're just a failed actress.* It was profound to be in Philadelphia, where I was born, where my father was born, where my mother was born, where so much of me grew from, to have this revelation that I could be whoever I wanted to be.

CHAPTER 10

Boys of Summer

ONE SUNDAY, shortly after I got the job at The Newsroom, a dozen roses had come to the restaurant with my name on them. I was standing at the host stand, checking my voicemail, an obsessive habit I had, the nineties version of scrolling through social media. A huge bouquet of the most stunning red roses I had ever seen were placed in front of me, right on top of the wait list. My coworker and by then good friend, Tremell, said, "These are for you. You're the only Jennifer. Ooh-la-la."

The card simply said *Love, Robert.*

I scanned the litany of guys I had gone out with since getting to California: Steve, Brooklyn, Richard, Paul, David, Todd. I didn't know any Roberts. I did know that one my mom had tried to fix me up with, but he didn't strike me as the type to brazenly send roses to where I worked, so I didn't even consider him as a possibility. At the time, I was getting a lot of gifts from men. I had started to gain weight in the few months in Los Angeles since that lunch with Robert. I was still exercising three hours a day, but I was sexy skinny as opposed to "deathly" skinny, and people know that difference well, especially in Los Angeles. Of course, at the time I thought I was getting fat. I wore tight skirts and I tied my T-shirt so my midriff was showing and I wore plastic black platform shoes to make me look taller and skinnier. I got asked out all the time and I got tips and presents from men. Books, bottles of wine, little giftwrapped boxes, cards with phone numbers on them, twenty-dollar bills slipped into my palm. It wasn't even that kind of restaurant. We served wheatgrass and egg whites. We weren't fancy, but we were popular. It was *the* place to be seen. Especially if you were Lindsay Lohan, Nicole Richie, Will Smith, Kevin Smith, Adam Sandler, Sarah Silverman, or Patton Oswalt. And I stood in the front of the place to be seen, in my long black skirt with the slit up the thigh and my plastic high shoes and my stomach exposed, and I tried to be seen.

Finally, *Robert, who Mom tried to hook me up with but pretended she didn't,* called me at the restaurant and asked if I had gotten the flowers. I felt like a jerk. I remember wondering if I should lie and say, "What flowers?"

"Yes, oh my god. I am so sorry. I didn't realize they were from you. I didn't think I knew any Roberts. I mean, I know you and you're Robert, but for some reason I didn't think of you. I am so sorry I didn't call you to thank you. Thank you. They are beautiful. How are you?" I stuttered and sputtered into the phone at the host stand, sounding like an airhead in plastic platform shoes and a belly button ring exposed for all to see as if it was my crowning achievement. *Look at me. I have a flat stomach. I am worth something.*

He asked me out.

"I just want to be friends" is what came out of my mouth. "Just friends."

AND WE WERE FRIENDS, sort of, for a year or so. I called him every once in a while if I was lonely and wanted a meal. I was young and broke, so don't judge. We exercised once at the Santa Monica Stairs, where I was killing myself by climbing them at least twenty times a day. There was a wooden set of stairs and a concrete set and I would alternate between the two. I took Robert to my exercise-addiction haven among the multimillion-dollar mansions by the Pacific Ocean and we ran up and down the stairs like the other ass-holes sweating and grunting in the sun.

I used to play this game in my twenties with men. It was called *I don't like you but I want you to want me.* I was insecure and wanted all the attention I could get from men, but I didn't want to have to give anything up for it: sex, intimacy, love. I wanted to feel pretty and desired without having to look into anyone's eyes or have them claim me as theirs. I felt ugly and short and I never left the house without makeup. I was a master at flirting. I could make men want me.

Then I would panic. I would check my ribs, and check my ribs, and check my ribs. I would avoid. I would not return phone calls or e-mails. I would hide. I would be distant. I would arrange my armor and tighten all the buckles and ropes.

I once agreed to go on a date with a guy I had been waiting on for years. I had known he'd had a crush on me and I wasn't attracted to him at all, but I was trying to get over heartbreak and I thought it would be a good idea to get out of the house. I wasn't interested in him, but the date was fun. He took me to a big famous Hollywood television producer's house for a Christmas party, and after we left he told me the big famous Hollywood producer kept asking about me. *Who was the cute little Jewish girl?* I'd felt flattered. And seen.

I was not into this guy at all, but I tried to force myself to be at-tracted to him because I thought he would be "good" for me. He was a successful television writer and he was smart and funny.

I just didn't want to kiss him. Ever.

We went out on a few dates. He told me he was allergic to tilapia. I ordered the tilapia. I slept at his house, but I slept on the sofa, fake sleeping as we watched a movie and then I acted like I was asleep.

I e-mailed him jokes. He e-mailed me back after I sent him a forwarded joke. He told me that he had enough friends. That he wasn't interested in me *as a friend* and I needed to be straight. *Was I interested in him or not?*

I wasn't. I stared at the computer, horrified. I couldn't bring myself to type the words. I admired him for his straightforwardness. I forget what I said exactly, but it ended with *No, I don't want to date you.* I never heard from him again.

I cringe when I think of the things I used to do for love. I hated myself and thought that if enough men wanted me, it could fill that hatred with something else. Even something I didn't want.

I don't want you but I want you to want me. Or even the *I don't like you but I can't stand that you don't like me. I want everyone to love me.*

The feelings are so ugly and horrible. But if I get down real low and look where I am afraid to look, *Want me want me want me want me want me* emerges from the darkest crevices you can imagine.

I WAS, by this point, four years into my "summer job" at The Newsroom, still talking about going back to college but not doing it. I was twenty-five years old, sleeping until eleven in the morning every day in the old pre-war apartment I shared in West Hollywood with a model who also liked to sleep. I was eating in my sleep, losing and gaining the same twenty pounds over and over, self-medicating with wine and alcohol and sex, and promising myself that tomorrow I would do something to get my life together. Tomorrow I would do something about feeling so stuck. *Tomorrow I will* was my great mantra of those years, alongside *I am tired* and *I am fat* and *I hate myself.*

When I first met Randall, I was waiting on him at Table 11 at The Newsroom, a tiny little two-top against the wall. He was having multigrain jumbo hotcakes (for dinner) and checking out my ass. After me giving him the wrong number, and him tracking me down at the restaurant, we started seeing each other.

I loved this not-boyfriend boyfriend. I went on the birth control pill for this not-boyfriend boyfriend. We'd been together a year, albeit a year where I was unsure of my standing with him because he would not let me call him boyfriend or admit that we were in a relationship. All I knew was I loved him and that he made me feel like I was crazy. He was funny. He'd dance in his underwear every morning in front of his closet and we had the best sex I had experienced yet in my twenty-plus years on earth. He also started pushing me away. He never took me out, I felt like he was ashamed to be with me, and that, precisely that, validated my forever mantra of *I am a bad person.* We'd fuck and I'd cry with the intimacy of it, and then he'd make me leave at seven in the morning. It was all I thought I was worth, and I was addicted to that feeling.

The first thing I remember about the garbage bag incident was that red wrapper invading me with its plastic face. The (unfortunately for him) clear plastic trash bag had fallen over. Inside, grays and whites of innocent *I will not hurt you* trash, and then there it was: a LifeStyles condom stuck to a chicken take-out container.

The significance of images, powerful enough to place two people right there inside my mind, naked on a bed. Maybe they're in a dark room, the blue glow of the television bobbing on the wall. The woman with him, imagined as perfect, tall, leggy. My father's

Eye-shadow Lady, only younger. But then when it was just us, all I could see were red LifeStyles wrappers like sheep jumping fences. Rows of them.

I wondered how many women lied in this way? Making love to someone with only their body while their mind drifts, *I'm fat, who else is he having sex with? What can I eat for dinner? I wonder what time the movie starts. Am I not enough? I'm not good enough for him, what's wrong with me? Shit, I never called my mother back. I have to remember to pay the electric bill. Damn it, is he done yet? I am good enough for him, he's not good enough for me! I wonder if I could fit into those jeans? Did I shut the stove? He smells kind of musty. Ouch, that hurts, what is he doing? I wonder if they have a class for men to become better lovers at The Learning Annex.*

All I could see was that condom wrapper. I was paralyzed with *not* wanting to know the truth. *You love me, right? You love me, right? Right? You love me?*

Everywhere I looked I waited to be convinced of *I love you*s and *You're safe*s and *Nothing bad will happen*s and *I am not going anywhere*s.

How quickly the mind latches on to what it wants to believe is the truth. How little it takes to seal the deal.

I used to think reality was relative and irrelevant. *Tell me what I want to hear. Tell me it wasn't yours. Make me believe.*

Mine, and perhaps yours, too, is a mind that filters everything through a vicious process of hypothetical situations, of beautifully formed sentences, of what-ifs. Images left in a room of the brain to ferment will create an alternate universe where no matter what time it was with my not-boyfriend, the time in my head was a red red world where he was having sex with someone other than me.

Of course he convinced me that it hadn't been his condom. That it had been old or that it was his cousin's and I'd nodded and said *okay* and shook from the *I'm going to be sick* adrenaline in my body, but I stayed.

And for as much as I wanted him to lie to me to make me feel better in the moment, I'd known the truth all along. We always know the truth.

If he hadn't lied, if he'd just said, *Yes, yes it's mine* and *I am sleeping with someone else*. Or, *Aren't you at least glad I am using protection?* I would have had to leave him. The lies gave me permission to stay. They gave me permission to hate myself more. The lies got me off the hook.

The truth will set you free, the platitudes say.

Lies will set you free, too. They will unglue you so much that you will have no idea who you are anymore as you float above everyone else with your own set of facts and knowledge. The lies hurt more than the truth but in that slow, painful, deathly kind of way.

Sure, the truth hurts, too, at times. But it's what keeps you knowing this one very important fact: who you are. The fact of who you are in the world. The truth was that I was a girl who didn't love herself enough to leave someone who hurt her again and again. The lie was that it was all I deserved.

Randall had been one of the most painful and dark experiences of my life. And. I. Couldn't. Stop. Fucking. Him. He made me feel horrible about myself. And. I. Couldn't. Break. Away. We had dated for two years, from the time I was twenty-six to the time I turned twenty-eight. I know the exact ages because he broke up with me on my twenty-eighth birthday. Over AOL Instant Messenger.

Read this carefully: on my birthday.

I couldn't seem to get away from Randall until I met Robert. Or until I met Robert *again*.

Save Yourself

I didn't trust Randall to save my life. I was sure he was sleeping with other people. He told me I was crazy and why couldn't I just enjoy the moments when we were together? He constantly told me that he didn't want to be my boyfriend and in the same breath he'd say, "But you love me, right? You love me? You love me."

"Yes, I love you. Of course I love you," I'd say. And I did.

I couldn't stand how he made me feel but I was addicted to the adrenaline. I had sex with two men in one day, because I was trying to feel something else. Anything else. The addiction to feeling worthless was so powerful it turned me into the worst kind of addict, the kind who will do anything for her fix: lie, cheat, steal, beg, fuck.

Him: *Sit on my lap.* I didn't see it then, the patriarchal desire to have women be tiny so they can be dominated, I just wanted to make him happy at any cost. I would do whatever he asked. He wanted money, I gave it to him. He wanted sex in the middle of the night, I gave it to him. He wanted me to sit on his lap. I gave it to him even though I was so self-conscious about my body that I thought I would crush him.

One morning, I stopped by Randall's apartment even though he warned me to *never do that.* I buzzed the intercom and a woman answered. I threw up in my mouth. He came down and opened my car door and got in. "I can't go out with you anymore," he said. He said that the woman was from another apartment and that the buzzer got confused. I told him to let me in to see. He said, *No, you are crazy. You are crazy. You are crazy.*

I ended up begging him to please take me back. Begging. Like a dog. Like I swore I would never do. *Please, I am sorry, please do not leave me,* I wept, banging my head against the steering wheel. I felt like my life up until then was begging men not to leave me.

In ancient Greek mythology, there was a purgatory for criminals. When Randall broke up with me that December, I went to that space because, as usual, I did not know where to go, where to put my feelings, or my body. I dated a guy whose car smelled like cereal and another I met on Myspace. I was in purgatory, trying to sort it all out. I sucked my thumb a lot. I lost fifteen pounds. Not having gone back to NYU was part of my self-hatred and yet I felt immobilized to move in any direction, especially toward going back to school. Everything felt impossible. I felt stupid and useless and like I couldn't write, except the occasional poem on my pink iMac in the middle of the night after work. In my mind, I had missed my opportunity, as if we only get one shot in life. I did not realize then, as I banged my head against the wheel, that I could have changed my mind about who I was, that being unworthy was a bullshit story, that I could have picked up the pen to write at any time and that it was never too late.

If I put the pain elsewhere, I shall not feel it. If I hurt you first, you cannot hurt me. Maybe on some level, I knew my father was about to die so I said *I hate you* to save myself. *You cannot hurt me if I hurt you first* was a mantra I carried in my head. The mantra was not true. It was a bullshit story I had carried for a long time.

A few months after Randall dumped me on my birthday, my childhood friend Joe from New Jersey came out to California to visit me, after having hiked the Appalachian Trail for six months. By himself. I remember thinking it was the craziest thing I had ever heard, and also being slightly jealous because I knew I didn't have the courage to do anything alone.

Joe told me he'd started with a huge backpack and that by the end it was almost empty. All the weight he'd shed during the hike. He said he'd gone to find himself and I remember thinking at the time that I didn't know any guys who talked like that. *Find himself? Find the truth?*

I asked him how he'd managed, though, at the end, with almost nothing in his pack? Didn't he need *stuff*?

Later, I would realize that nothing is lost when you dump the untruths. It's the letting go, the starting out with so much weight and ending up with water and a sleeping bag. The truth is your sleeping bag. It's your water. It's what carries you the rest of the way from here. It's what says, *Yes, I do love you* and *I have been here all along. Waiting. I've got you.*

It's what takes your quivering body lying there in the corner of your kitchen floor and picks it up. It's what turns you into the strongest mountain lion.

I wrote Joe a letter after he left and said how he'd inspired me to start living my truth and to start writing again. I wrote, *Speak the truth. You know what? Fuck that. Roar. Love, Jen, the mountain lion.*

I often think back to Joe and that backpack of his getting lighter and lighter. How he kept gently releasing things on his hike until he was left with only the bare necessities. *Carry only what you need*, I'll say, and I think of him, and my own overstuffed backpack, and my IA, also heavy on my back.

IT WOULD BE within the same stretch of my twenties that I would decide to go to a two-year acting school in Santa Monica that taught the Meisner technique, which focused on truthful acting, imagination, and a lot of repetition. During the repeating part of the class, I discovered that I couldn't hear well. I would repeat the wrong word or stare confusedly at my partner standing across from me.

"I said, 'I like your shirt,'" he would say, again, exaggerating the word *shirt*.

"You like my shirt?"

"I like your shirt."

So you have this one-dimensional dialogue about something obvious, like *I like your shirt*, but you start reacting to the person's behavior rather than *what* they are saying. You start responding to behavior, and this skill made me listen with my whole body. Once I realized that it wasn't about the words, I knew I could understand what was being communicated.

And as I sat in the audience watching scenes from plays, I understood that my hearing loss would be degenerative, that each year it would get progressively worse, as it had done in the last couple of years until that moment. The truth was, I wasn't really discovering I had hearing loss, it was something that had always been there that I had ignored. I was recovering it. I was finding something lost, and like all the other losses in my life, I simply pretended it was not there. I acted as if everything was normal. I was ashamed of this broken part of me and would not tell a soul. I vowed to never admit it. Or rather, my IA vowed to never admit it. And also, I ask you this: What is normal?

CHAPTER 11

Lessons from The Newsroom

I worked at The Newsroom for thirteen and a half years, and sometimes, while I am in the shower, I think I still work there. As I soap my breasts I'll get this anxiety attack that I am late for work and I've only shaved one leg and *I have to hurry or I will get fired*. Then I remember that I, in fact, do *not* have to go into the restaurant. That I, in fact, *can* shave my other leg with reckless abandon because I do *not* have to go into The Newsroom ever again except to eat if I'm craving a Tuna Deluxe.

The Newsroom has closed, so I actually can't get the Tuna Deluxe, which pains me more than I care to admit. Before it closed, I went in when I had a doctor appointment with a hand specialist next door at Cedars-Sinai hospital. (I would still park at the restaurant since all the same valet guys still worked there and were my buddies.) This waiter, the only one on the floor I still knew, whispered to me, "We're going to close any day now. Freddy hasn't paid the rent in three months and the sheriff has been knocking."

I felt as if he told me I was about to lose my job.

"No. Come on!" I said.

"I'm telling you," he answered as he grabbed what I immediately recognized to be the Grasshopper Smoothie (mint, grapefruit, and ice) and a glass of red wine from the bar to be delivered to a table. Table 11. I still remembered the table numbers but I couldn't remember my twenties.

A couple of days after that conversation someone posted a picture of The Newsroom with a sign that said "Closed" and tagged me on Facebook.

At The Newsroom I learned so much about how to be a person in the world, and also how to lose your personhood in the world. I loathed myself and stank of shame and wine. I drank with ex-gangsters who chopped tomatoes in the kitchen and who fucked child molesters in prison as punishment when they'd lost in a game of cards. (*It was just business,* he'd said as he drank his tequila and lit a cigarette on the back patio.) I lost and gained the same twenty or so pounds. It is where I first understood what a collective consciousness was. I saw the absolute hideousness in people, the gross entitlement and awful mistreatment of people they believed were less than themselves. I saw women who spoke in really high apologetic voices when they asked for extra dressing. They raised their shoulders into their ears as if they needed protection when expressing their own desires. I saw men respond to my body and my own response to that attention—*I am worth something! I am worth something!*

But it's also where I began to really see the beauty in humanity. Like the time after my nephew was born and he was in the NICU (neonatal intensive care unit) and no one knew what was wrong with him, just that he was classified "failure to thrive," that terrible term that implies it's somehow the baby's fault. It would take two years to figure out that he had Prader-Willi syndrome, a rare genetic disorder that seems like it is straight out of a science fiction movie—it is a condition that causes a person to be starving all the time. Blaise could eat himself to death. I was waiting on my favorite regulars, a couple who always ordered the same exact thing—the "special sandwich" of the day with a cup of soup, known as the Special Combo, the turkey meat loaf, two Arnold Palmers, and a chocolate chip cookie to split between them. Their therapist was in the building upstairs. Many people made a pit stop at The Newsroom before they sat on their shrink's couch. I was bringing them their Arnold Palmers, my mascara running down my face. I looked like a hysterical pale clown in, yes, those same platform shoes.

They asked what was wrong, so I told them as I put their drinks down on the table. The table rocked side to side.

"Raymundo," I called, "we need a wedgie for the table. It's unsteady."

As Ray squatted under the table and stuck the little triangle under one of the legs to even it out, the couple said that they were sending me to Atlanta so I could be with my sister and her baby. They said they had miles and they didn't need them and it was the least they could do. They said, "It's going to be okay. You're going to go to Atlanta." Ray looked up from below the table and smiled before he got up and went to bus Table 26.

There were those words again. *It's going to be okay.* The phrase that could mollify me even as I feared my baby nephew might die. The words I fantasized about.

There were people who came over to The Newsroom while loved ones were in the hospital next door. Moms dying, kids with cancer, people feeding themselves before they schlepped the halls of Cedars-Sinai, and I watched those people and imagined them bringing veggie burgers back to the hospital and the things they would talk about in the rooms with the dying people. Mundane things like how the burger had ginger ketchup and *should ketchup have ginger in it and wasn't that sort of a blasphemy* and *did they want a blanket, were they cold,* and *was the bed comfortable* and *did they take their last pill* and *how come the restaurant doesn't have fries?* (Later, after I quit, they would add French fries to the menu and I felt like I had been robbed.)

It was there at the restaurant that I first began to pay attention to the beauty, because if I hadn't, I would surely have killed myself. The landscape of self-loathing I traversed was so treacherous that the only thing that could have possibly saved me were those moments of beauty I hunted—accidentally at first, and then deliberately, and in earnest. Otherwise, the barbed edges of my self-hatred made everything wiry, dark, unbearable, particularly the idea of continuing on with my life and going into work each day wearing my dumb dirty apron. The years at The Newsroom have all melted together like a stew of self-loathing that sat too long on the stove and burned, filling the air with toxic fumes. I can hardly tell one year apart from another except for the moments that haunt me, and the moments when I took my head out of my ass and looked around to find a piece of something beautiful. A husband whose wife had a stroke, wiping the corners of her mouth with a wet napkin. Women who sat at tables with their lattes and wrote movies by the magazine rack. A couple, who'd shared how long they had been trying to conceive, walk in with their three-week-old baby in a stroller. Laughter coming from the patio, where children were eating their kids' menu quesadillas and drinking cranberry lemonades.

The Newsroom is where I learned to see people, even through my own fog. I listened to the produce guy's poems in Spanish and I had sex with a customer I served eggs to and I gave a flower to a girl who just lost her mom as she ate a Tandoori Chicken Salad and I didn't judge my friend the ex-gangster chef when he told me what he had to do while he was in prison and I learned which celebrities were assholes and which were kind, but mostly, I learned that people were faulty and that they would fuck up and disappoint us and die and forget us but that they would also send you to Atlanta while your nephew was in the hospital and they would ask you about your writing.

There was nothing to differentiate the years for me: no change of seasons (this is Los Angeles, after all), no personal or career growth, just a fluctuation of my weight depending on how much I allowed or denied myself, and the scars on my face from picking. In my workshops I tell people how difficult it is to break patterns, how persistent and ritualistic our habits of loathing and negative self-talk become.

Want proof? Here's the breakdown of the years 1995 to 2008:

1995

I started seeing Stanley, a therapist suggested by one of the girls who worked behind the bar. His office was far in the San Fernando Valley, but I went once a week because he allowed payment on a sliding scale. He looked like a teddy bear with a beard and a big beer belly. We talked about how I was about to be twenty-five years old and he tried to convince me I was not the old destroyed hag I thought I was. After I told him about my relationship with my parents and my dad dying so young, he suggested the attention my dad gave me was a form of psychological abuse. He explained that the way my dad turned me into an adult and tried to use me as a weapon against my mom was abusive behavior. Stanley specialized in addictions. He told me he thought I might be an alcoholic. He told me

I was anorexic, which I already knew. Just because I knew things about myself didn't mean anything. I wasn't asking, *Now what?* Now what am I going to do about this being anorexic? This self-medicating? I didn't need someone to tell me what I already knew. I needed a *now what*, but that would not come for years.

Stanley felt fatherly to me. I'd pay him to tell me who he thought I was, and it brought me comfort driving to the Valley to visit him, until it didn't, until he wanted me to look too closely at things I did not want to look at. I eventually stopped going, citing the drive, as well as the cost, even though he was seeing me on a sliding scale. I felt protective of my parents, especially my father, even though I knew he was a little bit right. I stopped going and never heard from him again until he sent me a Facebook friend request a few years back. I did not accept it.

1996

THINGS I OBSESSED ABOUT:

*The damage I thought I had done and how I could not go back in
    time to repair it*
*Wrinkles around my twenty-one-, then twenty-two-, then twenty-
    five-year-old eyes and who would love me like that?*
*I was convinced I had AIDS until three years later when I finally
    went, shaking with fear, to Planned Parenthood and found out I
    indeed did not have AIDS.*
*All the stuff I had left in New York in a black trash bag in some girl
    named Meghan's apartment*
My lack of willpower

The twenty pounds I had to lose
No, the thirty pounds I had to lose
My height (I was too short)
How I was starting to forget my father's voice
Why I was so ugly
Diet pills to get through the day
NyQuil to get through the night
When I would go back to NYU

1997

My head was up my ass.

1998

My head was still up my ass.

1999

1999 was the year of the world prepping for Y2K. I was twenty-five and wondered, *Who will want me like this?* I got drunk and hooked up with another waiter from work. After he came, I went into the bathroom and spit in the sink and then I cried about how I just wanted someone to love me. I looked in the mirror, cum in the corner of my mouth, and said, "You are so gross. You are so ugly. No wonder no one loves you."

2000

Y2K did not end the world or even crash our computers. My entire worth was dependent on whether or not someone told me I looked good, or looked thin. I held my breath for a year as I waited for people to open their mouths at me. I quit therapy. I self-medicated with wine, sleep, excessive exercise. I didn't go back to therapy.

2001–2004

I finally retired my Steve Madden platform shoes after each shoe ripped in four places. I got new platform shoes. Who would want a short person?

2005

Everything was my fault. I felt guilty and overwhelmed or else I felt nothing. One or the other. Nothing in between. I drank every night. I slept and then I would feel guilty. Everything was my fault.

2006

How did I end up working as a waitress at The fucking Newsroom in West Hollywood? I was once in New York at NYU. I was going to write poems, I was going to write. *What have I done? What have I done? What have I done?* became my mantra, tattooed on my mind: W H A T H A V E I D O N E? and I was sure everyone could see it.

There was a way someone would say my name where I could tell they had said it at least three times. A bark with a smirk, a half-kidding kind of irritation. I didn't hear the bussers behind me. I misheard orders. I practically lived on the floor of the restaurant because I was always stooping down to hear what customers were saying. My hearing was declining rapidly. I had the reputation of being moody and an airhead. I might have been moody but I was not an airhead. I just could not hear. I could accept *moody airhead* but not *hard of hearing. Moody airhead* was not permanent nor was it a disability.

At one point during one of my shifts, someone hung a picture of me in the back server station on the bulletin board. I was holding a big brown paper shopping bag. Someone had written on the picture, "Does this bag make my face look fat?" I laughed, but my insides felt like wet sponge because it was the truth. That was my legacy. When someone thought of me, that was the first thing they thought of. How much I hated myself. What if I looked back on my life and saw that what I had spent the most time doing was hating myself?

2007

I was at the bar waiting for my drinks for a table and I kept jokingly yelling to Javier and Edgar to "simma down now" over and over again, imitating Cheri Oteri on *Saturday Night Live.* I looked over after about three minutes of doing the terrible imitation and Cheri

Oteri was sitting at the bar eating a salad. I could hear the ringing in my ears, but really nothing else.

2008

I went to a new therapist, again referred to me by a woman at work. After our first session he said, "You're depressed. You need meds." *What a know-it-all,* I thought. Another dude telling me who I am. I asked my friends and before I could even finish the question, they all said, *Yes, you should definitely go on antidepressants.*

I was scared of antidepressants. I was scared to gain weight and I was also scared to write again. I was scared of everything. I started going to yoga classes at the little neighborhood gym next to The Newsroom where all the people who worked at New Line Cinema went to work out during lunch or after work. Pagan, the yoga teacher who taught at the gym, would come in to The Newsroom for a smoothie and insist that I try yoga because he saw me on the treadmill after my shifts for two hours at a time. He bugged me for so long about trying his yoga class that I finally went.

I called my regular doctor and asked him if he had any samples of antidepressants. I couldn't afford a psychiatrist visit and I did not have medical insurance at the time and I also thought I would just try it. He gave me a white paper bag filled with a month's supply of samples of a medication called Cymbalta. At first, the medication made me feel speedy, like I had taken Sudafed and drunk six cups of coffee. I couldn't sleep at night and I was sweating profusely, and when I did sleep, I would have violent and vivid dreams. I hated the drug at first and when I called my beloved doctor to tell him, he told me that the side effects would subside soon. They did.

Then I just felt good. The moment I knew with certainty that they were working was three weeks into starting them, when I noticed a few days had passed and I had not obsessed on my body. This hadn't happened since I was seventeen years old. I felt calm, which was a way I had never felt in my whole life, except while I was doing yoga. It was like I was in a dark hole in the earth and for the first time I could see a pinpoint of light. Someone was throwing me a rope to climb out. That rope was called Cymbalta.

I stopped the cycles I had been living in for years. Those self-destructive patterns that had me take two steps forward, five steps backward. After starting the medication, I started eating meals during the day, and stopped eating in my sleep because I was going to bed satiated. I stopped feeling like I had to exercise four hours a day or it didn't count. I started to enjoy sex because I wasn't so preoccupied with my body.

My sweet doctor kept giving me antidepressant samples. Every month I drove to Beverly Hills and stopped in his office to get my bag of free drugs. He saved my life. It was as if I finally understood what *being present* meant. I had heard it so many times in yoga classes but I had never experienced it. It was like a protective film that someone had forgotten to take off was peeled back from my brain, and I could finally see things clearly.

How I wasn't truly stuck.

CHAPTER 12

Yoga Finds Me

New Line executive offices were in the building across the courtyard from The Newsroom, along with loads of therapist and psychiatrist offices. I did Iyengar yoga in that gym, a practice that emphasized detail and alignment, next to producers, actors, locals I waited on at the restaurant. Pagan, a beautiful man with wiry muscles and dreadlocks, was my first and most cherished yoga teacher because he put me on the path of yoga. I don't remember what my first time having sex felt like but I remember the first time in Pagan's Iyengar class: how my muscles felt, how my grief untethered itself, how my mind felt still for two whole minutes. He wore what looked like a cloth diaper (and nothing else) and wrapped his hair in a big knot on the top of his head as he adjusted our bodies into triangle, headstand, shoulder stand. He had a deep love and respect for the practice and because of him, I fell in love with yoga.

The class was in the center of the gym and there were no walls or doors. We just did yoga with the weights banging and people running right there behind us on treadmills and the personal trainers talking way too loudly. I loved it. Pagan would turn down the television sets and ask the people throwing weights to keep it down and I learned how to focus in a shit-storm from him. Every time someone would sub a class for him, they would tell him they could never do it again, that it was too noisy and hard and they couldn't concentrate. When I was in his class in the center of that gym, you could have yelled *fire* and I would have stayed in plank pose.

My crappy therapist was also a yoga teacher on the side and I asked him if we could do yoga as he gave me therapy because I thought, *How cool, to be in a hip opener while talking about my childhood. It'll help me release.* But he just said, *Yoga schmoga.*

I had trouble breathing when people asked me what I did for a living. I started lying. I said, "I'm an actress." (If by "acting" I meant waiting for someone to discover me, then I guess I was not lying.) I hid so no one could ever ask me. I didn't make eye contact. I did nothing except go to work and come home. I was not writing, I was not taking acting classes, I was just a waitress. Hi, my name is Jen and I am just a waitress.

But I loved Wednesdays at The Newsroom. The guy who delivered produce came in and read his poems to me in Spanish. He recited them on his way to drop off boxes of lemons or artichokes in the kitchen and they sounded so beautiful even though I didn't understand a lick of Spanish (which was pathetic on my part, since most of my friends at work were Mexican). It was magic listening to his poetry.

I learned everyone's story who came into The Newsroom and what made them happy, where they grew up, how they liked their eggs. I leaned in and leaned down to hear better or to tell a joke, and I knew that the way out would be through this kind of connection. I had no idea what that looked like at the time, but I had spent so much time living in my head, obsessing on my body, replaying the past just so I could swim in a sea of guilt, that coming up for air meant looking at the beautiful people around me, the people with stories to tell, with poems to read and boxes of fruit to share, *Here, have a lemon, here, listen to my story, here, tell me yours.* I knew from the very beginning that I was a shit waitress but something was becoming so obvious that even I, Master Avoider, couldn't ignore. I could get people to open up. I began to share more of myself with people, and like I learned in Meisner acting class, I watched their bodies, I listened to their behavior, and I responded to that. Even though my hearing truly was failing, I never let on, and people thought I was the most honest server in the world. I became like a therapist to a lot of customers except I wasn't getting paid nearly as much and I didn't get to sit on a couch. I still forgot to get them ketchup nine times out of ten, though, when they asked.

Beauty on the Mat

I started to look for beauty but I hated L.A. I blamed it on the city that my life had turned out the way it had. I refused to take a look at my own choices. Instead, it was always my mom's fault, the city's, the restaurant's, bad luck.

I kept doing yoga in the middle of the loud and noisy gym, moving my body in a quiet space while chatter and noise just blended into background. I could feel—and even hear—my breath. I did yoga on my living room carpet. Twists and downward dogs and backbends right there in front of the sofa. I would sweat through *vinyasas* at a donation-based studio in Santa Monica. I became obsessed with moving my body in sync with my breath. I dreamed of upward dog, of handstands, headstands, pigeon pose. I could not get enough. I was out of my head for once. I focused on the alignment of my outer hip, and on whether my kneecaps were lifting, or my arms were externally rotated. I loved how strong I felt in yoga, but it was a different kind of strong than when I used to try and make myself believe I was strong. This felt like it was coming from the inside out, where the other was the outside telling my inside how to be in order to not feel. Yoga made me feel.

It softened me, and that softening would eventually lead to the epiphany that I could use yoga to get other people to feel things.

I started to notice more of the world, more beautiful things: How Lorenzo behind the bar always smiled even as he pushed carrots or lemons through the juicer. The way the palm trees swayed on the street and covered the sign that said "West Hollywood," separating it from Beverly Hills. How when I'd run I would stop and ask people what made them happy. One day there was this crossing guard listening to a little boom box he had set up next to his crossing guard chair and a plastic bag filled with CDs on the ground next to him. I heard the music as I ran by, so I stopped and asked, "What made you happy today?" And he told me all about his job as a crossing guard and how he was born in 1936 and the music he was listening to and how his father was into Vaudeville. How the mailwoman swung her hair around her shoulder as she pushed her cart and told me she loved her job and that her favorite was delivering checks early.

Like my father, I could engage people. But instead of making them laugh, I could connect them to one another. And when I connected them, as humans, magic happens. I see it every day now.

One of the greatest sources of joy for me now is to see how friendships sustain after my retreats. Women who met in Italy become best friends. They come back and share a king bed at another retreat of mine, this time in France. They call each other "wifey" (as I call Lidia Yuknavitch). They travel to Africa together, they talk on the phone, they celebrate birthdays and hold each other during deaths and loss and divorce. I have never seen anything like these connections, and I am reminded of the years where all I wanted was someone to want me. I have found it, except not in the way I thought. I have provided the space for these people to fall in love with each other. And they do. It's not a superficial yearning to be desired; these are deep connections that have bypassed years of bullshit and small talk. I see these women becoming close, especially as the years go on, and I feel proud as a mother would. This was one of the reasons that for so long I didn't think I wanted a child. I had my maternal fill, in this way. These connections sustained me.

BESIDES THE MEDS, yoga was helping me with my depression and it was helping me be in a better mood, which I realized was imperative at a restaurant. How contagious all of us were who worked there, all crammed in the back server station. Really, how contagious all of us are in life. Yoga made me a nicer person.

The collective consciousness—it'd be like this: nobody would order the chicken potpie. In fact, one of my coworkers used to say that it was "dry as Grandma's snatch." (She also said that about the scones.) So no one ordered the chicken potpie and I asked, *Why do we even have it on the menu? No one orders it!*

And then, on a Sunday morning, someone would inevitably order it. Say around eleven a.m. Then a table on the patio would order it. Then people throughout the whole restaurant would order it. This dry dish that people referred to as Grandma's snatch (which was sexist, but this was a restaurant, and that was the norm).

I'd be like, *Okay, maybe they saw the table next to them order it* and it was like the power of suggestion, but how to explain the others ordering it throughout the day and night? As if they called one another beforehand and agreed everyone would order it. A chicken potpie agreement. It was like a chicken potpie collective consciousness.

It happened all the time until I became accustomed to it. Someone started to order something that no one had ordered in weeks and I turned to my coworker and said, "Watch. Everyone is going to order that now" as I punched the order into the computer in the back and one of the busboys rubbed my shoulders. (There was so much *touch* in that place. I was always flinching when one of the guys in the kitchen grabbed me, but I never said anything because there was no other way to get what you needed for a table. Mustard? Touch. Rush on that order? Touch. Extra sauce? Touch. Medium rare? Touch. Dry as Grandma's snatch. *Touch.* Did you lose weight? *Rub.*)

I don't claim to understand my chicken potpie collective consciousness theory, but as I teach my few remaining strictly yoga classes these days, I remember that phenomenon. Some days I walk in and it's like a roomful of zombies—everyone yawning, frowning, picking their split ends. It's like leading the walking dead through downward dogs. And kindness and beauty are like that, too; all of a sudden, when you look up, they are everywhere. I think of those poor chicken potpies and how no one wanted any and then everyone did and how life is like that.

Moody, unpredictable patterns everywhere, complete, yet utterly indecipherable and vicious patterns. Those were my patterns for years, and yoga was the blip on the screen that helped me see them so that I could break them, change them, break them again.

Those initial breaks were crucial: if it is indeed the cracks that let the light in, as Leonard Cohen sings, with each pattern I broke, the brighter my life became. In Japan, there is a custom for repairing broken pottery called *kintsugi*. The method emphasizes fractures and breaks instead of hiding them. I began to think of myself as that pottery. Maybe I wasn't ruined.

Once I went on the antidepressants, I was able to recognize how much I was getting done in a day because my hours were no longer consumed with self-hatred, and with wondering what my boyfriend was doing and who he was fucking. But something else was also happening inside me: I was shining light in all my corners, and liked what I saw there. Maybe it was yoga, maybe it was antidepressants, maybe it was just being in the world, but things were shifting, changing, and I knew it.

I was working five shifts a week still at The Newsroom but I was happier than I had ever been, my mind no longer in a constant state of worry, fear, and obsession. I was doing yoga six days a week because I had so many injuries from all the years of overexercising. Naturally, my obsessive personality did too much, too many classes, too many days a week, but it was helping me feel calm. That in itself kept me going back to the mat again and again.

CHAPTER 13

Blast from the Past

TEN YEARS AFTER the day my mom introduced me to Robert at The Newsroom, there I was at the host stand, flipping through an *Us Weekly* with a pregnant Angelina Jolie on the cover. It was slow and I had no tables. *Tumbleweeds,* we used to say. I saw him sitting at a table by the magazines with another man. I recognized him and went over.

The last time I had seen him was eight or nine years earlier. We'd had dinner one night at a hotel in West Hollywood on West Third Street that is no longer there. It was a warm October night and we sat at a table outside and made small talk. He was working at New Line Cinema and I was still at The Newsroom, but by then I had been upgraded to server from hostess. He had a beer, I had a mojito, and it was one of those fine evenings, pleasant enough, but where you just want to go home and watch *The X-Files* and read stolen magazines from work in bed. At least that's what I wanted. I was distracted and obsessed with an actor who rode a motorcycle and who couldn't look me in the eyes, but with whom I'd had the best sex of my life. I was twenty-two at this time and I'd had sex with three people, so the competition wasn't tough. Robert pecked me on the cheek at the end of the dinner he paid for and I drove off in my 1988 Volkswagen Fox so I could dream about being fucked from behind by a guy who couldn't even look at me. And then, here walks in a man I'd met—and ignored—ten years earlier.

"Robert?" I said, peeking to see if he had a wedding ring. I didn't remember him being this cute from ten years before, I thought, but I didn't even remember myself ten years before, so how could I trust my judgment?

"Oh, hey," he replied, batting those lashes I remembered envying. His face opened into a big smile. All cheeks. Cheeks and sweet brown eyes.

"Oh wow, I haven't seen you in forever. How are you?" I said, sticking my hands into my dirty apron.

"I'm good. This is my friend Rick. I'm so sorry but I am blanking on your name," he said, seemingly embarrassed.

I didn't believe him. Why do people do that? It drove me crazy because I remembered everyone's name and what they ordered and how they made me feel.

"Jennifer. Jen Pastiloff."

"That's right. Jennifer." He introduced me to his buddy Rick and then I took their order. Rick got a Noodles Diablo. I still remember that.

I don't remember if he asked me or I asked him, but we agreed to get a coffee.

We didn't go out for coffee but instead went to a little Japanese place called Musha that was a few blocks from my apartment. We drank sweet unfiltered sake and shared a Negitoro Tuna Croquette with daikon mayo sauce and a lobster roll and tofu French fries, which are way better than they sound. We laughed and laughed and I remember being confused because I didn't recall the Robert my mom had tried to fix me up with as making me laugh. Or being cute. It was the best date I had had in a long time. Timing is everything.

We sat in his car outside of my apartment and talked for two hours after the dinner. I don't remember what we talked about, but I remember this: I got out of the car and shut the door and as I walked into my apartment building, called The Sands, I knew that I would be with Robert. It's that feeling you get when someone's hand is on your forehead, or your shoulder, or wherever a hand needs to be that says *I got you*. That feeling of safety I had been searching for my whole life.

In 2006, the first few months of my dating Robert, my sister, Rachel, was living on my sofa. She had just gone through a breakup and left Oakland, California, where she'd been managing a Jewish deli and going to college full-time. She dropped out, quit her job, put all her stuff in storage, drove her car down to Santa Monica with just a suitcase, and moved onto my couch to start her life over. It was miserable. For both of us. Of course, we would understand the true definition of miserable after she'd long left my sofa for Georgia and her first son was diagnosed with Prader-Willi syndrome.

It was like we reverted to being little girls again, sharing that room with the bunk bed.

I don't think I would've minded so much if we had more space, but for some reason it felt like we were living together in a tent with no air circulation. She had the TV on all the time in the tent and we only had one bathroom and a kitchen the size of a postage stamp. I had a fake fireplace, so we even had campfires for our tent-feeling lifestyle. It was like a pitiful version of glamping.

It wasn't all bad. Sometimes Robert came over and we ordered

Italian food and we'd have a picnic with my sister on the living room floor on a blanket, like true campers. I have a photograph: It's my sister, me, and Robert at the Italian neighborhood restaurant where we'd order pasta. It's kind of blurry, but I am wearing my favorite pink zebra top I got at the thrift store, where I got most of my clothes. My sister's big blue eyes are clear, her beautiful big lips painted red. Robert is wearing a yellow polo shirt. This was a moment my sister lived with me where we were truly happy, so I tacked it on the wall above my desk to remind me that nothing is ever one thing, that although there were moments where we hated each other and couldn't stand living together, there were also times like this. How many times would I need that reminder that so many things were "*and*" statements. My sister lived with me *and* we wanted to kill each other *and* we loved each other like no one else would or could. My sister lived with me in my teeny-tiny apartment *and* I wanted to weep with frustration *and* sometimes we laughed so hard I cried.

I never, and to this day I can say the same thing, had the desire, need, worry, or inclination to look on Robert's phone or computer. I never doubted him when he said, *I am going to x, y, or z*. With Robert I had someone who was content just to sit on the sofa where my sister had been living and watch my little TV. We'd put in movies on my DVD player and he'd sit in his socks and trousers, as he called them, as we watched *Goodfellas* for the millionth time or *Just Friends* with Ryan Reynolds, and we'd laugh about how I told him all those years ago I just wanted to be friends after he'd sent me roses at the restaurant. He'd drink a little whiskey and I would look over at him and wonder why he wasn't leaving. There was someone, right there, a real-life body who wanted to stay and I could not fathom it. I still had one foot in the Dark Years, even as I sat on my couch leaning on Robert's shoulder.

I often wondered if I had reconnected with Robert at a later age, would it have been harder to let that programming go? That bullshit story my IA had let me believe that I wasn't worthy of love, just of sex. If I had started dating Robert any later, would I have been able to quiet my IA that yearned for drama and disappointment and feeling panicky? I have a deep gratitude for the timing of meeting him at thirty-one, when I was old enough to recognize respect, and yet not too old to push it away because I thought I didn't deserve it after a long time of being told that. My own IA was the champ at telling me that I didn't deserve love. I had to work to let go of the old beliefs that had become tattooed in my mind from the Dark Years, and all the years before, but being with Robert freed up my energy in a way I had never experienced as an adult. I felt safe in the world. All of a sudden, it seemed I had more hours in the day, because all my time was not being consumed with obsessing on why my boyfriend didn't love me or on what he was doing.

The first time he spent the night, the first time we had had sex, after three months of dating, we lay in bed, the sun coming through the curtains my mom had made and hung for me. She may have quit the drapery business years before, but I would always get the Mom window treatments.

"Do you want to get breakfast?" he asked.

I almost choked.

"What?" I said, facing the window so I didn't have to look at him. It was all too much.

"Do you want to get breakfast?"

"Oh." I had not had this before.

We went to Jinky's in Santa Monica and I had about fourteen cups of coffee and two bites of a pancake and some of his eggs and potatoes because what anyone else ordered always, always looked better. We sat outside and he held my hand and looked at me. I was alive and eating eggs off someone else's plate and I was not dead and it was 2006. I'd made it very far in life. I was seven years away from thirty-eight. And what was more shocking was that I didn't want to think about death.

CHAPTER 14

How May I Serve?

There's Enough for Everyone

In 2008, I was self-identifying as a yogi, and the yoga teacher training I wanted to take was a month-long intensive rather than the typical ones that were spread out over six months. I had no patience. I wanted it done and DONE. I come from an impulsive line of people whose favorite word is *NOW*. After Pagan, I had been practicing yoga with Annie Carpenter, known as the "teacher's teacher," and I wanted to study with the best if I was going to go through with this plan, if that's what it was, not so much a plan but a thing. Of course, I had no idea how I was going to go through with "this thing," because I had no money and I had to work and I didn't think I actually even wanted to be a yoga teacher in the slightest but I knew I loved yoga. I felt safe while I was doing it.

For the first time in more than a decade, I saw a possible escape route from the self-obsessed and self-loathing monotony that was my life, and I would be damned if I would let something like money stop me. I loved doing yoga and I hated waiting tables. It was like I had been thrown in a well and I was finally climbing out because someone had tossed a rope called Cymbalta down for me. The light at the top said, *You need to write. You can write your book and work on your poems and teach yoga instead of waiting tables.* I said back to myself, *But I don't even want to teach yoga.* Now, what I say in my workshops is that the IA and fear will always be there, just as it was for me then. The work is getting it (my IA is a he, not sure what gender yours is, if it even has a gender for you) to get quiet. If the IA is taking up less space and making less noise, we can start making moves in any direction. If we let it be the dictator, we get stuck. I ask people what their *now what* is, meaning what step do they need to take in order to start quieting that pesky IA? At the time, my *now what* was figuring out a way to take a yoga teacher training.

My self said back, *Yes, but you'd rather die than wait tables any longer so what the fuck do you want? Choose. You can teach yoga and make less money but you won't be refilling goddamned coffees anymore.*

But what if I suck? my IA said loudly.

Well, you suck at waiting tables and yet and still, here you are.

This is true, I said to my IA and shook its hand as it got quieter, finally.

So, we had a deal. We (I, us) were going to do Annie Carpenter's yoga teacher training.

I stopped seeing a therapist once I signed up for the teacher training. I had intended to go back until I started getting honest about the fact that he wasn't doing much for me, except he gave me the phrase, "Get out of your head. It's a bad neighborhood." I still use it as a mantra all the time, so perhaps I can thank him for that.

I met my actor friend Holt in 1996, during my first summer working at The Newsroom when I was twenty-one, through a mutual friend, and we remained good friends. When I was thirty-three years old, I asked him if he could help me with the money for the teacher training since I had to take a full month off work and I wouldn't survive without that income.

He said, *Of course.*

I was pretending to be an actor for so many years but there he was, out there, really doing it. Working on movies and television shows. And making a good living! I was in awe that someone had found something they loved doing and actually made money doing it, that I had a friend who got paid for their art. There was great comfort to me in having someone to call who could say *of course* without batting an eye. This was the first time I had friends with financial means. He'd known me all these years and had seen how miserable and stuck I felt at The Newsroom and I was finally going to do something to change that. But I was not doing it alone. I asked for help and I was open to receiving it.

Holt gave me the money and said it was a gift. I was able to get my shifts covered for a month with that gift and sign up for the yoga teacher training. It is a moment of beauty and generosity I will never forget—it paved the road that opened up to the rest of my life. Those small moments that answer *now what* add up to a lifetime of courage. The gestures of kindness from people who say *I got you*, who not only say it but embody it, the gestures of self-care that allow you to receive the help—it can change your life if you let it. The three thousand dollars allowed me to not have to think about the customers at The Newsroom for the month of July and that was worth my sanity, even if it was only a month. I would miss my lovely regulars, but I was thrilled to be away from the people who wouldn't look at me while they ordered, who snapped their fingers at me, the people who thought they were owed something.

Once I decided to take the yoga teacher training, I felt proud of myself in a way I hadn't since I was writing poems at NYU. Those rainy-night readings where my mom would drive all the way from Cherry Hill, New Jersey, to come hear me stand at a podium and read my poems about my dead father, about the flab that hung from my Bubbe's arms and her Yiddish, about hunger, about not being able to save my sister. Everyone would stand up and clap and wait in line to talk to me. I had not felt anything like that in all those years since I left college. What was that feeling? It was so simple, and something we forget so often. *I did something I feel good about and I am sharing it with someone who appreciates it.* But mostly it was the first part: *I did something I feel good about.* The truth is that it doesn't matter what *it* is, whether it's a poem, or taking a yoga training or quitting your job or making a great cappuccino. It's just like that lesson I learned in acting school: it's the behavior behind it, the feeling. The *damn, I don't suck after all. Taste this cappuccino, it's delicious and I made it.*

The only time I felt anything remotely close to that feeling was when I was kind to people, when I looked customers in the eye and asked how they were, when I *meant* it. When I waited for them to answer and only then took their order for a smoked turkey sandwich with cranberry mayo and a side of vegetable chips, or when I understood the way they averted their gaze to the palm trees out the windows that the person they'd been visiting at the hospital next door wasn't doing well. When I said hello to every guy working in the hot airless garage downstairs from the restaurant and learned all their names and how they liked their coffee.

The only time I felt that surge of being awake was when I was paying attention to other people and letting them affect me. Essentially, when I was *doing love* was the only time I felt worthy. I hadn't coined the term yet, but this was when I understood the idea of being fall-in-loveable. To not only let someone in to see you, but to see them back, fully.

I would be in the back refilling the iced tea pitcher at work and I'd tell my coworker Ricky how I was taking off a whole month to do a yoga teacher training. *Did you hear me, Ricardo? I'll be gone for a whole month!* It was less that I was proud of the actual yoga training and more that I was able to show people I was doing something for myself. *I heard you, Jenny,* he'd say, patting my back. *Table 21 needs to order, they're in a hurry.*

CHAPTER 15

Seen and Heard

Stop Hiding Who You Are

ANNIE CARPENTER IS the best there is in the world of yoga. A former Martha Graham dancer who weighs about as much as a peach, which my recovering anorexic brain was slightly jealous of when I first met her. I decided I wanted to get serious about my yoga practice and Annie happened to teach in my neighborhood at YogaWorks in Santa Monica. I bought a monthly membership and went to every class of hers I could. If I wasn't going to therapy I was sure as hell going to go to yoga and try to work through my shit.

Annie had eyes in the back of her head and she was tough as nails. I learned more from her than from any other yoga teacher I had ever taken, except Pagan in that funny little gym next to The Newsroom. He taught me how to begin to find quiet in the noise, how to build a room for yourself even when you had no walls, even when you had clanging weights and meatheads doing pull-ups next to you, grunting away like they were approaching orgasm. Annie said she had been looking at bodies for over forty years and the things that she could spot from across the room seemed impossible sometimes.

"You're hyperextending your elbow," she'd yell from the other side of the studio. Her superpower was that you couldn't bullshit around her. I wanted that, too, if I was going to learn how to teach. I had left college, but Annie made me feel like I was back at university. She reminded me of that tough professor you love to hate, the one who makes you work harder than you think you can, who makes you earn every damn thing you think you want. She was a genius. Well-read and well-spoken: she was terrifying to me. I loved her. She didn't give out compliments lightly, and when she did, I felt like I was walking on air for days.

"Good job, Missy," she said as I attempted to hug my right hip under the bone (whatever the hell that means, I still don't know and I am a bona fide yoga teacher) in a half-moon pose. "Good job. Nice external rotation."

Missy was her term of endearment. I felt strong in her classes. I felt present and capable.

The training was held near my apartment in Santa Monica, close enough that I could ride my bike. We practiced and learned in a rented space above a Mexican restaurant called Tacos Por Favor on Olympic Boulevard, a busy throughway connecting West Los Angeles to the rest of the city's sprawl. I didn't care what kind of restaurant it was as long as I didn't have to work there. I felt like an adult not working at The Newsroom, even though I was essentially back in school with my big-ass binder and sharpened pencils.

Annie co-led the training with another teacher, named Sonya, and they had two assistants, Kia and Gigi. There were about forty students, a mix of all ages and levels and class, but I can't remember any people of color.

In the last ten years, yoga has gotten a little more diverse, but boy was it *white*. Working at The Newsroom, we were like a Benetton ad, so I felt very aware of this lack of diversity. Nonetheless, I continued on because I was determined to make a change finally and also because: privilege. I was very lucky to be able to take a month off of work to study something that wasn't even white people's to begin with. But at the time I was only thinking, *I can't wait until this is over and I can start making money.* I had my eye on the escape route: the ultimate prize.

I did love the learning, though. My favorite was the philosophy. My least favorite were the meditations.

Annie would ask us to close our eyes and I would have mini–panic attacks, where my heart would race, I would feel like I couldn't breathe, my ears burned. I didn't understand why until I got honest with myself. I couldn't hear.

This was the second time in my life I had really come face-to-face with what was happening to me. When Annie asked us to close our eyes, I could no longer read her lips. I realized then just how much I had been relying on lip-reading and context and people repeating themselves. And simply pretending. I was alone in the dark when she asked us to close our eyes. I was alone in my body, for so long the enemy. Alone with the mantras of my childhood *BE STRONG BE STRONG,* which were crumbling in the silence and I was afraid.

What was happening? What are they saying? How will I know what to do? I am scared.

Being in that space, in a room with all those other sweaty people for eight hours, investigating our bodies, our karma and dharma and our backbends, made me really vulnerable. I found myself crying for what seemed to be no reason. I found myself getting honest about things I had been lying to myself about for years.

I was deaf and I could no longer hide it.

The disempowerment that comes with not being able to hear is incomparable.

My hearing had been progressively getting worse, but it was during the teacher training that I finally stopped being in denial. The shame I felt that part of me was broken, my ears, was insurmountable, and I did not want to admit that I was weak. *I am strong. I am strong. I am not broken.*

Except I was. My ears didn't work properly. I heard ringing in my head twenty-four hours a day on top of the hearing loss. I couldn't fake it anymore, and in that place, with those bodies, for some reason, I decided that it was okay. It was the first time I saw how softening can happen when we allow ourselves to fully inhabit our bodies. I began to let go of the mantra *I am strong.* It became *I am soft.*

"Annie, I can't hear you if I close my eyes," I said one day after class.

"Why not?" she asked.

"Because I have a hearing problem and I have to read lips." I had never said that out loud.

"Oh, I always wondered why you stared at me," she said, which made me feel self-conscious. Did everybody think I stared at them oddly? Did everyone think I was a freak who looked at mouths instead of eyes? Then I remembered one of my favorite quotes: *It's worse than you think. They're not thinking of you at all.* I let that become my mind tattoo for the rest of the training.

"Is it okay if I keep my eyes open?"

"Of course," she said. And from that moment on, she went out of her way to make sure I could hear, that I was in the front of the room, that I was taken care of. She may have been tough but she was also like a den mother. I loved her.

The previous ten years, when my hearing had started to really decline, I could never have imagined a time when I would accept it. One Thanksgiving a few years before the teacher training, my friends Jen and Shana had an intervention with me to try and get me to admit I had major hearing loss. I fought them and cried and said I just had a cold and I was congested and that's why I couldn't hear. Until finally I said, *Okay, I'll go to the audiologist,* as long as they promised to come with me. They promised and then I still didn't go for years. My bullshit story: *I am not deaf. This will go away if I ignore it.* Both were incredibly vicious bullshit stories that proved false. I was going deaf, and it was getting worse.

There in the teacher training, I felt a safety I hadn't felt, the feeling that I could finally stop pretending to be someone I wasn't. I felt seen and taken care of. Annie would constantly ask, "Can you hear, Jen?" "You okay, Jen?" "Did you get that, Jen?" and I did not feel like a burden or I was annoying or that I was deformed. I felt like there was someone who cared, someone who wanted to make me feel like it was all going to be okay. Robert was the same. Whenever we went out, he kindly told the waiter that I was hard of hearing and I read lips. He would get headsets at the movie theater so I could hear, but I was too embarrassed to wear them. Robert did not get frustrated with me when I asked him to repeat himself six times.

Part of the training was breaking off into groups and "practice teaching." I was terrible at adjustments but very good at speaking and giving directions and at making people laugh. I was scared to put my hands on people. I never quite got the hang of how to give a downward dog adjustment or to help someone in a backbend. Couldn't I just talk?

I would always let my partner go first when it came to adjusting each other so I could copy what they did, as if I didn't trust my own hands or the knowledge in them. The truth is, I didn't care that much. I liked things that felt good and I was good at that part—adjustments during *savasana*, pressing someone's shoulders down or rubbing their feet or their head. I liked the kind of touch that said, *I'm here, I got you, you're safe, it's going to be okay,* but the adjusting of someone's left outer hip, meh. I always felt like I wasn't pressing firmly enough, I was turning their shoulder the wrong way, I was pushing too hard. The truth was that I wasn't ready for the truth yet, which was, that although I was there to learn how to become a yoga teacher, I sensed that this wasn't my end game. I always wanted to touch people with words. I didn't know then, during that first teacher training, that I would eventually find a way to weave it all together, that the vulnerability I experienced from doing the yoga opened something impenetrable in my chest and found its way to my heart, and also: my ears, which perhaps were always the same thing.

"Okay, now grab your partner's heels and pull them down toward the earth."

"Push on their lower back as you gently rotate their triceps away from their ears."

"Slide your hand under their shoulder blade and externally rotate it."

During Annie's training I went and took a class somewhere else one Sunday. I was doing a pose on my back called "happy baby," where you grab the outside edges of your feet and pull them toward the ground. The male teacher started walking over to me with a grin on his face. I was down low. He was above me, smirking. He bent down and said to me, "You look around too much. You're always looking around."

I got red, my face burned, my eyes welled up. Did other people hear him? I was mortified. I was vulnerable, lying on my back like that, looking at him expectantly—I had thought by the way he was smiling that he was going to flirt or say something that I (sadly) would feel validated by. Nope. *You look around too much.*

He walked away and I wanted to sink into the yoga mat, into the floor, into the center of the earth. I thought: *I suck. I can't even do yoga right. I'm a failure.*

As I walked out, I said, "I look around because I can't hear. I have to look around to see what to do. I cannot hear." He seemed embarrassed as he reached out to touch my arm, "Well, you still pick your feet too much." I guess he was trying to be funny, but he wasn't. I didn't laugh. I never went back.

I decided that when I became a yoga teacher, if I did, I would vow to make my class a safe space. I knew that you could never know what's going on with someone. How many times had people judged me because they thought I simply was not listening when really I had an invisible disability? How many times had I judged someone in the past? I promised myself to not shame anyone for looking around too much and "not being present" when in reality they might be deaf. I vowed to have compassion. Empathy.

As I walked about with my sweaty mat rolled under my arm, I thought, I will not judge someone for "looking around too much" because I will have no idea what they are looking for. I will just be there to hold their hand and their heart. *Fuck you, shame,* I said, looking back at the yoga studio I had just walked out of for good. I wish I had said to the teacher, "Will you help show me the way? Or shame me for looking?"

During my training I also realized that I'd never experienced silence. Because of the tinnitus, a ringing, a whirling, a whooshing, and a hush sound were present in my head all the time. It's never been quiet. In that month off from The Newsroom and delving into my deepest places of myself in yoga training, I realized that perhaps my silence was not other people's silence. I started to think: *What is silence? What does it sound like? Feel like?*

I unfolded my body and took a *vinyasa* and collapsed into a child's pose. My mind was racing: *How did I not realize this before? All this time I took for granted what silence meant when I've never truly experienced it. Or maybe that is my silence? Who is to say? Isn't it astounding how we never know what someone else's experience is? Not fully, anyway.* Little glimmers of knowing other people's experiences filled my body as if they were all a part of me. Like when I talked to my sister on the phone. I wondered, how could I keep this feeling? How could I turn this yearning to want to know other people's stories into something bigger? I had to go back to waitressing as soon as the training was over and I vowed to pay attention to my customers instead of my own IA as they spoke, to really listen to people as best as I was able and to hunt for beauty, but I wondered how I could do something with my life where I could learn about other people and help heal a wound by seeing them. I didn't know what that would be as I rested in child's pose but my arm hairs stood up. I started shaking. We all have scars, some invisible, some not so much, but most of us hide them. What if we didn't? What if we started to share more, without shame?

DURING THE TRAINING it felt like a fish-eye view, where you can see everything at once: your whole future unrelenting and nimble, as quick as an idea forgotten before it's spoken. How you can see it all mapped out: irreversible veins raised and ready for puncture. This geometry of your life: blue, ingrained, vainglorious. How your eyes can adjust to things—the inside of an apartment after an eyeful of sunlight. How you can see part of the moon when it isn't really there anymore: that hanging sliver, white as pearl on black. It's fullness still faintly visible: an illusion, the whisper of its former body. A palsied arc, the fingernail piece of moon that hangs like it's missing something of itself. Waiting out its own cycles.

What I would not realize until my forties was that the moon is never missing any of itself. We just can't see it. People are like that, too.

Yoga was so weird to me because one minute I was in a balancing pose at the top of my mat and the next I was in child's pose plotting how I could quit waitressing for an idea I had that made no sense yet. How did yoga do all of this? I was dreaming up ways to make a living that didn't require me taking an order. I was letting go of people long stored in my muscles. I was crying. I was feeling. To me, yoga was magic. What else could it be? I cried for my father. I raged and breathed through twisting triangle pose and warrior two. I hissed breath of fire and I kicked up into handstands like I was weightless, and yet, I didn't think about my weight as I was moving my way through the poses and Annie's meditations. I was releasing through all the sweating and bending and work and even the softening. I was letting go.

I felt myself unclench.

Learning to Soften

Robert moved in a few months after we started dating. He was giving up his apartment and didn't want to renew a lease because he wasn't sure if he would stay in L.A. or move back to London, where his parents were. He had been living in an overpriced studio apartment in Marina Del Rey and his rent had gone up some ridiculous amount, as rents do in Los Angeles. I told him to stay with me for just a few months. But knowing my classic "few months" or "summer job," I should have known that that was *it*. It was a done deal.

It was terrible in the beginning, just like it had been with my sister, except for different reasons. I felt like I had a guest. With my sister I simply felt like there were two of me and I hated even just the one of me, so I certainly hadn't wanted two of them in my small apartment. Robert was like a really polite guest. I kept telling him to act like it was his home, too, but it never felt like he did. I always felt aware that I had a formal visitor in my apartment. A visitor I had to entertain. I told myself bullshit stories that he needed to be talked to all the time or given permission to open the fridge. At first I couldn't stand it. I was so used to being alone. But I was also comfortable around him, which was an odd feeling.

Once he moved in, I couldn't keep up with my pre-antidepressant self-abuse tendencies. I couldn't drink a bottle of wine and then sit on Myspace all night. I couldn't as easily sleep until noon or pick my face.

Living alone allows you to self-destroy in private, with no accountability. Living with someone forces you to take better care of yourself, or at least fake it.

I had a real-life person in my space who I had to try and allow to look me in the eyes; this was still nearly impossible for me. But I was starting to let go of the bullshit story that I was only worth sex and that I was a bad person, because Robert treated me with kindness and dignity and respect, and, every night, he was still there. He wasn't leaving. I stopped trying to deaden myself all the time. I began to believe I was worthy, because I saw myself through the eyes of this person who loved me. I remember at the time reading Caroline Knapp's *Drinking: A Love Story*, and balking at the line,

. . . the way women (at least women like me) use alcohol to deaden a wide range of conflicted feelings—longing for intimacy and terror of it; a wish to merge with others and a fear of being consumed; profound uncertainty about how and when to maintain boundaries and how and when to let them down.

I felt like I could have written those words. I was stuck in between the battle of wanting intimacy and being deathly afraid of it.

In 2008, two years into dating, I finally relaxed, or he relaxed. Or we both did. It also coincided with me going on antidepressants. It finally felt like we lived together rather than him just visiting every night, seven days a week. Three years in I farted in front of him. I was horrified. I had never done that in front of a guy. But then I kept doing it. It made me remember when my father used to fart and then pretend it was me. I was a grown-ass woman, but every time I farted I wanted to pull a Mel and say, "Robert, was that you?"

Robert and I lit my electric fireplace and curled up on my couch, watching TV with the subtitles on. The subtitles didn't bother him. *This,* I thought. *This is love.*

Four years into dating we were walking to the movies on the Third Street Promenade to go see *Inglourious Basterds* and Robert nudged me to the other side of the sidewalk. He always insists (still) on walking on the side closer to the street. I wasn't expecting it, so when he pushed me, I almost lost my footing.

"So, um, would you ever want to be Mrs. Taleghany?" he asked, and he shoved me, which I equated to pulling a girl's hair you like on the playground.

"Are you asking me to marry you?" I said.

"Well, would you want to?"

"Wait. Is this how you are asking me to marry you?"

It sure was. The next morning I woke up to a velvet jewelry box from a local jeweler on my pillow. Inside was a small diamond engagement ring.

I opened my eyes and rolled over onto the jewelry box. He said, "I waited for you for ten years."

He had. But he did not remember my name despite my ego telling me he was just trying to save face.

I wanted to keep my last name. I felt like it was my only connection left with my father. I am always going to be Jen Pastiloff, Melvin's daughter. Daughter of Mel the Jew, his nickname when he hung on 5th and Wharton in South Philly as a teen.

I avoided planning the wedding. You know how when you ignore something, it just goes away? Like your hearing loss or grief or your toothache or the fact that you hate your job so much you want to pull all your hair out?

I had a root canal once when I was in my early twenties. I never put a crown on the tooth and it started to give me trouble after a couple of years. I ignored the toothache until, eventually, one day, the tooth broke as I was brushing my teeth. I hit the toothbrush against my tooth, and the tooth broke in half like it was taking a stand against my inertia. *Enough*, the tooth said as it cracked in half and fell down the drain of the sink. Even then I didn't go to the dentist. I was scared and thought that by avoiding the situation it might magically rectify itself. My tooth might grow back like a child's might.

So I waited.

One day, the rest of the tooth gave in and dangled by the root as I ate a pickle. I let it hang for two days before I finally went to the dentist to have it pulled. I am missing a tooth to this day. I am an Avoider, not a Facer. And that is a classic bullshit story. I am deafer, my tooth is still missing, I still have no college degree, the patterns of holding my grief inside my body have created neural pathways that cause me to binge-watch Netflix for hours on end under the covers instead of facing what is really going on. None of the things have taken care of themselves simply by avoiding them. I tell people in my workshops: This stuff takes time to unwind. It takes your whole life.

I equated wedding planning with going to the dentist. I didn't have any money, and traditionally the wife's family pays for the wedding and my mom sure as shit didn't have any money, so I suggested we just get married in court. My sister was married by this point, her oldest son, Blaise, had just been diagnosed with Prader-Willi syndrome the year before, and another baby boy, Maddock, had just been born. She was living outside of Atlanta and my mom was living in Tehachapi, California, with my stepfather, Jack, on an ostrich ranch. We all talked multiple times, daily.

I was really into Wayne Dyer at this moment in time and I kept thinking of him saying, *How may I serve?* My mom had tried to get me to read him and Suze Orman for years. I was a hard *no*. Until one day I heard Wayne on PBS and realized my mom perhaps knew more than I gave her credit for. I downloaded all his talks onto my iPod.

But the first time I heard him say those life-changing words was in an auditorium with thousands of people. I was in the front row because I was determined to meet the man who was changing my life, and also so I could hear better. When he said those words, I shuddered. *How may I serve?* It made me want to barf in my mouth because at the time all I was doing was serving people all day. Veggie burgers and eggs and chocolate espresso no-nut brownies and decaf coffee and *fuck serving*.

Then it hit me. I never woke up in the morning and asked, *How may I serve?* If my friends booked acting jobs, even though I did not genuinely want to be an actress, my first thought was always my IA saying, *What's wrong with me? Why am I not enough? I am never going to get out of this restaurant.* I was living in a desert of lack and a city of not-enoughness. I listened to Wayne speak and wondered, *What if there really was enough? And what if I am enough? And, oh my god, I have been such an asshole for so long.* I suggested to Robert that we turn our wedding into an opportunity to serve other people.

I had no idea who was saying the words coming out of my mouth. It certainly wasn't my IA. Who was I? Having a wedding to serve other people? Did I think I was Wayne Dyer of the yoga world?

"What do you mean?" he asked as we sipped pinot noir on my hideous gray carpet.

"I mean, I can ask if they will let me cancel my Sunday yoga class and instead have a party and invite everyone but tell them they can't give presents. We can ask them to bring donations and if anyone wants to sing or speak or play music or whatever, they can. It'll be like a yoga party wedding thing and we won't have to spend any money. Maybe we can get someone to donate wine. Oh my god, this is such a good idea."

"Okay," he said.

That's Robert. Okay.

Okay. *It's going to be okay.*

We got married at the Beverly Hills Courthouse on February 25, 2010. I taught a yoga class at the donation-based yoga studio that morning, where I rushed out yelling, *I have to go get married now* and almost forgot to collect my donations in the box, which always reminded me of getting tipped like I was still a server. I ran home to shower and change. I had thirty minutes. I wore a black dress I'd borrowed from someone, and a little mascara. Robert wore a dark suit and a maroon tie. The judge who married us, a funny and warm woman, had us take each other's hands as we stood under a huge wreath of beautiful white flowers to take our vows. Besides Robert and I, there were four other people present. His mom and dad had flown in from London, Robert's friend Jason, and my friend Loren.

After the ceremony, the six of us went to a hotel in Santa Monica called The Huntley, where from the penthouse restaurant you can see the whole coastline. We had martinis and champagne and French fries (with mayo for me). It was just as I always imagined my wedding would be, which is to say, like any other day. Only different.

I had never imagined myself getting married, since I could never imagine the future. I hadn't thought I deserved one. My mind would still, even at thirty-five years old, freeze up when I tried to think of anything beyond one month into the future.

IN MY WORKSHOPS, I talk about how unbelievably hard it is to break patterns. How we can't beat ourselves up when we struggle. We all struggle. Always. It's part of being human. I would see someone come to my workshops again and again, the same person, and she would write the same things down when asked what she wanted to let go of. Every time.

I didn't judge. I was, in my late thirties and early forties, doing the exact same thing. Moaning how I needed to let go of the belief that I didn't deserve a future, that I couldn't plan anything. I would panic when I had to think about any moment beyond the one I was living in. I'd hear these women (it wasn't just one woman, we all do this) repeat the same things over and over. It was from the listening of them that I saw myself.

If I wasn't asking *now what?* after every pattern I claimed I wanted to break, then I was just making a list of reasons why I sucked. I saw these women doing this, paying a whole bunch of money to come to a weird yoga workshop and just make a list that they would stick in a drawer and forget about. It's what we do. (Which is why I hate New Year's resolutions.)

I started asking them to ask themselves that question. And not for the litany of what they perceived as their flaws, but one at a time. If I was asking them to do this, I absolutely had to do the same thing. I thought about how, despite my complex relationship with my mom, she has taught me so much. She introduced me to Wayne Dyer's work, and without him I would have never started the journey I am on. When I started dating Robert and I was deep in the cycle of overexercising and starving myself (yet another pattern that came and went over the years like a virus), I called my mom and said, "I don't know, Mom. He's so great, but I am not sure I am ready for a relationship. I like my routines. I like coming home from The Newsroom and being able to go and do my walk and exercise and not have to talk to anyone and sit on the computer all night if I want to. If I have a boyfriend, I can't just do whatever I want."

She said, "If you keep doing what Jenny Jen P has always done, you'll keep getting what Jenny Jen P has always gotten."

"Oh my god, Mom. Did you really just call me 'Jenny Jen P'? But, ugh, you're right. Why are you always right? I love you. Bye."

Jenny Jen P was my nickname and my AOL Instant Messenger screen name and e-mail address at the time. Essentially, my mother was asking me to ask myself, *now what?* I would have talked myself out of allowing myself to be in a relationship just so I could keep up my self-destructive patterns.

Turns out being in a relationship did interfere with my patterns.

Thankfully.

Now what? would be my challenge for the rest of my life, as it will probably be yours, too.

Even though things hadn't ever shown themselves to be A, I wanted A. They had only shown themselves to be B and C and D, and yet, I wanted A and wished for A and starved myself in hopes that would bring me A. Whatever A was. In whatever situation. Love, my father, acting jobs, my body, my apartment.

Allowing myself to enter into a relationship with Robert, and then having him move in, helped me break the cycle. The first step was asking myself *now what? Now what* became *yes, I will go out with you.* Then, *yes, I will marry you.* Both things terrified me. And yet, moment by moment, I entered into them as if entering cold water. And look, it did not kill me.

Each time I thought about breaking a pattern that wasn't serving me, I took a breath in, asked *now what,* and then waded into water. And there was always someone holding my hand. I didn't get there in a vacuum and neither will you. Look around for the folks who will call out your bullshit stories, who will help you not only to identify your bullshit stories but to call them out. Look for those who will ask you, like my mom asked me, "Do you want to keep getting what you've always gotten?"

Breaking Patterns (or Trying To)

I had spent so long not allowing myself to be present, drifting off and leaving when things felt like too much, that I didn't even know when I was physically hungry or not. I wasn't ever sure how I felt. I was married. *Oh. Okay, I am married now.* I remembered when my dad died and I said, *I don't care.* That was not the truth but that's all I could allow myself. One rice cake. One grape. Only *I don't care.* I smiled really wide for pictures and I made jokes but I wasn't 100 percent there. I can see in the photographs I was indeed there, but I was not inhabiting my body.

I was terrified that if I really accepted the beautiful scene in front of me, it would all vanish, so I kept a part of me at bay, locked in my time machine, fiddling with the dials, trying to escape. I looked over at my stepfather, Jack, and my new father-in-law laughing with each other and I closed my eyes and imagined my dad in there, too, trying to smoke inside as if it was still the eighties, making everyone laugh even though he wouldn't have wanted me to leave him. He'd discreetly look at me and press his finger into his nostril and say, *You know what I mean?* our secret code, and I would say, *Yes, of course, I know what you mean.*

I wished I had continued therapy through the years. I had only gone a few times to a few different therapists over the span of twenty-seven years. It's always felt overwhelming, like dating. Having to go and retell your story again and again and hoping you found the right match. (I've never been good at dating, either.) The closest thing I had to working through my shit with my dad was listening to Wayne Dyer and doing yoga. I had never dealt with my grief, my eating disorder, my relationship with my mother. And yet, there I was, married. A real adult.

I posted a blog about my upcoming wedding and why it was special—and it wasn't about how much money (that we didn't have) that I'd be spending, but about something much greater that had started to come together for me as a yogi, and as a leader of yoga retreats, and finally as the writer I always wanted to be.

I wrote:

This is such a special occasion. Not only is it marking my new life, but it is a sign of the yoga (meaning "union") of the human spirit. When I told people I was donating the money to Haiti earthquake relief for my wedding, they wanted to be a part of it.

The pots and pans and dish towels will always be there.

I would really love a wok, though.

AT THE WEDDING party at the yoga studio, little kids walked around with white buckets and collected money from everyone for the Red Cross relief efforts in Haiti. A woman who had taken my yoga classes for years did my makeup as a wedding gift and I didn't wear shoes, since there was a "no shoe policy" in the yoga studio. I painted my own grubby toenails. Not surprisingly, I didn't plan it very well, because I only had wine, cheese, and crackers. My friend Gabby ran out and bought tons of burritos and tacos from somewhere on the Third Street Promenade and came back with them thirty minutes later. We ate Mexican food with the donated wine as we collected money for Haiti and celebrated my new life in our bare feet. We ate leftover bean burritos for a week.

I asked anyone who wanted to perform music or read poems or get up onstage to do so. A friend of mine played the cello, another sang. Someone read poetry, some said prayers. Someone offered a blessing. My friend Annabel gave a speech. I stood onstage and spoke although I have no idea what I said. My mother-in-law was impressed. She'd never heard me speak publicly before and couldn't get over how I could just get up there and project my voice and speak without having planned anything out. She still talks about it.

I remember thinking I had to get up and speak. I hadn't planned to, but as soon as I got up there in my silky dress and bare feet, the words poured out of my mouth. It wasn't the donated wine I had been drinking, either. Being in front of people and speaking, or connecting with them, was home for me. Once I was up there, I never wanted to get down.

The next day I walked into the local Red Cross with our donations. I don't remember ever feeling as good. *How could I keep doing this, this idea of serving?*

In life, we have so much shit and we constantly collect new shit on top of the old shit and we mostly don't even remember the shit we already have, so when we get a new espresso maker we act delighted and we use it for a while before we stick it in the cupboard with the other things that don't fit on the counter and then forget about all of them because they're hidden.

Isn't it funny how we house so much crap that we aren't even consciously aware of? We do the same thing inside our bodies. So much pain piled on top of pain and memories on top of memories that we just shut the door to our minds and pretend there is nothing in there. That we are fine.

After I brought the money over to the Red Cross office, I couldn't stop thinking about the idea of *stuff.* I'm a stuff person. The kind who always has an indentation in her shoulder where the big heavy bag digs in. The kind who always leaves a trail and is always knocking something over because there's so much stuff around her.

When I worked at the restaurant, the guys who worked in the kitchen used to put things in my bag. Melons and cast-iron skillets and bottles of hot sauce. The Newsroom made a fantastic cast-iron skillet blue cornbread in a cute little mini–iron skillet that always ended up in my backpack. I wouldn't realize until I got home because my bag was already so heavy and filled with unnecessary things like shoes, bottles, hardcover books, sneakers, underwear, bottles of water, bananas. Sometimes I'd be happy because, *Hey, I needed a cast-iron skillet,* but mostly I felt embarrassed that I hadn't noticed, that I walked around with so much that I didn't notice when someone added their own stuff to my life. That's how it is, though, isn't it? When you have a lot of crap, it takes a while to notice that more is being added, however slowly. *This guilt? Not mine. This hot sauce? Not mine (but I'll keep it). This shame? Not mine. This drama? Not mine.*

It's hard to not realize you have the cast-iron skillet before it's too late. Once you get all the way home with it, you might as well keep it, right? Because, let's face it, it's kind of embarrassing to come back with it explaining that you didn't steal it, that someone stuffed it in your big-ass bag and you just didn't notice. Or maybe it's not embarrassing and you just want to keep the cast-iron skillet because you think you should have one. Maybe you think you deserve one. That's what we do, right? *I know it isn't mine to take on but I'll keep it because I probably deserve it.*

The things we take. The things handed to us that we walk around with as they dig into our shoulder and cause us pain and yet we say, *No, I'm fine. I got this. I can carry it all. It's mine.*

When you carry so much shit you don't notice when other people add their shit, truthfully, I was glad to have not gotten more shit. As I walked out of the Red Cross, I remembered those days with my backpack at The Newsroom and remembered my friend Joe on his hike: carry only what you need.

After Robert and I got married, I thought about what I could carry. I decided to take an assessment of what was on my back and in my car and in my heart, and to imagine what it would be like to be free of it all. If I imagine myself free of my dad's memory, I want to vomit. So *thank you very much* but I will keep that one. The rest, though? The guilt and the drama that doesn't belong to me or that once belonged to me? *Good-bye.* I am putting you back with the cast-iron skillet and melons that aren't mine.

You think as you get older the weight gets lighter? It doesn't. It gets heavier and heavier until you are buried in a pile of it and you can't even reach the front door. I did get a bunch of woks, though. But what I got more was: the power of community. I saw how I was able to bring people together, not just at my retreat, but at my wedding, and on the internet. I wanted more of it.

CHAPTER 16

Embracing Change

ONCE I HAD started teaching yoga, the restaurant started to slip away like a mirage in the desert. It was only three months after I finished teacher training with Annie but I gave up one of my six shifts. Then two. Within a year of finishing the training, I only had one shift left. The mirage became only faintly visible, just a couple of squiggly lines above the asphalt. Like those years my mom and Jack, my stepfather, lived in the suburb of Vegas and I'd walk out into the street in my bare feet and hop foot to foot because it was so hot and then I'd run as far as I could with that heat under my feet before I'd stop and look back. All I'd see were moving lines, which reminded me that everything was always moving.

For a year I worked only on Wednesday afternoons. I didn't really *need* the shift anymore, I was teaching so many yoga classes and hustling (I put my yoga business card down with every tab that I dropped off) that I probably could have quit. I could've let go of that one shift. Except I was terrified. That job was all I knew. For thirteen years I had only known those four walls of that restaurant. I had spent almost my entire twenties there and some of my thirties. (Funny thing: if you ask me what those walls look like, I can't remember.)

I'd come home during so many of those self-loathing years and sit at my lopsided kitchen table by the window in the apartment I shared with my roommate. The only light came from the apartment across the way, where a creepy television commercial actor and rumored sex-offender lived. My feet would ache, my whole body would burn, and I would cry silently as my elbows leaned on the wobbly table with the broken leg. I would pour a drink to take the day away, but the day never went away and I'd stay up until four a.m.

The idea of not having my restaurant job made me feel like I was a piece of driftwood at sea. Bobbing and lost, without any idea when I would see the shore again.

My friend Amy got asked to be the yoga teacher for a retreat in Mexico but she was moving away to Texas and couldn't do it, so she referred me instead. The idea that I could lead a yoga retreat just barely being out of yoga teacher training made me giddy, like I'd just stolen something and made it out of the store without getting caught. *Look what I stole!*

I took the meeting with the people hosting the retreat. They asked me to take the job, to come to Mexico with them, and be the yoga teacher for their "life-coaching" retreat. I played it cool when we met for lunch in the Southern California Valley, like, *Yeah, yeah, I do this all the time,* but I nearly let my iced tea spill from my nose. *Boy, did I pull the wool over their eyes,* I'd thought. *If only they knew I am so new at teaching yoga! I can't believe I am making this kind of money doing what I love.*

Over iced teas, they explained that they would want me to use my database (I had no idea what they were talking about but I nodded, *Yes, of course,* as I squeezed lemon into my tea). What database? My poems?

"We will pay for your flight there and your room and board, plus one thousand dollars," they continued. "All you have to do is teach a yoga class every day and tell your database about the retreat. Just one, one-hour yoga class a day. And anyone extra you bring, we will give you two hundred dollars per head."

We shook hands and I agreed to alert my database immediately.

Look what I stole! My hands were itching.

I was going to get away with it.

I walked out of that Italian restaurant in Encino after shaking hands and agreeing I would be the resident yoga teacher for the retreat in Mexico and I cried.

It wasn't a sad cry. I was waking up and waking up can be exhausting. The kind of exhausting where you have to pull over on the side of the road in Encino and ask yourself, *Is this happening?* and *Is this happening to me?* and *Am I ready? What if they find out who I really am?*

Who do you think you are?

RIGHT BEFORE I left for the Mexico retreat another one of my teeth broke. I had a missing tooth *and* a broken front tooth. My IA is a teeth grinder, it clenches and my teeth pay the price, as do my recurring nightmares of teeth falling out.

It was a Tuesday night and I had to work my one lonely little Wednesday shift the next day. I was leaving for Mexico Thursday to lead my first yoga retreat. Like that Talking Heads song "This Must Be the Place": *"Feet on the ground, head in the sky."*

Take that, apron! Take that, measly tip! Take that, rude customer! Take that, sticky hot sauce bottle!

Obviously, I couldn't go to Mexico with a broken tooth, nor did I want to. I tried to get my shift covered so I could go to the dentist even though going to the dentist was one of my greatest fears and I avoided it at all costs. No one could cover for me, which made me roll my eyes and say *figures* and *typical* into the air as if *no one anywhere* had *ever* done me a favor before, which was not true at all. I called and told the manager that I had tried to get it covered to no avail and that I had to get my tooth fixed because I was going to lead a retreat in Mexico.

The transition from me starting to teach yoga to the moment when I told them I had cracked my tooth and couldn't come in had been only one year, the trajectory in my career had moved so quickly that I became invisible to them.

Did you hear that, guys? I made it! I escaped. After thirteen years, I am finally doing something with my life! I am getting out! I am free!

They only heard t*ooth* and *broken* and *can't come in.*

The manager wished me luck getting my tooth repaired and hung up on me because I called during the lunch rush and they were slammed. I thanked the manager even though he had hung up and I was speaking to a dial tone.

CHAPTER 17

It Was in You All Along

DURING THE RETREAT in Mexico with the life coaches, I had one responsibility. On paper, at least, which was: teach one yoga class a day. Other unspoken ones were sitting in on the numerous coaching sessions they led with the participants. I was supposed to sit there and absorb everything. I truly do not know why I was asked to sit in like a silent auditor on people's innermost fears, but it was part of our agreement. I found it challenging to be a fly on the wall. For the first time in forever, I wanted to let my feelings out. I watched all the participants share their stories and cry and have breakthroughs, and all I felt was a lump in my throat. I wanted an outlet, yet I wasn't invited to share. Per my agreement with the retreat. And per our agreement, I was paid two hundred dollars for each person I brought through my database. I brought three from the classes I was teaching around Los Angeles, so my database was getting therapy as I sat and watched.

Sayulita is a village on the Pacific coast of Mexico, just north of Puerto Vallarta, full of vibrancy and color and waves that will knock you on your ass. (For real, do not go out in the water there alone. I almost drowned.)

In the southwest part of the peninsula, there are humpback whales and dolphins. We were staying in a big house on the remote part of the beach, about a twenty-minute walk to the center of town. I taught yoga every morning under the thatched roof of the *palapa* for shade. In their Lululemon tops and yoga pants, the attendees put their hands in prayer position whenever I asked them to and adjusted their pink and purple yoga mats to face me, depending on where the sun was.

I thought I had no idea what I was doing. Isn't it astonishing how we trick ourselves into thinking we don't know what we are doing when it's actually right there inside of us? (This retreat is when I started to recognize and call out bullshit stories.)

They had no idea I had just started teaching yoga a few months before. We tell ourselves, or rather, our IA tells us, that we should just quit while we are ahead because we are garbage and have no clue what we are doing and we should just go back to refilling green mint iced teas, but then something else clicks in, something bigger takes over, call it whatever you want, and it moves through you like a jolt, or like three espressos, and all of a sudden, you're a big shot, telling people to lift their leg in the air and to stand like a mountain and to rotate their outer hip and you actually do know what you are doing despite a whole life of saying *No*. Out of your mouth comes a *Yes* and that is the something bigger than yourself.

So that's what happened in Mexico. I opened my mouth, and can you imagine my shock and awe when I discovered that although my IA was telling me I was an ignorant dumpster fire, I actually knew a lot. I was a wealth of knowledge and I was a really good teacher. I may not have been the best at yoga, I can barely touch my toes still to this day, but I was a damn good teacher. I could communicate what I wanted to whomever I wanted to hear me, I was teaching yoga poses, but I realized it was my words that felt powerful. I could move people with my sentences, my voice. This was the place I discovered that power. I led them through a practice of holding space for grief, letting go, for gratitude and joy. Asking them to move into positions, into yoga asanas, was a way of asking for their trust.

They trusted me. And through their belief, I began to trust myself.

So even though I had moments of being terrified of the perfect life coaches with their weird eating habits and never ever taking anything personally, I was deeply indebted to them because my IA took really long naps on that beach, and on the Day of the Dead, when the sun went down on October 31, I looked out at the Pacific Ocean and thought, *Good-bye, asshole.*

Of course it wasn't a final good-bye because is anything? Ever? But it was enough of a good-bye that I was able to continue teaching that week with confidence. The pool was shaped like a lima bean and I would float on a big pink raft in it as my face freckled up like it used to when I was a kid frying my skin. I wore a fanny pack and a pink top that said AVON WALK FOR BREAST CANCER I had received as a gift from a beautiful Mexican woman with breast cancer, to whom I was offering free private yoga lessons back home as part of my commitment to serving others. I was happier than I had allowed myself to be in years because I was drinking tequila and I was calling the shots. There I was, walking home across the beach at night with my newfound friends, barefoot, singing Tom Petty's "Free Fallin'" like drunken sailors, off-key and obnoxiously. I felt that big thing inside of me again, that voice that threatened to drown out my IA. I felt it in the back of my throat and knew it was the start of something.

My IA was beginning to slip away because I was beginning to believe I had value. I was beginning to realize that no one was coming to save me, and there I was, saving *myself* on a beach in Mexico.

I began to see how powerful I was. If I was powerful, I thought, then it means that everyone is. The feeling that I was part of something was bigger than my IA. I was no longer just a waitress simply slinging veggie burgers and pressing my ribs.

I saw glimmers of the belief that said, *You are not broken.* I started to realize I was not as alone as I had always believed myself to be. I realized I needed to be around people in all their messy glory.

I may not have wanted to be a yoga teacher when I took that yoga teacher training but *something led me to this beach*, I thought. And for all the years I beat myself up, there I was drunk on a beach in Mexico being paid good money to teach people how to move their bodies and *I did this*, I thought. I took action and did something and there I was so maybe I could cause other things to happen besides "bad things."

As I walked on the beach in the early mornings after I taught my yoga class by the pool, I thought, *What are they doing that I can't do?* My IA got quiet just long enough for me to get the courage to decide to lead my own retreat.

There Is No Such Thing as the Perfect Time

Want to know something? There will always be something to stand in the way. Something to tell you, *No, absolutely not. This is not right. You mustn't.* If you wait for things to speak, they will. Everything and everyone has an opinion. You know what they say about assholes and opinions: everyone's got one. Including our own minds.

There's never really a good time for anything. Something in the way, someone coming to visit. Someone leaving, someone showing up, the weather, the football game. Your mother. Death. Whatever it is, there will always be something saying, *Wait! This isn't right! Do it later. Now is not a good time. Now is bad.*

Sometimes you find yourself in the midst of a life and you think, *I don't remember starting this, yet here I am*, and sometimes you literally have to wake up and say, *It's time. Despite everything pointing south, I must go north.*

People ask me all the time how I did it. How I made this life. How I went from A to B, from waitressing and being stuck for so many years to doing what I do now.

I woke up and decided I'd had enough, and despite the timing being utterly horrible, I was going to go for it. And even though I had no idea what *it* was, and some days I am still not sure, I kept rising to the coffeepot and looking into the cup and you know what? It spoke back to me. It said things like, *What are you doing? Who do you think you are?* It was my very own Inner Asshole and I gulped it down quickly and drank cup after cup until it stopped talking and I no longer had to hush it. If it did decide to speak again, I would ask it, *Who do you think you are, asshole, you don't exist. You don't get to tell me what I can do. I created you in my imagination.* And then finally the coffee started agreeing with me as if it saw the sense in what I was saying. Sometimes it was the eggs that spoke or the wine or the customer at the restaurant, but always it was me who got to choose who I listened to regarding my life and my own personal clock.

The timing is never right.

Don't believe me? Go ahead and name some perfect times for things. There's always going to be something in the way and it's always going to be up to you to make it the right time. Your IA will most definitely always tell you that now is a terrible time.

There will be people, too. You might have your own Randalls. People will remind you how bad things are and how bad of a time this is. Much like the coffee or the eggs, you have to look those peo-ple in the eye and say, *You may be right but I am going to do this any-way.* And if you decide not to, which is always your right, just make sure it's because of what *you* want to do and not what others want you to do.

I have spent a bulk of my life thinking that the timing of the earth is off. That perhaps I had just experienced too much death for someone so young and the only way to justify such loss was by ex-plaining it away with a problem in the earth's rhythm and cadence.

I'd always told people that I couldn't have a baby because I was just too busy, I couldn't slow down my schedule. I couldn't go back to school. The timing wasn't right. I couldn't quit The Newsroom *just yet*, I couldn't leave my apartment, I couldn't travel. The timing was always bad. I couldn't deal with my grief. I couldn't face my hearing impairment. No time! Too busy! Too stressed! Too whatever.

I finally realized that timing is an invented thing, an inherited trait, and that along with depression, my height, and a penchant for sleep and for coffee, I will have inherited the ability to create the life I want for myself. Just like you.

Don't wait for the coffee or the eggs or the shmuck in the front row to tell you how it is. You'll wait your whole life and then end up in an embankment with a heart full of sorrow and *I could have done it better*s.

The way I see it, time is the con artist. The con artist telling you that *this isn't a good time, you should wait.* The right time will never exist. Like so many of the things we think are perfect and in the end turn out to be just ordinary.

It was time to lead my own retreat.

CHAPTER 18

Bringing People Together

A FEW WEEKS after I graduated from yoga teacher training, I attended a yoga retreat in Ojai, California. The retreat was held at a gorgeous old house, and in my fantasy brain, a place I believe we should all visit frequently, I had imagined that I would leave The Newsroom and lead my own retreat either there or in Italy. My fantasy brain, like the TV show *Fantasy Island*, was very specific. Ojai or Italy. I didn't dream of Costa Rica (although I would eventually lead a retreat there, and in Mexico and Bali and the Galápagos Islands and Stowe, Vermont, and the Berkshires and France).

When I was twenty, I had gone to Italy with my Scholars Program at NYU. It was during the time when I was trying to disappear via eating only baby food and puffed corn, but Italy was so magical that I still managed to fall in love with *Italy*, not South Philly's version of Italy, the only Italian I had ever known up to that point.

That first time in Italy, I pretended to be Italian, which was easy to do: I was good at pretending and I had long dark hair. I ordered espresso, and unlike my deprivation at school, I let myself have bread there, dipped in olive oil and salt, and blood oranges from the outdoor market. I wrote poems near the Coliseum and I was as happy as I had ever been. Ojai had that same feeling for me, like I was coming home. How I could come home to two places I had never been didn't make sense to my brain. Only to my body, which felt safe.

In 2010, I wanted to do my own yoga retreat without the life coaches. I'd been teaching for just over a year. I figured I'd start with a local one before I went big. The only place I knew of was the house where I had attended a retreat in Ojai, an hour and a half north of Los Angeles. I decided to rent the same house where I had been a paying attendee, only this time without the sexist yoga teacher who slapped women on their asses as he said, *Damn, look at that thing. Good job, honey.* He had given me a massive discount, so I went because I was eating and breathing yoga and the idea of a yoga retreat was better than anything.

Leading my own retreat scared me more than feeling my feelings or facing my hearing loss, but I was determined. I announced the retreat at every yoga class I was teaching (and I was teaching upward of twenty times a week), I posted endlessly on Facebook. I asked all my friends and family to post endlessly on Facebook. Twenty-seven people signed up. Twenty-seven people I had fooled into wanting to come with me for my Yoga + Wine + Food weekend. Twenty-seven souls who had no idea what a mess I really was.

I had stayed at The Newsroom all those years because fear was making all my decisions. Was I fearless when I did the retreat? No. But I was fearless-ish, and that was enough to get me where I needed to be.

I made this terrible flyer on shiny paper that was way too big, so you had to fold it into tiny squares or crumple it to fit in your pocket or purse. There was a picture of me in knock-off UGG boots, a flowery off-the-shoulder top from Ross Dress for Less, yoga pants, and the words *Yoga Wine Food Weekend* written across the top. On the bottom half was a description of the property and what would be included in the weekend. A wine tasting, two yoga classes a day, hiking, massages, free time. I put an exclamation after *Free Time!* Who had free time? We were all so busy in our phones and schedules and it seemed to me that we were all equating worthiness with busyness, so I wanted to accentuate *Free Time*, even though I secretly wondered if it would make people nervous, not having anything to do. I wondered if I needed to have every minute accounted for so they would feel like they had gotten their money's worth. I copied the schedule of the yoga retreat I had attended there, because I had no idea what I was doing. I was a terrible planner and scheduler. I couldn't even schedule an upcoming weekend, let alone a retreat for other people.

Another bullshit story. So often we say that we have no idea what we are doing when, in actuality, it was in us all along. But that revelation did not come until after, or at least during. Before the retreat, my mantra was *I have no idea what I am doing. What have I gotten myself into? What have I done?*

I was teaching yoga at a studio near my apartment called Tru Yoga at the Yahoo! Center in Santa Monica. It was nestled inside the office building, so you couldn't see it from the street, but inside it was like this secret beautiful yoga room with expensive wooden floors and green wallpaper and Buddha statues. There was a little tea lounge where you could get your hot green tea before you got your *vinyasa* on. I loved it. Most of the people who took my classes there worked in the Yahoo! Center and would come to class during their lunch break or right after work to my evening class. They became regulars, just like I had regulars at the restaurant, except they didn't ask me for a chicken potpie or coffee, and they listened to me like I had all the answers to life besides having a good playlist. I didn't have any answers but I did have a fantastic playlist: P!nk, Snow Patrol, The National, The Beatles, Cat Stevens, Jay-Z, Michael Jackson, Kenny Loggins, Nick Cave, Bill Withers, Simon & Garfunkel, Journey, Krishna Das, and Missy Elliott were among some of the artists I played in classes. I even played my old college roommate Stephonik, formerly knows as Stephanie.

I mentioned my upcoming retreat at every class I taught all over town. I was also teaching at the donation-based studio on the Third Street Promenade in Santa Monica. To this day, it was the most beautiful studio I have ever seen. I had two classes in the big bright room upstairs, where I had my wedding party, and one in the smaller room downstairs.

I also discovered how community could be built and sustained through social media. With Facebook, I'd found a tool and I wouldn't put it down. I was, by nature, a connector. My whole life I had been the person who kept in touch, who didn't let things or people go. But now I had an actual site to help me do what I was already good at doing.

I took down people's names and e-mails if they took my classes or when I waited on them and I added them on Facebook. I kept adding and posting about my classes and the retreat I had coming up in Ojai. I didn't care if people thought I was self-promoting (I was), I got people to pay attention. They started asking questions about the retreat. They started e-mailing me and messaging me on Facebook.

"It sounds intriguing," the people who took my class said as they rolled up to a seated position after *savasana*, final resting pose.

"It will be amazing," I replied, although inside I was constantly second-guessing myself, the constant asking of *What have I done?* After I did anything.

"Yeah, it's going to be amazing. You should come." I'd smile, rubbing lavender oil into their palm or massaging their temples.

"I think I will. I deserve this. It sounds like exactly what I need," they would say. It was always fascinating to me how many people would say, "This is exactly what I need," yet they didn't truly believe they deserved much. Me being one of those people. Nonetheless, I had no idea what I was doing, but I was planning on changing lives in my Yoga Wine Food weekend. I just didn't know how. I also didn't know one of the lives would be mine.

Most of the people who came were from my yoga classes. I had been so incessant in my selling it and my posting about it on Facebook, that after a while I think people gave in and came just out of curiosity and because I made it sound so enticing, just like I did with that second glass of wine or how good cheese would be added to your veggie burger as well as avocado and a double side of chips and salad. I made it sound too good to resist. Like my father, I could sell a dream, only this time the dream was real.

No One Saved Me, and Other Truths

I was still a brand-spanking-new teacher, but I had twenty-seven people signed up to come away with me to Ojai.

In the end I winged it. I made the retreat up as I went along.

I counted on my improvising skills learned from my years of acting class and people skills from years of waitressing and my impulsive mother's skills to help me through the weekend, as well as the schedule I had been forced into making because people wanted to know what they would be doing when, which seemed unreasonable to my unorganized brain. But I conceded and made a schedule.

I listened to my Wayne Dyer recordings on my iPod (thanks, Mom) and went over my yoga teacher training notes and prayed to my dad and bit my nails and asked myself what in the hell I was doing, but I got in the car and drove to Ojai with a cup of coffee in the cupholder next to me, which was sticky for some gross unknown reason. I was on my way. Was I afraid? Yes.

But I bought my fear a cup of coffee and showed it what to do (even though I had no clue). I pretended. Thankfully, fear didn't know the difference. Hence, my expression: *Buy your fear a cup of coffee and show it how it's done.*

Robert came with me on that drive. He was so proud of me, of what I had accomplished and who I'd become in such a short period of time since we'd gotten together. From being so miserable at The Newsroom to going on antidepressants and then taking the yoga training, to doing the retreat with the life coaches and then my own retreat. All in a year. It was antidepressants and yoga and the willingness to love and be loved. All were contingent upon the rest. Robert was my greatest champion.

He called me Pasti, short for Pastiloff. "You got this, Pasti. I believe in you," he said all the time. If it wasn't for him I am not sure I would have gone through with it, at least not then. His support meant I went from standing at the host stand reading *Us Weekly* and *Shape* magazines at The Newsroom to standing in front of a yoga room and leading retreats. I did not get there on my own. He was my *I got you* person.

That first day of my retreat, I was standing in front of the yoga room at ten a.m. and the itinerary said *meditation* because I thought there had to be meditation at a yoga retreat. I had only been to one yoga retreat, where we had all kind of pretend meditated. I figured I should at least do that if I wanted it to be an authentic yoga retreat. So we were doing meditation.

It dawned on me I actually had no idea how to teach meditation or what the meditation should be on. I didn't have a meditation practice. Why had I decided to include a meditation? What was I trying to prove? Maybe I could say it meant the meditation would be self-directed? Quiet time for everyone else to meditate while I took a break? *Fuck. Fuck. Fuck.* Everyone was waiting for me to say something.

I turned around so no one could see me frantically thinking and F-bombing. I faced the Ojai Valley right there out the window with its lemon trees and calming vortex and mouthed the words *Fuck me.* I spun around, and much to my surprise, this came out: *Let's meditate on what we want to manifest in our lives.*

Manifest? Where did I get that word? What the hell was I talking about? What did I, Jen Pastiloff, know about manifesting? Wasn't I "just-a-waitress"? What did it even mean, to manifest? It sounded woo-woo and ridiculous. I looked down at my absurdly wide little feet and my botched cheap pedicure, and I figured those twenty-seven people were about to find out I was just a regular person who struggled with depression and had no idea what she was doing. *They are going to hate me,* I thought. *Once they see who I really am, they will throw rocks at my head.* But they didn't. They sat and waited and listened. They *listened.*

Being deaf, and especially in the years after I started being honest about my hearing loss, I was extremely self-conscious about being heard. Everything sounded like it was underwater. I was careful to enunciate clearly and to speak loudly. I didn't have hearing aids yet and I wasn't as open as I would become later about my disability. I was filled with shame and frustration.

But there, in the room in Ojai, it was quiet. Everyone waiting.

Let's. Meditate. On. What. We. Want. To. Manifest. In. Our. Lives. I was using my overcompensating "poetry voice," that voice poets sometimes use when they read poems, a lilting cadence that annoys most people I know. Poets, myself included, adopt it the minute they open their mouths to read. I am not embarrassed to admit that I was using that voice. There, leading the manifesting meditation, my voice did not wobble even though I had no idea what was coming out of my mouth. I couldn't even hear my own voice—and yet, no wobbling. I had no idea where the words came from or where I had gotten the confidence, something moved through me and pushed past the fear. I was speaking from my heart, I was speaking the truth, not just parroting some shit I'd read in a self-help book about how to transform your life or live it well or let go of this or that or here's the path to freedom. Nobody knows the right path, but we can all use our imagination. And we have the stuff—the raw material—of our lives and myriad experiences. Suddenly, in that moment, I realized the value of what I'd been through and who I was. And I thought about a writer I had just discovered, Lidia Yuknavitch, and how she posted on Facebook a lot about time not being linear. Perhaps my greatest wish of all time. Maybe it was true?

"You can't manifest it if you can't imagine it," I said to the class.

"I used to never be able to even imagine a few months into the future, let alone what I wanted to *do* with my life. When I was pretending to be an actress all those years at the restaurant, and yes, I was pretending. I did nothing about it (except take some classes and be in a crappy play this one time), so when I was claiming that I was an actress, I could never actually imagine myself on set. I would close my eyes and try to see myself as the star of a TV show or in my dressing room, and I couldn't do it. I couldn't even visualize myself as having just one line. That should have been a red flag to me that I didn't really want to be an actress, but I kept on saying *yes* when people asked if I was one. And I would get the dirtiest feeling. You know, the one you get when you lie? It's not that I felt I was lying, because I was saying I was an actress and I just wasn't booking any jobs, I wasn't equating success with landing gigs. I simply wasn't doing anything to pursue that so-called dream. How could I explain to the customers who had seen me in the restaurant for years on end that I really didn't want to be an actress at all, that I was depressed, that I had no idea what I wanted or who I was? So I just kept saying that I was an actress and I kept waiting for someone to come in and discover me or rescue me so I didn't have to do the work of doing it for myself. *Someone save me,* I would pray as I delivered lattes to tables.

"I still didn't know exactly what I wanted, but I had stopped saying, *I don't want to be here.* I just kept doing things. I call them my *now whats*. I got out of bed. Most days. I took a yoga class. I went on a walk. I started a blog. I didn't want everything to be in my head, to be so woo-woo. I wanted to take concrete and literal steps. Little *now whats* and not so little ones. And then, I started to pay attention to my fantasy brain. In other words, my imagination. If you can't imagine it, you can't manifest it. I started to 'make shit happen.' That's what manifesting is, right? Making shit happen. MSH. I like to use acronyms. And I like to curse. And to drink coffee and wine. And I'm still a yogi. I refuse to live inside any kind of *Just-A Box*.

"In my fantasy brain, I saw you all here in this place and I kept imagining that every day. You all here. This place. Me and you. Me doing *this* instead of feeling sorry for myself. Even on the days where a customer treated me like crap or I was dead broke or I slept until noon, I kept seeing all these people coming together, a community. I had no idea how and I'm not suggesting that you get things in your life by simply visualizing them. That's dangerous and lazy thinking. And please don't worry, if you don't know what you want to manifest, if you have absolutely no clue, welcome to being a human being, *Hi!* Ask for clarity. Being a human being is mostly having no clue, anyway. At least it is for me. But we do it together, right? We have no clue together and it's so much less scary. We can help ourselves have no clue together. Or we can find clues together."

I talked about how I'd started to finally believe in myself; how I married the kindest man I'd ever met just a month prior to this gathering; how I stopped obsessing on everything I put in my mouth. I talked about accepting my hearing loss, even though it is the worst. I talked about being able to hold those two things in my mind at the same time: acceptance of something that seems unfair, and acknowledgment of its unfairness.

I talked about the time I realized that it was okay to change my mind. That just because I had held the bullshit story that I was a bad person in my body for so long did not mean I had to keep it forever.

I talked about myself, but really I was trying to give permission to everyone else. To put language around the thoughts that I knew they'd had, too, because they were human.

People were taking notes. Nodding their heads. Wiping tears away. All those words came out of my mouth as if I had spoken them hundreds, if not thousands, of times before. They were all listening. They were *hearing* me.

After I was done talking and channeling the Ojai Valley or whatever it was I was channeling, I asked them to write what they wanted to manifest on Post-it notes and stick those desires on the wall. A wall covered in wishes, a bona fide wish wall born of the imagination of this group of gathered strangers.

I'd been gifted the idea a few months earlier when a man had suggested it as he was doing my hair with some new chemical straightening process. He offered it up for free if I would be in his hair show, so I sat in his chair for six hours. My hair was down to my butt so it took forever. I told him I had just started teaching yoga and was about to teach a special class for Thanksgiving. He wore a leather jacket and Doc Martens and suggested I had the class write what they were grateful for on sticky notes and then stick those notes to the wall. He was one of those people who did everything. *I do hair, but I am also a painter and I sell houses and I am a writer and in a band and I also preach in my local church and I am an inventor.* I was desperate for ideas and I thought the sticky-note idea sounded like a good one, so I said *thank you* as he straight-ironed my hair for the third time before swiveling me around to check out his work. Since that time, I have used the sticky-note idea for every single workshop and retreat that I do. It's amazing how inspired you can get if you (a) sit your ass in a chair for six hours and (b) really listen to people. Thank you, Hair Straightener.

After the students wrote what they wanted to manifest on their notes, I asked them to think of the idea of serving others. I had them go to the wall, grab someone else's sticky note, place it on their heart, and come back and sit down.

I decided to tell the truth about my life. Fully. I told them about my jealousy—of other people's bodies, of their lives, their money, their living fathers, and big fancy houses, and fancy degrees from fancy colleges.

"You have someone's sticky note on your heart. You literally have their dream on your heart. Close your eyes and want that for them. Even though you probably don't know whose note it is, it doesn't matter. This is about wanting happiness for others. Supporting others. Remembering that there is enough, despite our Inner Asshole telling us otherwise. This is our meditation."

Everyone pressed their fingers to the notes on their hearts.

"Those of you who struggle with feeling supported in life—and I get that—remember that right now, in this moment, someone has you on their heart. You are supported. Can you feel that? Even though the sticky note will come off, the feeling will be tattooed there. Someone is saying, *I got you*. This is the experience of being *gotten*."

The rest was yoga, or "traditional yoga." Downward dogs and planks, pigeons and headstands. All the stuff I had been trained to do, mixed with the stuff I'd been struggling with all my life. This was the alchemy, this was the magic.

I had them start in child's pose. Toes together, knees apart, forehead heavy on the mat. Back when I started, most of the people who were there were from the yoga classes I taught locally in Los Angeles, so most of them knew at least the basics of yoga. Many, in fact, were pretty advanced practitioners. That would change over time. Nowadays, most people who come have never done yoga or don't practice regularly.

On this day in Ojai, I led them through sun salutations and other poses, and I played Journey and Elton John and Snow Patrol and we meditated on the things they had written on the notes that had been stuck to the wall. We sang during "Purple Rain" and "Don't Stop Believin'," which eventually gave me the idea of Karaoke Yoga after I saw a sign for a cycling class with karaoke. It was the first time since I read my poetry at NYU that I felt worth something. I was sort of using my poetry voice, but people were digging it, and I read poems at the end of class before we broke to eat organic spinach pie and drink wine. I still couldn't cook or thread a needle or hear that well, but *fuck*, I thought, *look at me*. I felt like I was a person for the first time in a long time.

CHAPTER 19

From Connector to Leader

TWO YEARS AFTER the retreat I did with the life coaches, I returned to Mexico to lead a retreat at a place called Xinalani, except this time on my own. I thought back to that meeting I'd had with the coaches in California when they decided to hire me and how I thought I had tricked them and how far I had come in two years. I thanked them as I climbed the endless stairs to my room. *Without the people who led me here, I would not be here*, I thought. *May I be a Human Thank-You.*

There were hundreds of steps to get up to the rooms, so you felt like you were living in a treehouse overlooking the ocean on one side, jungle on the other. Each room was open-air and had a hammock. You had to take a boat just to get to the retreat center. It was paradise. I had a small group, including the comedian Steve Bridges, who was on the flight with me from Los Angeles. Steve had recently started coming to my yoga classes and then started coming to my retreats, one after the other. He was an impersonator, famous for his impersonations of presidents George W. Bush and Barack Obama, among others. He was the funniest person I had ever met, besides my father. As we boarded the plane, he turned to me and said, "I love my life. I have a great life, Jen." I wish I had recorded it so I could play that sentence all the time and tattoo it in my ear for when my IA takes the reins.

I asked everyone to bring journals to that retreat. I was getting braver and more creative and more outside the (Just-A) box with what I was doing in my classes and what I was saying. I had never really wanted to be a yoga teacher, so any opportunity I got to veer away from that felt truer to me than teaching the poses. We did a lot of yoga on that retreat, but I would have the particpants "stop, drop, and write," as I called it. I would get them hot and sweaty, with *I'm strong* mantras in thcir minds, and too tired to have their guards up, and then I asked questions and gave them prompts I dreamed up while serving vegan hotcakes after listening to Wayne Dyer on repeat. *Who would you be if nobody told you who you were? In order to be where or who you want to be, what do you need to let go of? What would you do if you weren't afraid?* And they would stop, drop, and write the answers in their journals.

I asked them to bring journals because I had been using sticky notes in my shorter retreats so they could write what they wanted to manifest into their lives and stick it on the wall. A sticky note would not be enough for an entire week. I wanted to go bigger. What would I do for a week with these other humans who had come to Mexico with me? I wanted to write, but I got them to Mexico under the guise that it was a "yoga retreat," so I didn't think I could very well say, *Hey, y'all, we are actually going to write instead of doing yoga, 'kay, thanks.*

I had an idea that I thought might work. It wasn't yoga, but it was yoga-ish and it was largely inspired by the life coaches after I saw the breakthroughs the people had at their retreat as well as my own retreat and my rekindled writing practice. In yoga teacher training when we had our notebooks by our mats to take notes about poses or anatomy, I always ended up writing poems and lines for essays and blogs. Ideas came to me while I was in the poses as if I was somehow more alive. Fully present. I decided they could bring journals and maybe I could get them in that same inspired place that I was able to get to while I was doing yoga. Then, I could cheat and actually have them write. I figured if I did yoga and writing, no one could claim I tricked them into coming to a yoga retreat. I would use yoga as a way in.

I thought about how I used to have to get drunk to eat or to have sex. I'd down two glasses of wine on an empty stomach and only then could I allow myself the vulnerability to have sex, or to at least be less self-conscious. I would drink the wine and then feel free enough to allow myself any kind of pleasure. Or how I used to eat in my sleep and how those things occurred because I was in a more vulnerable or altered place (asleep or drunk), so I suggested to my groups that I wanted to get them to that kind of place without having to get drunk or fall asleep or literally fall out of their living bodies and minds. I just wanted to get them hot and sweaty and tired so they were less in their cerebral minds and were more willing to be honest. I would have them do some *vinyasa*s and then tell them to drop down and write from my prompts.

Why am I so afraid? What am I waiting for? What would happen if I loved myself? What if I told the truth?

ON THE LAST MORNING before we left, Steve and I sat across from each other while everyone else went down to the beach for a photo shoot. He called me *Gin*, with his Texas accent. We made funny videos where he kept saying, "Give me some ass water," instead of *ice water*. I thought I was falling in love with him.

I could look at Steve and allow him to see me. We talked about love, and having children, with him definitely wanting kids and saying how awful it would be if he never did, and me saying I did not think I wanted children. I felt both vulnerable and safe with him and I wanted more of that feeling. Three days in, I wanted him to lean over and grab me by the hair and put his mouth on my mouth. I was married. It was neither sexual nor romantic. I just wanted his body near mine so I would know he was not leaving. He made me laugh and it was hard not to pretend he was a little bit my dad. The two funniest men I had ever known.

He didn't have a hammock in his room, so I said half invitations to him like, "You can come to my room and use my hammock." But he never did. Had I known he would die on his sofa two months later, I would have kissed him.

After I'd gotten back from my Mexico retreat and lain on my sofa feeling pancake flat, Steve had texted me saying, *I am lying flat on my friend's couch and I can't stop thinking about our trip. I wish we were back there. Wow.*

I wrote back *me too,* and then I stood up and put on shoes to go teach my yoga class, but I knew something had shifted, something was gone. Maybe that was why I felt flat or maybe it was natural after a trip like that to feel so much of that *I want to be back* feeling.

After he died, I texted him *I want to be back I want to be back* even though I knew that he was dead. And how did I know? A woman who had been on the retreat texted me *Steve died* the evening a bunch of us were all going to go out for a Mexico reunion dinner. The worst way to receive heartbreaking news like that? Through electronics.

When I got back from that first retreat to Mexico, I'd still planned on going back to work. I thought my safest bet would be to keep that one shift. *Just in case.* I had a back-up plan. A plan B. I still didn't know what my plan A was but I would keep my plan B.

Safety, safety, safety.

I called to ask what time I was scheduled to come in for my Wednesday shift. The manager paused and asked me to bring in a doctor's note for my tooth from the day I pulled a no-show.

A doctor's note?

And so, after thirteen years, after customers asking me out and being equally awful and kind, and after all the jumbo hotcakes and hummus plates and birthdays in an apron, I got fired.

AFTER ALL MY BITCHING about The Newsroom, it surprised me that I missed my people. The people who stiffed me a tip and then stole magazines from the magazine rack (which I also did). The women with the men who would sniff while telling me, "He's a poet. He wrote this in, like, five minutes. On the spot."

"Isn't it beautiful?" she'd say.

It said things like *your friendship is bigger than the ocean* and I'd silently barf a little in my mouth, but hey, this guy was writing and I wasn't, so who was I to judge? I was taking his order for a stupid simple chicken sandwich with mustard and a side of bad stanzas. But when I look back, I can see the amalgam of despair and loathing and how eventually I couldn't maintain that chemistry any longer.

I was charming to tables, mostly, and when no one was watching I hated myself. I made them laugh when I took their orders, and inside I thought I was garbage. When no one was watching, I ate off the plates in the back and I wrote notes to myself on my notepad about how gross I was.

But I hated myself so much that the only way I could feel any sense of joy was if I could make a customer feel good. This was the beginning of beauty hunting. Eventually, it would collapse as I realized that trying to make others happy all the time will suck the living shit out of you if you abhor yourself, and I would have to learn how to make myself feel good, but it was a start. It was my start, in any case.

I would put my hand on people's shoulders, I would remember what they liked, I would listen to them tell their stories. It was here I learned that all people really want is to be heard, which is the crux of the work I do now in my workshops. *Fierce listening. I got you. How bold one gets when one is sure of being loved.* I practiced all these things while I was a server.

It is also where I learned to be a *Human Thank-You*, as I call it in my workshops now.

I think about the wrong turns I've made, which, who's to say if they were *wrong* or not? Who's to say that if I had stayed in New York and gotten an MFA, that I'd be some professor at some university, writing my eighth book, drinking brandy out of a shot glass from a Jackson Hole, Wyoming, tourist shop? Sometimes, to torture myself, I like to think that my turns have been wrong, but hell, I don't know. I'm just over here trying to do the dishes.

After Steve passed and The Newsroom closed, I wrote a thank-you letter. To the restaurant I worked at for thirteen years and to all the fucked-up people I waited on, all the wonderfully peculiar and quirky customers, all the big-hearted ones, the overtippers, the assholes. I wanted to thank them *all*. I wish I had written more down from that era but I was half-asleep, so it was hard to pay attention to anything other than my survival and Tables 32 and 43. I do think, however, that they all left imprints in my DNA, or rather, I pray that they did, because without those imprints, I have no proof that I existed. I have no journals of all the times people were rude to me or said awkward things like, "Is there something wrong with your ovaries? I have a feeling you have a cyst. I can feel that by your energy," or the exact words they said when they insisted on buying me a plane ticket to see my newborn nephew across the country. I wondered, if I was that professor drinking brandy from that weird Wyoming glass, would I be happier? Would I have written down all the moments that led me to whatever moment I was in, in my professorship or famous authordom? Maybe. But wouldn't I at some point still weep at the sink? Doesn't everyone?

It was then that I decided to say thank you to my past. Thanks to all the weirdos and inappropriate old men, and also thank you to all the kind people. Thank you to my coworkers, the ones who escaped and the ones who still haven't, who are off working at other restaurants, with another slew of demanding hungry customers. Thank you to those who believed in me and thank you to those who didn't. Thank you to the talent manager I met at the restaurant who told me to lose ten pounds. Thank you to the guys in the kitchen who would make me food when they weren't allowed to. Thank you to the douchebag who, just because you had a hit TV show, thought you could humiliate me. Thank you. I loved running into you recently when you couldn't place me and said, "It's so good to see you. You look great. Really great." Thank you to Kevin Smith, the director (also from New Jersey), for always *always* tipping 100 percent of your bill. Every. Single. Time. And to Patton Oswalt, Titus Welliver, and Sarah Silverman for being great customers, big tippers, and treating me like a human being. That helped. Thank you to the lady who told me she thought *I would've made something of myself by now.* Thank you to the people who paid attention. And those who didn't. Thank you to the women who couldn't ask for what they want, who let their voices get really high as they sing-songed, "Um, can I, like, get extra dressing?" Thank you. Thank you forever to Laura Louie, Woody Harrelson's wife, who told me my pants had a big slit in the back and that my ass was showing. I would have done the same for you, for anyone. Thank you to those who made me laugh or sit down at the table like I was an equal. Thank you to those who said I looked good. Thank you to the lady who asked if I had herpes. Thanks to the guys who asked me out and thanks to those I went out with. Thanks to the famous songwriter who always asked for plastic cutlery.

But mostly in those years, I learned how easy it is to confuse grief for body fat, your job for your worth, your lack of knowing who you are with the fact that you are nobody and nothing. I wish I could go back because I remember all the table numbers and how to put an order in and what was on the menu and I would not wear high shoes or makeup or sneak booze in the back or hide myself in all the ways I did back then. I would let myself get *slammed, in the weeds,* in waiterspeak, when you are utterly unable to catch up, and I would ask for help. And I would realize that it wasn't that big of a deal, asking for help or being stuck. That the world was going to keep spinning. And I would slowly make my way out.

Somewhere in me those experiences and memories have an inner life, and somehow, despite the pathetic head banging in the walk-in freezer at the restaurant, I made it. Not only had I re-created myself as someone who was not dead inside, but I was teaching other people how to feel more alive. I was married, I was teaching yoga, leading retreats, writing. I no longer believed that I didn't deserve to take up any space on the planet.

I sat on my living room floor and rolled back until my head hit the carpet. I stared up at the ceiling of my apartment and wondered who I'd thank in fifteen years. Of course there was no way to know that I would be thanking my son, so I simply said, *Thank you, Robert, thank you, apartment, thank you, ceiling, thank you, sink. Thank you, everything that is anchoring me to this.*

Thank you. May I be a Human Thank-You. And not an asshole.

CHAPTER 20

Fearless-ish

I Am of Service, or, Fear Doesn't Own Me

AS IT TURNS OUT, I didn't fool twenty-seven people into anything on that first retreat of mine. I did a service by making room for their imaginations, by making their hopes and dreams come alive not just for them, but for the people who held those dreams against their hearts.

I don't know what I'm doing was another bullshit story I'd been walking around with for decades. I knew what I was doing. I just had to tell the truth. And listen. I was teaching myself to hear with my whole body. I was paying attention.

It wasn't all smooth sailing. That first retreat, the first few, really, I was desperate to get people in the room. I made a lot of mistakes, the kind that desperate people make. The *love me? love me?* kind where you don't care who it is as long as they say, *Yes, I will come* and *Yes, I love you*. The kind of mistakes where you don't question who is in your bed because *Hey, at least someone is in my bed. At least I am not alone*. I didn't know how to teach meditation or what I wanted to accomplish, I just knew that I wanted to fill the room. I felt an immense pressure to not lose money after growing up without money after my father died. I just wanted bodies. I wanted to feel like it was all going to be okay, that I wouldn't wake up and have everything gone, a box of doughnuts in lieu of a life.

But even though it wasn't perfect, it was change. Big change. I was softening, and instead of being unable to imagine a future, I was looking out into it—not without fear, but with less fear, which was something I had never been able to do. It was one of the first times fear had not been calling the shots. I was undead for the first time in years.

Who Do You Focus On?

I'd started to write again. I wasn't writing poems like I used to, but I was putting words together. I started to blog on a website called Elephant Journal and I saw Facebook as a way to share what I was writing, which at first I thought would fill my yoga classes and, I hoped, my retreats. I was so used to living in scarcity, so used to being in hustle mode, that I didn't think I could just teach yoga or lead retreats without forcing it. In other words, I rarely let it be, as I was fond of telling other people they should do. I did not trust that people would come, that things would work out. I thought I had to work every second of every day to fill those classes, because if not, I would end up being a waitress for the rest of my life on Robertson Boulevard in West Hollywood.

The truth was this: I had never given anything my all. I had never tried to succeed at something.

Tomorrow. Tomorrow I will stop hating myself, I would say, bent over the trash can where I had thrown the muffins I felt bad about eating.

I thought, *What if I got really honest?* What if I stopped caring if my blog posts made people sign up for my classes or retreats and just wrote for the sake of writing? What if I let go of attachment to any outcome of what I was writing? What if I trusted that I was enough and I could write whatever I wanted and the people would come *or* they wouldn't, but that the writing itself was the thing, rather than just being a means to an end?

I was getting excited. I had a lot to say. I decided that I would be fully myself, honest and human, messy and truth-telling. And I would share that fully because *that* was who I was.

I was scared, but then I remembered my younger self sitting behind that desk in Hayden Hall at NYU, writing poems next to my roommate; or sitting in Italy daydreaming about being an author; and I remembered how alive I'd felt in those imaginative spaces that made me feel present *and* as if I had a future (another "and" statement). Sure, once I published a piece or once I closed my notebook and left the café or stopped daydreaming, I was scared again, but while I was writing, while I was telling the truth, I was unafraid. I wanted that again. Fearless-ish. Afraid and not afraid. Scared and doing it anyway. Holding more than one thing. Two things at once. More than two things at once. Everything became an "and" statement.

And it began.

Being Wrong as a Way of Being Right

I started to write about my depression on my Facebook page and in blog posts and for a website called Positively Positive that at the time had a couple million readers. It was there that my "following" really started to build, even though I have always hated that expression. It reminded me of cult leaders and their "followers." I had a weekly slot on the site and took it very seriously. People were sharing my articles all over the place and e-mailing me and telling me how my words made them feel less alone. So, who started to feel less alone, less like a trash bag and a failure? Me.

I felt connected to something powerful and real. I had spent almost my whole life feeling disconnected and half-dead and now I couldn't stop doing. I posted on Facebook all the time. I craved how important and valued it made me feel, and I started to have moments where I thought that perhaps I wasn't a bad person after all. Maybe I had been wrong about myself?

What else had I been wrong about?

I talked about taking antidepressants, which at the time were unheard of for a yoga teacher to be publicly talking about. And there I was hitting *share share share*. Every time I hit the share button I wanted to throw up in my mouth (the research professor and writer Brené Brown calls it a "vulnerability hangover") but I kept doing it. I was done letting fear rule my life. I started making videos where I just talked to the camera the way I wish someone had once talked to me.

And people e-mailed me hundreds of times a week thanking me.

At first, I didn't know what they were thanking me for until I realized that by my letting go of the shame in who I was, I helped them to do the same. I kept getting messages like, "I feel like you give me permission to be myself."

I certainly was not giving anyone permission simply because I was talking about being depressed or the fact that I never even started to grieve for my father until I was thirty-five years old and how much destruction that had caused me, how much pushing everything back inside my body and locking everyone out made me feel like I was not even worthy to be a person. I talked about how I drank too much wine and I cursed and I didn't think I was very good at yoga per se but that I was a good teacher. I think people felt like I had changed the rules. *Oh, I can talk about the fact that I do yoga and it doesn't help? I am still paralyzed with depression? I can talk about how I was suicidal? I can talk about anxiety?* It was like I was saying *yes* to all of them with my words.

I *had* to write. I was coming back to where I had always wanted to be, even though the road was crooked and I had fallen off and ended in a ditch called The Newsroom wearing platform shoes, and my writing was being done on something called Facebook, so what? I was back on the road, with no idea where it was headed, only that I was driving and that I was leading the way this time. Fear was no longer driving my Hyundai. And I had taken off the damn platform shoes because I was never *not* going to be short, I was never going to be more worthy because I was tall, so I might as well take off the cheap heels and put on some sensible shoes.

The more people responded to my postings on Facebook, the braver I got. I see the danger in that, and also the humanity. It's hard to not respond to love and validation and people eating up your words. It is hard to not get addicted to that kind of need and want. It can be mistaken for love. At first I thought it was love. I'm grateful for those people, though, because it allowed me to keep going. *How bold one gets when one is sure of being loved,* that Freud quote I am so fond of, guided me back then even though I wouldn't hear the actual quote until years later. I felt like something bigger and heavier was holding me down, or at least guiding me. I can see now that it was *me*, my voice, which had been drowned out for so many years by my IA and all the grief and self-loathing I had force-fed myself instead of eating actual food. At the time, though, it felt like I was channeling something. I allowed whatever (or whoever) was coming through to come on through. My IA was quiet, for once. It was my turn. I had found a platform that weren't Steve Madden shoes.

I became obsessed with Facebook, which at this point was already garnering the reputation that it was for old people. *Facebook is for dinosaurs. My parents use Facebook.* I had Instagram for years before I knew what I was doing. I would just put pictures on it and use the cool filters to make them look prettier. *Rise. Valencia. Mayfair. Early Bird.* I had no idea that people could "follow" me on Instagram or I could follow them or what a hashtag was. I didn't understand, but I tried to because apparently it was *the thing*, like Facebook had been *the thing*, and I had started to be known as a social media person, so I felt like I should get with the program.

I knew I wouldn't be a bendy yoga handstandy type of Instagram person (because: I am not), but then I realized I could indeed add my words in the captions and it felt easier to navigate. I also found I had to be succinct, since there is a word limit, so I started to edit down what I wanted to say. I never followed any rules, I hardly used hashtags, I didn't post shiny perfect pictures of me doing arm balances mainly because I suck at them and can't hold a handstand. I just posted my thoughts about real life, like I had been doing with Facebook and my blogs. Real motherfucking life. Years later I would turn that into a hashtag, but at this point I was just sharing what it meant to be human, according to me.

I would post my thoughts and talk about not being able to hear and how hard that was, or not wanting children, or being ambivalent about it at the least, or how I didn't practice yoga that much or how I lived in a tiny apartment or how I had sat on my ass all day and then, at the end of the posts, I would say, *See you next week at so and so place in Philadelphia,* or *in May in New York,* or wherever my workshop was to be held. And the people would tag their friends, saying, *Let's go!*

I was always scared that no one would come. Did I even know what a workshop was? But then I thought, *Wait. I can make a workshop be whatever I want it to be. I can do whatever I want.*

I contacted yoga studios in Philadelphia and New York and asked if I could come and do my three-hour workshop at their studio. At first, the agreement would be that they paid me 70 percent of whatever we charged for tickets and I would fly myself there. I didn't care about the money. I just wanted to see if I could pull this traveling thing off.

I could and I did.

CHAPTER 21

Gifts, Unexpected and Otherwise

Retreats were different from workshops in that they were either a weekend or a week. I rented the house or retreat center and the participants paid me. It was all based on trust because I could never guarantee that people would actually sign up. And since nothing is guaranteed in life anyway, I went for it. Another generous friend lent me the initial money to rent the house in Ojai. After that, I had enough money on my own from teaching to do it myself and to pay back my friend.

After one of my retreats in Ojai, I started carrying around a small purple journal, which an attendee had given me as a gift. One of the participants who had attended before had been so impacted that she brought her teenage daughter Rachel with her on the next retreat.

And right away I could tell the daughter hated it.

The daughter, who was probably sixteen, was dressed entirely in black and kept her hair in her face. She wouldn't share during opening circle. We usually just share our names and where we are from and anything that feels like it wants to be said. This girl was all, *No,*

I don't think so. She was a *no way, uh-uh, hell no* kind of girl. She was all cross-armed and looking for a way to escape. I recognized this. I knew what it was like to always look for an escape route.

She shut herself into the back bedroom while we had a wine tasting. Her mom had given me a brief history: she had an eating disorder and suffered from depression and she was a *cutter.*

I left the wine tasting and went into the bedroom where she was sitting on the bed, sulking.

I have everyone bring a "gift" for closing circle. A token of love, as it were. Something, anything really, that you give the (arbitrary) person sitting next to you to remember you by. Bought, handmade, a flower, a poem, a bottle of wine. Whatever.

One time a man had given me a bag of coffee beans and said he wanted me to have it because I made him feel awake and alert, and he wanted me to remember that. Plus, he knew I liked coffee. Things like that. Thoughtful things.

Hi, I said.

Hi, she said. She was working on her "gift." A tiny purple book. In it, she was writing all her favorite quotes and song lyrics and beautiful intricate drawings.

The thing is, you never know what you are going to learn from people, right? I mean, my mom couldn't get me to stop being anorexic when I was seventeen or eighteen (or nineteen or twenty-two) even though she tried. But me talking to this teenage girl? I'm a stranger. I am *not* her mom. She could hear me in a different way. She saw me. I never saw my mom back then. Perhaps not even still, because we see through the lenses of all that has come before and our childhoods and our pain, right? But with a stranger? It's like you are right there. In that moment. And nothing has come before. No history to interfere.

I went on to tell her about my history and the stuff I put myself through and how I wanted to die and she listened. Big, beautiful wide eyes. I was firm but loving. She told me that she didn't trust herself and was scared that she would hurt herself. *I get it,* I said. I sent her an essay I had written about my anorexia for The Rumpus. I left the room. I told her about "Dear Sugar," by Cheryl Strayed, also on The Rumpus.

She emerged from the back room a few minutes later and hugged me. Hard. A crack of a smile appeared on her face. She didn't leave the retreat. She swore that she would rather be dead, however, than sing out loud during Karaoke Yoga, which was a blend of what I was already doing: getting people out of their comfort zones through movement and, now, through song.

You know what I am going to write next, right? Guess who was singing her face off and dancing her ass off by the end of the retreat? Yeah.

By Sunday morning, her mom told me she was worried that the daughter wasn't eating breakfast. I told her mom that that sounded about right. Sure, she was making strides. She was doing some *now whats*. Yes, this retreat would be pivotal in her healing (she went on to an in-patient program after) and yes, the retreat would show her what was possible with connection and vulnerability and some good old-fashioned singing out loud. But.

There's always work to do. This was a tiny step in the stairwell. A windy, loopy, never-ending stairwell that I myself was still climbing.

The end of the retreat came and the girl, Rachel, told me that she did not want to sit next to "just anyone" because she had someone special she wanted to give her purple book to. *I need to give it to you,* she said.

It's beautiful. I carry it with me everywhere. Even still.

She has left her in-patient facility and is doing really well. I helped her. She helped me. You never know, do you?

Now in my workshops I encourage everyone to remember that it is all about helping each other. So stay. Stay and don't walk out the door. Listen. Listen when the woman who is leading your retreat sits on your bed and says, *I have been through this and you are going to be okay.* When the teenage girl dressed in black hands you a book filled with quotes that sometimes, on certain days, like the ones when it's really quiet and you're trying to make some big life decisions, look, because that book will often bring you solace. That little purple bible.

Here is what the opening pages said. And keep in mind that when she first started making the book, she didn't know who it would be for. She was just looking to help. To connect. To make a difference.

Hey there,

I don't know if you're struggling with depression, an eating disorder, anxiety, PTSD, addiction, etc. If you are, I am so sorry. I am too and I know what it's like—it's fucking hard and can even seem impossible sometimes. If you're not, then also know that doesn't mean that you don't have any bad days and you don't feel sad and anxious and overwhelmed sometimes.

So here are some songs, quotes, poems, and passages that help me when I am in "that" place. I hope they will help you too— whether it's getting through a meal, getting through an urge or getting through a panic attack, or just getting through a bad day.

Then she drew a heart. A great big red heart.

My favorite quotes that she had written in the book:

And now that you don't have to be perfect, you can be good.
—JOHN STEINBECK

Think of all the beauty still left around you and be happy.
—ANNE FRANK

I wonder what would have happened if someone hadn't believed my bullshit story and come to me when I was a teenager? I now find compassion for the younger me who hated herself for making her father die—so much that she wanted to die herself. I wanted to put my arms around the young starving girl I was. I couldn't, but I could put my arms around the girl in front of me.

So yes, *I* decided I could make a workshop be anything I wanted it to be, but it was not and never would be entirely on my own. The people on my path, the stories, the pain, the shame, the singing helped me do it. I did not get here in a vacuum. I did not get here on my own. I got here with every single person who came. With your pain, your beauty, and your unique and unrepeatable bodies.

CHAPTER 22

Bullshit Stories and Other Lies I Believed

Fuck the Myth

THE WRITER EMILY Rapp Black says we met because I grabbed her crotch. She came to my yoga class and I am positive I did not grab her crotch (it was her leg), but whatever. She has a better memory and she swears that's the way it happened, so let's go with Emily's version.

Emily Rapp Black came to my yoga class at the fancy gym where I teach and I grabbed her crotch while I was helping her get into a handstand at the wall. We bonded, and whether it was a crotch or a leg, there was some unspoken understanding between us that we had been through hell with our bodies and were simultaneously repulsed by them and also completely unafraid of just getting up in there. It was like a silent code, a secret handshake, recognizing someone who had been through anorexia. We knew each other and if we had made it to the other side there was always a fear of sliding back, because there is no such thing as completely healed, not ever—so don't fool yourself—but if you found that person across the yoga room or classroom or subway, and you gave the silent agreement with your eyes, you knew you had a friend for life. Emily and I were like that. It was immediate.

I had heard from someone that she was a writer, but I didn't know she was a *writer* writer until we started to spend time together and I saw her book *Poster Child*. I assumed when I heard that from someone at the gym that she was a blogger or someone who called themselves a writer (I'm looking at myself here) but this chick was the real deal. She had been a Fulbright Scholar and had published a book whereas I was all, *Let me post an update on Facebook!*

·She encouraged me to start writing again. I had started a blog called The Manifest-Station (I was obsessed with the idea of manifesting back then, like everything had to be about that word, people even called me Jen Manifestiloff), and Emily encouraged me to keep going, keep generating. I compared myself to her a lot in my head (and sometimes out loud to her, which she would swiftly shoo away and tell me I was being ridiculous) and imagined that if I hadn't dropped out of NYU I would be just like her: teaching classes like she did and knowing how to type for real instead of my *two-finger, let me give myself carpal tunnel* way.

I had by then developed a following on Facebook, so once I would share the posts I wrote on The Manifest-Station onto Facebook, they would spread like wildfire. Social media seemed to be the key. Until I posted the posts on the social networking site, it would hardly have any readers, but once on there—bam! Viral.

I had an audience. I had all these people who wanted to read what I had to say, but the bullshit story that I wasn't a real writer haunted me. I couldn't stop obsessing on the fact that I didn't finish college, that I was a yoga teacher and therefore no one would see me as a real writer. I felt like a fraud and yet I also got extremely irritated when people called me a "yoga person" and not a writer. It mattered so much to me how I was seen, what I was called.

I put a call out asking other people if they wanted to guest-post on, The Manifest-Station. I saw how many people were reading my words, so I thought I would share the wealth. I would give away my real estate to people who were looking to get in front of others. I thought of *How may I serve?* This felt like a way I could say, *Like this.* I wanted to share what I had. If the main thing a writer wanted was to have their words read, I could help with that.

I had two friends help me run the site once it became too much for me to do alone. Let me be perfectly honest here, with my unorganized ass, it was *always* too much for me to do. I couldn't keep the e-mails straight, I would forget to reply, I would post things with typos, I would forget to post something I had scheduled. I had no system. Thankfully, my two whip-smart friends Melissa Shattuck and Angela Giles helped me read the submissions and decide which ones to accept. They would let the writer know. They helped me create a beautiful beast. Angela did all the formatting and scheduling because I broke out in a cold sweat even at the mention of those words. They both loved the chance to read through the gorgeous essays. We were getting stunning submissions from teens and young writers, from retired school teachers and published authors, from people who had never written a word in their lives. This is what I had written on the site under "Submissions":

We are looking for fantastic writing. Period. We don't care if you are a well-known author or a computer programmer who secretly writes at night.

We want honest and brave writing.

We are interested in risk-taking. To be shown what beauty is. What love does. What inspiration means. What the power of language and words can do.

Other Voices

Emily Rapp Black and other established writers guest-posted on the site. My sister wrote about being a special-needs mom. Women wrote about losing their babies. People wrote about suicide, depression, autism, eating disorders, racism, rape, grief, hopelessness, and hope. Men started submitting to the site, too. It was not a yoga blog, it was not a vehicle to get people to come to my retreats, it was simply a place writers could tell the truth.

I began thinking, *Why all of a sudden are people paying attention to what I have to say?*

The reason was simple: because they were seeing it. There was no magic to it. I was the same me, I just had many more sets of eyes looking at my sentences and poor grammar skills.

In the past, no one but a couple of select people were seeing my words. I'd call my mom and ask her if I could read her what I just wrote. Or my friend the writer Karina Wolf in New York. But now I had real-life human beings with feelings and fingers and eyes reading what I was putting out there. Whether they liked it or not wasn't the point. And to be clear, there will always, always, until the end of time, be those who don't like what we create. Or write. Or wear. Or say. Or do. And yet, we must keep on creating, writing, wearing, saying, doing. It is what I now call *The 1 and the 100*. There will always be The ONE.

I was battling with Facebook because I wanted to change my public page name to "Jennifer Pastiloff." At the time, it was called "Jennifer Pastiloff Yoga." I wanted to drop the "Yoga." I got it into my head that the "Yoga" part of the name would deter people and make me less of a *real* writer. (My IA was working overtime and my bullshit stories were laughing at how susceptible I was to their sneaky influence.)

My friend said something that I liked about this. She said that yoga is what brought me an audience. That nature knew how to organize itself. Yoga was a way in.

I realized it probably didn't matter if my page name said "Ralph the Penis" or "Jennifer Pastiloff Yoga." It was the content. It was what I was saying. And yes, it was what I had wanted my whole life. *Hear me? Listen to me?*

The Power of an Audience: Of 1 or 100

We all need an audience. Whether it is one person or one million. We must feel heard to thrive.

Whether it was through my writing, or retreats and workshops, I was finding my voice, and community, and that led to less self-loathing. I was finally moving toward self-acceptance. Finding my voice and finding a community were essential to loving myself. This is why my workshops work so well, still. It combines these elements and the equation is beautiful and true math. Your voice + a community = connection and self-love.

Randall, whom I was dying to have love me, never used to read my writing. I'd write a poem and ask him if I could read it to him. I didn't write much, a couple of poems a year at best. As we were lying in bed, just having had sex. *Can you e-mail it to me?* he would say without looking up at me. I'd be hurt but I'd do it because I wanted someone, *anyone,* to read what I wrote. Anytime I had written something, even as a child, I wanted it to be read or spoken aloud. I may not have been able to be vulnerable with my actions, but I was on the page. I needed someone to bear witness.

He would never respond to the e-mail.

I had no audience with the man I loved. Looking back I think, *There is no way that could have been love,* but who am I to judge at a vantage point of all these years later? Who I was back then settled for anything. Any nod in her direction that said, *Keep going.* But there was nothing except *You need to stop waitressing. You need to figure out what you want to do with your life. You need to stop sleeping so late. You need to make a plan.*

Can you just read what I sent you? I finally wrote something, Randall.
I will. I'm busy. Later.

Sometimes it felt like a fluke to me that I was doing so well, that people were reading my words and submitting to my website and coming to my wacky workshop. They would come up to tell me, *Thank you, I feel less alone.* Or, *You have changed my life. Thank you, I never felt like I could talk about being depressed out loud before.* Then they would say things like, *You must be used to it* or *You must get this every day.*

Let me tell you the answer as plainly as I can: *No.*

No, I was not used to feeling awe at the resilience of the human spirit, nor was I used to feeling like I was making a difference, and I never will be, just as I will never get used to the beauty of nature. A beautiful alternate-leaved dogwood in full bloom, a young forest with so much to offer, so much new life and old life intertwined— the shagbark hickory sighing, its arms muscling at the sky.

I want to keep being surprised at how holy this all feels. And if I ever stop feeling profoundly grateful and utterly surprised and like a five-foot-two Human Thank-You, I will be done.

CHAPTER 23

We Must Have Tools

ONE MORNING AFTER my yoga class at Equinox gym, Emily and I went walking to the Santa Monica Farmers Market, and as we sampled apples, I knew she was pregnant. It was just a feeling I had, but I was usually right when I got that feeling. I was excited for her and her husband. I didn't think I wanted a child, but I was thrilled for my friends who were having them. Of course, the IA in me panicked when my friends told me they were pregnant and I would wonder if I was making the wrong choice. I would worry I was going to get left out, left behind, left eating apples alone while all the other women pushed expensive baby strollers and sipped lattes as they walked through the farmers market. *Wait, what about me? How will I know what the right choice is?*

"I am so happy for you guys," I said, eating my fruit. And I was.

After Emily and her husband moved to Santa Fe, New Mexico, and Ronan was diagnosed with Tay-Sachs, I went to visit a few times, wishing I could take away some of their pain, even for one minute. I was bereft and all I wanted to do was smell Ronan's head and hold his tiny body.

So after what felt like a million flight delays, I found myself in Santa

Fe, sitting on a love seat with a sweet baby propped up on pillows next to me as I wrote on The Manifest-Station. He had drool sliding down his chin, eyelids heavy and soft. He purred like a cat every so often.

A book on the shelf caught my eye: *Which Brings Me to You*, by Steve Almond and Julianna Baggott. It was nestled in between copies of Emily's book in the office. I was sleeping in the office they had converted into my bedroom, equipped with an air mattress for me on the floor. A dying baby was that which brought me to you, Santa Fe.

It was winter in Santa Fe. The weather in their little adobe house had been winter dark for the last nine months since Ronan's diagnosis. Losing light at four thirty p.m. and dead trees kind of dark. Dying baby dark.

Ronan was peaceful. He didn't know what was happening to him. It was hard for me to conceptualize that soon, perhaps months, he wouldn't *be* anymore. He would sit next to me in his little plaid shirt, in what looked like a lotus position in yoga, and I would think, *Look at him, he just is.*

The mathematics of this equation refused to register in my head. He was there and everything felt good on that brown couch. The rise and fall of his chest a reminder of what was constant in the world, of kisses and baby things and deep full breaths of mountain air after you'd been trapped in a dirty city way too long. He was so peaceful that it was hard to imagine that with his death would come such an uprising, such pain, such a loss.

I used to think perfect didn't exist. Not the word, not even the idea of something so without faults that there was no room for growth or improvement. It did exist in Ronan. He was sitting next to me in Santa Fe. Whining just a little, so I knew he was there. He would not improve or grow. That moment is who he would be forever in my mind, and he was perfect.

I visited Emily and Ronan several times. We visited El Sanctuario in Chimayo, we went to Taos and drank coffee at cute cafés where I took endless photographs of Ronan.

The last trip I took there while he was still alive, before we headed off to the miniature airport in Santa Fe, she asked me if I wanted to say good-bye to Ronan. I went into his room where he slept on his side with a stuffed tiger between his legs, his eyes half-open and drool coming out of his mouth. I said, "Good-bye, buddy, good-bye. I love you." I kissed him a hundred times. Maybe a million. I left the room and then went back in again to say good-bye one more time. I did that twice. I knew it would be the last time I saw Ronan. And it was.

On a flight home I decided to compile a list of what I learned from Ronan.

1. How to Be Present

Ronan just is. He knows when love is present. He knows when he needs to be fed. You feel silly when you find yourself worrying about the what-ifs of life when you are in his presence. He is present for his life in a way that is at once disarming and beautiful.

2. How to Love

The love you feel for this child is impossible. Can't you feel it, even having never met him? What if we let ourselves love in this way more often? Without any expectations, without regret, with only the here and the now and the openhearted abandon that comes with knowing how fast the clock is ticking.

3. How to Go with the Flow

Ronan was such an easy traveler! He came with us everywhere; his little head propped up with stuffed bears and tigers. He was happy to be there in the back seat. I wish I could take that lesson and store it in the pocket of my being, so if I started to feel nervous or antsy about how life was going, I could reach into that pocket and take out a piece of Ronan's sweet acceptance. I am sure he would want that. I am sure he would want us adults to take away the best parts of him and carry them, a small torch throughout the world with his name on it.

4. How to Be Patient

I don't know if he knows what is happening to him. How can we really know these things? How many times do we set ourselves up in life to be disappointed, or else, by pretending we know what's going to happen? Ronan just sits in his chair, being fed his prunes and bananas, and waits. He isn't truly waiting, not in the sense of *I am waiting for something to happen with my life,* but rather a waiting for the next breath and the next moment. A more primal waiting. He is patient with whatever knowledge he has. Whatever knowledge of love or bananas or mothers and fathers or stuffed tigers.

After Ronan died in February 2013, Emily and I decided to lead a retreat together but really, at first, we just wanted to go on vacation together. She had lost Ronan, her marriage to Ronan's father had ended, and she was in love with a new man named Kent, whom she would later come to marry and have a baby girl with. Emily wanted to go to Vermont and see foliage and horses and drink hot chocolate. She wanted to go far away from Santa Fe.

I thought she was the best writer of anyone I had ever read, so the idea that she wanted to lead a retreat with me was mind-blowing and of course I said yes even though I was terrified and we had no idea what we would do. We didn't plan a thing and it was perfection. We did it four years in a row until her daughter, Charlie, was a toddler and I was pregnant with my own Charlie. We had a good run with our *no clue how we will pull this off but watch us pull this off* retreat. It always sold out with a wait-list. And as she taught her workshops during her portion of the retreat, I sat and listened and took notes and wrote my face off. She, and later Lidia Yuknavitch, helped me to understand that being a writer had nothing to do with how many awards you won or what degrees you had, but what you put on the page. They helped me let go of my bullshit story that a real writer had to write every day or had to look a certain way. They helped me understand that what lived in my body needed a way out.

Writing was the way out, just as yoga had been the way in.

And then there's this: no matter how many bullshit stories you have or don't have, there are no guarantees in life. Nothing is owed to us. That "not knowing" is scary, but the tools to help us—writing, breathing, yoga, connecting—are all we have. And honestly, sometimes the tools are Netflix and coffee as well as breathing and yoga and writing. But we must have tools.

He Has It

Before my nephew was diagnosed with Prader-Willi syndrome, someone sent my sister a rude letter suggesting that maybe he had the syndrome—a rare genetic disorder that gave you small hands and left you starving all the time. We were horrified. We'd never heard of this condition before, and we began to do research. It sounded like something out of a science fiction film. Poor muscle tone. Failure to thrive. Lack of eye coordination. Poor responsiveness. Food craving and weight gain. Poor growth and physical development. Learning disabilities. Delayed motor development. Behavioral problems. Sleep disorders. Scoliosis. High pain tolerance. Constant hunger. Unusual food-seeking behaviors. The stuff of nightmares, for the parent and for the child.

My mom and my sister and I all said, *There was no way he had this and how dare this person suggest this, how wrong they were! He was just a little delayed. All babies develop differently. He was behind. He was fine. There was nothing wrong.*

Blaise had it.

That's all the text from my sister said. *He has it.* My cell phone was on the floor, and as my hand reached down to pick it up, I dropped it. My sister later told me she fell in her driveway and just sat there for hours trying to digest the diagnosis.

Despite all the praying, wishing, begging, and bargaining, when the cell phone beeped to signify a text coming through I knew what it would say and the world cracked open. *Why do you hate my family, God?* I yelled a voice that sounded like an eight-year-old's voice because I hadn't asked that question in a long time and I didn't even know if I believed in God, but there I was in some dark wet pit yelling up to some long-bearded vindictive asshole who killed people and gave them weird genetic disorders.

I loved my nephew Blaise more than I thought I knew how to love. *How is this even possible?* I used to wonder until I realized the things I didn't know how to do—how to love, how to keep going—were my greatest accomplishments, just like my mother's. Loving was perhaps the only kind of magic worth practicing or even partially believing in. Watch me pull a rabbit out of a hat. Watch me keep going after death, loss, betrayal, the loss of my hearing.

This was not the first time words altered the course of the world for me. The first, of course, was all those years ago in the kitchen, hearing "he died," and knowing the last words I said to my father were "I hate you." Now, the words "he has it" literally steered me away from land, right to the middle of the sea where they'd leave me wet, confused, and without a compass. But this time, the words were about someone who wasn't me; they were about a helpless boy.

Just like that C. K. Williams poem, Cleveland was gone. *There is no Cleveland, I adore you,* and, as you'll remember, *there was no last summer:*

the world last summer didn't yet exist, last summer still was universal darkness, chaos, pain.

But unlike my starving twentysomething self, I mulled these words and began to understand: we would navigate through the darkness, chaos, and pain, until eventually we would find dry land and begin to rebuild Cleveland. With hammers and nails and growth hormones and speech therapy and special doctors in places like Gainesville, we would look head-on into the eyes of Prader-Willi syndrome and do what we could with the tools we had.

CHAPTER 24

All Very Normal

THE THIRD TIME digital words altered my world after Steve's death and my nephew's diagnosis, the words were: *Pregnant.* Just like that.

Robert and I had been talking about it. I had been going back and forth with the *when*, with the *not yet*, with the *I just don't know*, with the *what about my career, my retreats, my book that I haven't published yet?* Everyone I talked to seemed to be certain that it would take a long time, *six months to a year*, most said. *Better start now*, they said. *You're thirty-eight*, they said. *You're no spring chicken*, the evidence-givers said. I wasn't, but I was also ambivalent.

Get an ovulation kit, they said. I did. I peed on a stick and when it said *Go*, we did.

And I got pregnant. That easy. One time.

And that was that.

I knew before I knew. I was anxious in a way I hadn't been since being on antidepressants, which I had just stopped taking for reasons I now feel are unclear. I felt like I was reverting into what I referred to as the "old me." The demarcations of my life clear as a line on a pregnancy test. Old me/new me. Bad me/good me.

I collapsed when I saw those words on the stick. Right there in the bathroom, my knees went weak in a way I thought people only said to exaggerate a story. There was that *He has it* text from my sister about Blaise and the *Steve died* text after my retreat and that same feeling of *Wait, I am not ready for this news. I have not had my coffee yet. I have not prepared myself. Take these words back. Take them back into the electronic void from which they came.*

Look what words can do, I thought once again, except this wasn't poetry to me and I was thirty-eight and way past the point of being a college student. This was my life and I felt that within the span of two seconds or so (how long it took for the word *Pregnant* to form on the pregnancy test kit from CVS), my life had gone from being mine to being both mine and no longer mine at the same time. How something could be two things at once, more proof right here in my bathroom.

I wasn't ready. I wasn't thrilled. I was ambivalent.

I felt guilty for my reaction at the news. Wasn't I supposed to be overjoyed? I did not want a child. It was too soon. I walked through those first few days in a trance. Hadn't I just found my way after such a long time fumbling in the dark? I couldn't believe I had gone off my medication and this was the first thing that happened. I was off my antidepressants at the time because I thought:

My life is better now, so I will be better.

I wasn't completely convinced I wouldn't try and get pregnant, and the meds I took were not okay to take while pregnant.

If I inherited the trauma of my ancestors, which I believe we can do, I inherited depression, and not the "I'm in a bad mood" kind, the crushing, life-altering, chemically violent kind. So to think that just because my life was *better* that I would be *better* was naïve at best, suicidal at worst.

I thought I could use all my tools I was teaching in my work-shops, and my depression would vanish. I thought I no longer needed help. I could not have been more wrong.

I shouted at the word *Pregnant* there on the stick, *No, wait! Take it back. I'm not ready.* I felt angry at the evidence-givers, the friends, the therapist I had been talking to over the phone for the last two months, another one I would not stick with as per my pattern. I understood crying when you found out you were pregnant as a teenager, but at thirty-eight? I felt like I needed a slap in the face, a hard drink, a map of the future, my meds.

I crawled in bed and stayed there for two days until I had to board a plane to Seattle to lead a workshop to be "the one who in-spires." I had to be two things at once. A scared, guilty mess who wanted my husband and weird Thai shrimp soup, and also the one who bellows at the front of a room, *What do you want to create in your life? What are you afraid of? Be a Human Thank-You. Fearless-ish. You Get to Change Your Mind.*

What a crock of shit, I thought. And yet I did it, and I did it with humor, honesty, and coffee. I stood up there and told not one lie. I allowed myself to be two things at once: voiceless and booming, truth-telling and scared, unfeeling, and also very much alive. Bro-ken and whole. Pregnant and not pregnant. Because, as it turns out, my pregnancy was ectopic.

The spotting started in Seattle. I was with my friend Rachel at her brother Matt's concert. They were up there singing the song "I Need My Girl" from their latest album. Matt was singing, *I keep feeling smaller and smaller* and I'm imagining myself pregnant and not pregnant, my belly expanding and my life—the life I felt I had carved from nothing—disappearing. I knew how much my mom had to sacrifice. I couldn't do it. I had a cramp and I was gripped with panic, as if my words might cause a catastrophe, as if I were a magician, capable of doing life-changing hat tricks. *Watch what I can do.*

I sat next to a man on the flight home from Seattle who was looking through hundreds of sympathy cards. He had a pile in his lap, a bag on the floor, a Jack and Coke on his tray. *You must be really loved,* I said, desperate to connect to anyone.

I imagine his wife had died. He was older, handsome and in his sixties. *My mother passed away,* he said. He lived in Jacksonville, had two daughters, wore a tan leather vest and had beautiful brown skin. I was in two places at once—with the man grieving over his dead mother at 13,000 feet and also lost at sea without a raft.

I looked out the window and saw Cleveland below the clouds even though I know this was impossible, as I was right above Washington. I felt myself grow smaller.

We discovered the pregnancy was ectopic soon after I returned from Seattle. Robert and I went for our fifth visit in a row to the ob-gyn, and when did she the ultrasound: *Ah, there it is. See that black dot? It's in the wrong spot.*

As usual, I had known before I had known. Like most things.
Your father died.
I know.
He has it.
You're pregnant.
You're not pregnant.

I felt nothing at first. I pulled my pants down and let the nurse inject my butt with methotrexate after she hugged me and cried.

She'd just had a baby. Tears were in her eyes as she injected my ass with a powerful cancer-killing drug that would also kill the pregnancy stuck in my fallopian tube. I felt two things at once: grief and relief.

The e-mails and alerts on my cell phone kept coming because I had forgotten to cancel them. *You're nine weeks pregnant! Thirty-one weeks to go.*

What to expect with your body this week.

Alternatives to popular baby names.

How to ease gas and bloating.

Back in the Dark

The pain came days later. I hemorrhaged in a hotel room in Lenox, Massachusetts, where I was a guest speaker at Canyon Ranch. I had a regular gig there doing Karaoke Yoga for health-conscious weekenders watching their calories, getting massages, taking drum classes, and zip-lining through the Berkshires. The powers that be had seen me do Karaoke Yoga on *Good Morning America* and invited me a couple of times a year after that. I brought Karaoke Yoga there and also did my workshop and it had become a deep and unexpected love for me.

After I started hemorrhaging, I sat on the toilet in the dark. I was afraid that if I turned on the light I would see a tiny baby, or something grotesque that resembled a baby, floating in all that blood. So I just sat on the warm toilet seat in the darkness. The pain was blinding. I got off the toilet and lay on the bathroom floor, my face pressing into the bottom of the toilet bowl.

I wondered if I could speak to them, the guests at Canyon

Ranch, about my not-pregnancy pregnancy. Would I tell the truth, as I always promised to do?

I imagined it like this: *I was pregnant last Tuesday, folks. I was ambivalent. I did not want to be pregnant. I got a shot that would terminate the pregnancy and then I went for sushi with my husband on Robertson Boulevard in Beverly Hills on the way home. I wasn't pregnant anymore, so I could have raw fish and wine and I did. I am here as your guest speaker to talk about manifesting what you want in life, about being human, about being vulnerable! I was pregnant on Tuesday. I was not pregnant later that Tuesday. After that, my body went away as it has so many times before when I don't want to feel a thing.*

And, dear guests, my body never came back into the doctor's office. I don't remember leaving. I thought I heard someone say, "The baby will always be with you," but I can't be sure.

So, what do you want to manifest in your life?

I crawled to the front door and put my legs up the wall.

I didn't want to be pregnant anyway.

I made it happen. I deserved the pain, I thought. *I am a bad person* floated through my head, that long-ago mantra given to me by my IA.

The morning came, and I didn't know how to tell if I was still alive except to start talking. "Hello, I'm here. Hello, I'm a person in the world." I e-mailed my regular doctor, who had given me the free antidepressant samples all those years ago, instead of my ob-gyn. He had been my doctor for over sixteen years. I e-mailed him at 4:27 a.m. EST and asked, "If I go to sleep, will I die?"

He wrote back (not surprisingly), even though it was also late in California. He is dedicated and hard-working. He told me I wouldn't die, but he said that it was time I considered going to the hospital since the pain was so bad and he was concerned.

I didn't want to be pregnant anyway.
I made it happen.
I deserved the pain.

I decided to go to the hospital in case I was, in fact, dying. I heard the *thump* of the suicidal student from NYU. I visualized my father's two left descending arteries, 85 and 90 percent blocked. The main one, the LAD (left anterior descending) artery, was the one that was 90 percent blocked. Those arteries bring blood to the heart, so as I looked at my own blood on my legs, I thought about his coronary atherosclerotic disease and how hard they supposedly tried to save him at the hospital the night he died. The LAD is often called *The Widowmaker.*

"YOU SEEM ANXIOUS. Are you always this anxious?" the ER nurse asked me when I started to cry after she couldn't get a vein for my IV.

I didn't say anything. Tears fell from the corners of my eyes onto the linoleum floor. I counted them until the anxiety medication and the pain medication took effect, and then I stopped counting. I exhaled. The pain was gone.

They wheeled me into a room to get an ultrasound.

My friend Katie, who came with me, told me later that she had cried while I was getting the ultrasound because she had never seen a uterus without a baby in it. I couldn't see the screen since my head was too far away but even if I had, I was numb.

A nice doctor with a beard and a nurse were there and they were telling me things, of which I caught only *Percocet* and *You're going to be fine.*

I placed my hands on my stomach and leaned forward just enough so I could see the ultrasound machine behind the doctor. My uterus was up there on the screen but nothing was in it. No baby. No black dot, as my doctor in Los Angeles had called it. I remember when she said it how it made me think of Pink Dot, this iconic grocery delivery service in the late nineties in Los Angeles, and how we'd get booze and chips and condoms from there late at night.

Then, and later, I waited for a jolt of something to shake me into the revelation that I indeed wanted a child. It would make me say: *Yes! Give me my chance back! Give me my black dot back and I will turn it into a baby! I take back all those little notes to myself that said, "I don't want to be pregnant." Who was I kidding? I was thirty-eight years old. I was the age of death! Bring my baby back because I wouldn't get another chance.*

The jolt didn't come. I just closed my eyes and let myself be wheeled back into the hospital room. Maybe the jolt would come in a few months. Maybe it would wake me out of a deep sleep and I would find myself reading the e-mails I hadn't canceled from Baby-Center and *What to Expect When You're Expecting*.

The jolt didn't happen in the hospital in Lenox. It didn't happen ever. No jolt. No certainty. Not ever.

It was all very normal, the doctor assured me. *This is what the methotrexate does. All very normal. You are not rupturing.*

All very normal.

I got back to Canyon Ranch and canceled my workshops and poetry reading for the day. I felt guilty, which in hindsight is ridiculous because: I had been in the ER. I slept, took pain pills, and bled. When I woke, it was dark and someone had put some wine and chocolate by my bedside, so I ate that and poured a glass, and still, felt nothing.

After Canyon Ranch, no longer pregnant, I flew to the Galápagos Islands to lead a yoga retreat. I was shaky and nervous and anxious and the flight was hell. We had to stop in Miami, so I watched an episode of *Breaking Bad* on my iPad and drank two beers. I convinced myself on the flight that I had arthritis, cancer, and carpal tunnel. My hands were numb. I was anxious, unmedicated, and depressed, but I was not pregnant.

When I got back from the Galápagos Islands, I felt broken. I wanted to quit retreats in far-off places. I convinced myself my "magic" was gone and that the gig was up. I did not want to admit that I was depressed or that I needed my meds back or that I had just gone through a really hard thing such as having an ectopic pregnancy. I was still able to lead the retreat, but I felt like a fraud because I felt so flat. It exhausted me in a way few things have.

I said to my husband, *I will go back to waiting tables. I can't do this anymore.*

I MET A WOMAN on the retreat who came because the Galápagos Islands were on her bucket list *and it was a good deal, for the Galápagos.* She had no desire to connect to anyone else or learn anyone's name even though there were only thirteen of us.

The last day of the retreat during our closing circle, she refused to participate and, instead, went around the circle telling everyone what was wrong with them. She told me that my retreats didn't work because, "look at her," she sneered, pointing at another participant, an eccentric young girl who had been on a previous retreat of mine.

There was a man on the retreat who smoked cigarettes and started drinking at ten every morning. One afternoon, when I returned from swimming in the ocean, he grabbed the hose near the outdoor shower and said, "Here, let me do that for you. I'll rinse you off." He also said, "Damnnnnnnnn" (with several extra n's on the end) when I came out in my bikini and he kept trying to fist-bump with my husband like they were bros.

See? I told myself as I coerced myself out of my bed every morning with the island's magic coffee. *Who were you to think that you could build a life that was happy and meaningful?* My Inner Asshole was unleashed and out of control. The Galápagos Islands, and especially Semilla Verde, the boutique hotel where we stayed, were otherwordly. There was even an adorable one-hundred-year-old tortoise who roamed around like an ancient badass vertebrate. My depression, however, had the kind of grip on me where the precipice between wanting to live and not caring if I got out of bed ever again became indistinguishable.

I didn't quit, and the next retreat, my New Year's retreat, brought me back to the land of wanting to be alive in the world. It was beautiful. We had a blast doing Karaoke Yoga, singing "Don't Stop Believin'" and "Stand By Me" and "Let It Be" and "Livin' on a Prayer" by Bon Jovi. We had a sound bath with Tibetan singing bowls from a healer named Fawntice, and the people, all so fall-in-loveable, fell in love with each other. I didn't want it to end. I found a glimmer of hope there in Ojai. I was outside myself and my body, but the people there kept me tethered with their stories and pain and, mostly, their joy. Maybe I could keep going after all? Maybe life was just bumpy and constantly surprising?

I realized on that retreat that I don't have to be Positive Patty or even "happy"—I just have to listen fiercely, pay attention, and tell the truth. And I can do that even when I am depressed. It's harder, but I can do it, and therein lies a danger. I didn't quit, but I was falling into such a dark hole that I could barely get out of bed. I was in the darkest place I had been in since I dropped out of NYU and I was soaring in my new career.

CHAPTER 25

Make Room for the Possible and the Impossible

One Pain Triggers Every Pain

FIVE MONTHS AFTER that New Year's retreat, I was back at that house in Ojai leading another retreat. I lay flat on the ground after I'd fainted as a woman fed me honey from a spoon. I was already writing about the experience. I was in my body, maybe more so than I ever have been, but also I was writing about it. Two things at once.

"Can you eat honey?" One of the women attending my retreat was standing over me with honey in a spoon.

"Yes, give me honey." I was desperate.

The woman lifted my head and fed me honey as I shook uncontrollably and someone else had to press down on my thighs. My psoas muscles were locking up, so someone was pressing on my thighs, and a woman I had never met before that night was feeding me, she said she was a nurse and that it would be all right. I felt less scared about labor, not that I was pregnant, but the way I was gripping in my thighs and the people all around me were all higher than me, looking down and telling me to *breathe breathe*. I thought: *This might be what it's like, but also I don't want to know what labor is like.*

And also: *I think I am dying.* But loudest: *I am a fucking asshole. I can't let these people down. I'm not ready to die.*

And if you think I am being dramatic, then you have never fainted.

Let me back up.

It was 2014 and I was leading a retreat over Mother's Day weekend. I had forty-five people there, some who had flown from as far as Chicago, Toronto, Maryland, and New York. We were laughing and I was thinking: *trust this.* We were outside under the pink sky tasting the various wines produced by the winery. We were on the cabernet merlot blend. Ojai is lined up with an east-west mountain range and the mountaintops become a gorgeous pink on the east end of the Ojai Valley as the sun begins to fade. We moved on to the rosé, and the pink reflected off the Topatopa Bluffs made everyone look a little buzzed. It's a great light for photos, so everyone was snapping away, pink filling their bodies. A friend of mine, Claudia, had moved to Ojai and happened to be hiking in the hills just beyond the winery where I held my retreat. She told me that she'd heard loud laughter coming from the house and had said to her husband, *It must be Jen Pastiloff's retreat.* I was proud that the laughter made her think it was my group, especially since the first thirty years of my life I'd been told I was too serious and too sad and that I should smile more. I may have been sinking into depression, but I could still create a joyous community, filled with people listening to each other and laughing so hard wine came out of their nostrils.

I hadn't seen Claudia in a year. I offered her a glass of wine and we clinked glasses.

"Look at what you've done, Jen. Look around at all of these people. Look how happy they are."

"I feel good in this moment," I truthfully replied.

She said I should move to Ojai and I laughed. But under that salmon-colored sky, every night I would stand and look out and reflect on what was required of me to be happy.

I was feeling content there under the pink sky, with my friends and my retreat and my wine, and in that moment all the anxiety and depression I had been dealing with in the last couple of months seemed far away, like it was somebody else's pain. I thought about bravery and how being brave looked like so many different things. How we couldn't really quantify it or compartmentalize. And also about an explosion that had just happened in New York and how a Japanese student had died. The student's mother told a translator for the *New York Times* that her daughter had written home and said, "It's beautiful here and I like it."

I thought, as I stood there under the setting sun, about how happy I was and fuck that fear I always had that the other shoe was about to drop, that good things don't last, that I don't deserve to be happy, that if I am happy it will get taken away, *fuck that*, I thought. It's beautiful here and I like it.

Earlier in the day, as we were first arriving to the retreat, one of my recurring retreaters (she jokingly calls herself a "groupie") asked how I was doing as we stood on the great lawn under the hot noonday sun. She said she had read an essay I'd written on depression that had gone viral and saw my schedule, how busy I was, and was wondering how I was making out.

I said, "I'm good. I am trying really hard to be present. I am putting one foot in front of the other." She said something about slowing down.

Later, during the wine tasting, someone else asked me how I did it.

"Did what?"

"Your schedule. You have so much going on. I mean, how do you manage?"

I said something about how I wasn't sure and then we laughed and toasted glasses and took a sip of the pinot noir. I said, "I just put one foot in front of the other and stay present as best as I can." I was saying the words and I wanted to believe them but I didn't. I was lying. Something was wrong.

When it was time to eat, we all went inside and stood around the island in the kitchen so that Caspar, our incredible chef, could explain what the meal was. The ritual was that we would all stand around and hold hands and after he explained the meal, which was always gorgeous and colorful, we would jump up and down and sing a song which went, *Yummy, yummy, yummy I got love in my tummy and I feel like loving you.* We'd sing it three times holding hands while we jumped up and down, and on the last refrain we'd drag out the *youuuuuuuuu* and throw our hands in the air. It is an amazing prayer, this silly child's verse, originally from a 1960s rock song. To see a group of grown-ass adults get so into this truly lights my heart on fire. Caspar was trying to get everyone's attention, but with forty-five people it can be hard. Kind of what it's like for me to hear all the time.

I ran outside to grab a Tibetan singing bowl so I could strike it to shut everyone up so Caspar could explain about the quinoa pasta and the greens that were just picked two hours ago and how they were still alive. I ran in my flip-flops, very much *not* putting one foot in front of the other, and there was a crack as my foot turned on the little step from the kitchen to the patio.

And I fell.

I got up and went back into the kitchen and stood there around the island with all the beautiful people I had gathered and the delicious food that I would not get to eat because I would be at the ER and I said: *Floor. I need floor.*

There was a wave. I couldn't tell where it started, but it was in my body and I couldn't hear any sound. The wave had rendered me fully deaf, not even with the 10 percent hearing I usually had. The ground started to lift up. I slowly headed to a man standing near the kitchen table and said, *I just need to lie down*, and then I was lying down and I closed my eyes and that was that. Blackness. I was gone.

I thought about one night a few months earlier when I was in the ER in the Berkshires, in Massachusetts, going through the ectopic pregnancy. At the time it was the scariest moment of my life. But no, this night, where I was lying in my own sweat and forty-five people towered above me as I had no control over my body or my mind or my hearing, trumped that. Having no control over your person is by far the worst thing I have experienced. Not knowing why. Just having to surrender to what is.

I thought I was having a stroke, and even though I knew I had hurt my foot, it didn't register that the foot injury had caused the wave and complete deafness and fainting. I thought I would die on the floor, so I asked the man who caught me: *Please, please, it's very important to me that they still sing the Yummy Yummy Yummy song.* So they did. And as I lay there, shivering. I fainted again.

Somewhere in the distance I heard laughter and footsteps and forks against teeth.

What the body will do to protect itself is flabbergasting.

I had always thought I had a high threshold for pain, but after that happened I Googled: *Why do you faint when you are in pain or shock?* and found this: *PAIN is the body communicating with the brain that something is wrong. IF the amount of PAIN is far more than what your current pain threshold can endure, the Brain will shut down your conscious mind so that it can continue the fight for survival without the "conscious you" being in the way. IF your pain threshold is very high, you will NOT lose consciousness.*

I don't know who wrote that on Wiki Answers, but it intrigued me.

I was trying to protect myself without knowing it.

People bent down and asked me if I had shook like this before. Was this something my body did? I said *no, yes, no.* Yes, when I have been very upset or excited. Like my body no longer belonged to me. When I found a condom at Randall's that wasn't from me, my body shook for twenty-four hours.

I asked for a Xanax. *Somebody get my bag and get me a Xanax,* I said. I couldn't hear anything in that moment and I could only see fuzzy shapes instead of faces. People were eating dinner and drinking wine. Most didn't even know anything happened and were confused by me splayed across the tiles, a sweatshirt under my head, one flip-flop on and my face drawn and white and frightening.

This is what came into my mind: *I will get fat. I will not be able to move and I will get fat.* It's all my brain could think. I could only hear the endless remarks from the last few months about how good I looked since I had lost weight, the same remarks that had been killing me because they sent me into a tailspin with my eating disorder demons. (I look good *now?* What did I look like before?) Being off my antidepressants, I'd started back with old patterns and behaviors and overexercising. The medication stopped the obsessing, but since I was not taking it, it was like a free-for-all.

I was triggered by all the weight comments. Why couldn't people just say, "You look beautiful" without the connotation that you look different than you did before? Why the endless commentary on women's bodies? How it hooked me into thinking: *How will I maintain this?* And there I was, on the ground, not knowing my foot was broken yet but knowing that something was off, and all I could think of was: I will not be able to maintain this, I will not be able to maintain this.

What *could* I maintain?

People immediately said things like, "This is a sign from God." To which I scoffed.

Or: *This is a sign you need to slow down.* Things like that. You can guess the things they said. Platitudes.

I don't believe in signs. Did I eventually turn the incident into an opportunity? Yes. Did I need to slow down? Probably. Maybe not. But I broke my foot and I was forced to slow down. I don't think the universe was conspiring to take me down so I would get its message. I can say I wasn't paying attention (I wasn't). Or I can say it was an accident (it was). But what it brought me back to was my demons and my fear of them.

The fear of what would happen was worse than the pain. Just like the dentist. The fear of anything beyond that moment was debilitating, so all I could do was be in that moment on the ground, being spoon-fed honey from a woman who said she was a nurse and used my magic words, *It's going to be okay.* I didn't know what was happening and if my fainting was separate from my foot injury, but I knew I was helpless. I was pinned to the floor and I couldn't hear so I closed my eyes and drifted.

When I opened them, I was back on the ground by the big oak kitchen table, giants above me. The voices were far away. There was a hand under my head. I was convulsing as I closed my eyes and let a person's fingers cradle my scalp. They were small hands. I was not sure who was holding me but I was not dead yet.

I thought, *How weird that I'm dying and I also just hurt my foot.* I wondered if the foot was a warning, a bell alerting me to what was about to happen to me.

Your life has come to this, the foot spoke. I'd gotten back up after the crack of my right foot, but the room had looked smaller, as if I was looking through the head of a needle, until I was lying by the kitchen table or under it.

I wondered if my father had received a message like this before he died.

A week before he passed away, he'd been in the ER with food poisoning. Later, after his death, my mother told us it was the speed. The doctor warned him, she'd said: *Use again and you'll die.* He didn't listen. As if he knew it was coming, the day before, he gave away all his beloved hockey paraphernalia to Paul Napoli, Uncle Johnny's son. Blood had stopped flowing to his heart because of the blockage in the left anterior descending artery, caused from too much speed, four packs of cigarettes a day, and who knows what else that made them say his thirty-eight-year-old body was that of an old man.

I couldn't speak while I was lying there on the ground. I wet my pants. I saw people I hadn't seen in years, and rooms, and lids to jewelry boxes, and the small ruby-hearted rings inside the boxes, and brown Chevys and meals I ate and the pink sky from just before I fainted.

Not Dead

I was not dying. I fainted from the shock of my fifth metatarsal breaking. My body had been attempting to protect itself. The lengths we will go to not feel pain. *You are not mine.*

You will not feel this. Protect yourself from this. You are strong.

I TOLD THE DOCTOR that the pain wasn't that bad.

"Is that normal?" I asked.

"It is. What it is," he said very slowly.

I said, "What are you, the Buddha doctor?"

He said that people come in and ask, *Is this normal? Should I be feeling this? Is this what I am supposed to feel?*

It is what it is, he told me he says to them.

It is what it is.

Laura, one of the women from my retreat, came to the ER with my mother and me. My mom came to almost all my retreats and thankfully was at that one. I was embarrassed by what was coming out of my mouth in front of this woman, but it would bond me to her for life. I spoke of getting big and not being able to run. I worried about gaining weight. My mom had heard me spew all this shit before, but not in many years, so she was concerned. I was delirious with shock and medication and fear. I slithered around on the table as a technician came in to give me an EKG. He said, "You're too young for an EKG" as he administered it. They had to check everything, since I had fainted.

I let myself float away a little because if I came back I would remember that I had forty-five people who I was responsible for at a craftsman home a few miles away up the road in Ojai, that I had to be in Seattle in a few days for two sold-out workshops, then Portland, then three weeks in Europe, that I taught yoga for a living, that I wouldn't be able to drive or run and mostly that I was absolutely out of control.

AT THE HOSPITAL, one of the nurses tried to give me a crash course on how to use crutches on my way to the bathroom. She had no patience, which I couldn't judge because I have none. She got frustrated with me. *Swing past this line,* she kept saying, or something like that. I couldn't hear her. I had no idea what *this line* meant.

I said to her, "I read lips," which didn't change any of her communication tactics. She was standing next to me and talking quickly, so I had to basically teach myself as I hobbled to pee. My retreat attendee and immediate new best friend Laura commented on how no one seemed to understand that I was hard of hearing. I was like, *Story of my life.* I was young and I spoke like a hearing person, so I passed for a hearing person. Invisible illnesses and disabilities: something to be conscious of. Compassion: something to always have.

When the doctor had me on my stomach to put the temporary fiberglass cast on, I had no idea what was being said. I kept trying to half lift up and turn around, but then the exhaustion of that became too much, so I just lay my head on the paper of the table and trusted they'd relay all the information.

It is shitty not to be able to hear things. Especially important things about your body. The helplessness of having no control over your body or what they are telling you about it, so you have to surrender and let go.

The foot is broken, he said.

He also told us a story about how he put a cast on the wrong arm of a little girl because that's the arm she held up to him when she was in the ER. I must've missed most of the story, but I laughed anyway when he told the punch line even though I am not sure what it was, which was something I did every day of my life. Played along like I heard, like I understood, like I wasn't on the outside. Still, looking back, that story doesn't seem very funny to me.

Back at the house where the retreat was being held, I tried to go to sleep. I wasn't sure what I would do in the morning since I had an eight a.m. class scheduled, but I knew I needed to try and sleep. My mother was in the bed with me. I took a Percocet the Buddha doctor had given me. I couldn't sleep. In the middle of the night when I could no longer hold in my pee, I hobbled on the crutches to the toilet, but once I sat down I wanted to faint, so I fell onto the ground and lay there. My mom couldn't hear me. I couldn't reach the crutches, so after two hours of lying there on the bathroom floor, I crawled with my pants down, back to the bed, got on my knees and hoisted myself back on. I didn't sleep all night.

I decided to teach my class anyway. I decided I would tell the truth about how I was feeling. It's what I am always going on about, anyway: *What if we just told the truth?*

The night before, a few people had written on Facebook and said things about how *this foot breakage was a gift blah blah* and yes, I agree, but come on—it is a lie to have something happen and immediately see the gift in it. *Oh, my foot broke? Yay. Here is a learning opportunity. Here is my yoga. Here is a gift.* Bullshit.

Would I get there? Yes. (I hoped so.) But I'd be damned if I would lie about how I was feeling. So I went and taught my workshop and did my best to have a sense of humor and not be an asshole. I had to be carried down to the yoga studio by Chef Caspar. I was sad and also exhausted, so my energy was razor-focused. I was present. I was without antidepressants. I was vulnerable. I was dirty, too, not having showered in two days.

It was one of the most beautiful experiences of my life. The group surrounded me and sang and I taught the whole thing either on a chair or scooting around on my butt. Everyone kept saying, "We got you, Jen."

I kept hearing about a concept called "spiritual bypassing." What I took it to mean was that people thought, because they did yoga or meditated or simply thought of themselves as "spiritual," that they got to bypass what they were really feeling.

I did not want to do that anymore. I may not have been spiritually bypassing, but I had been bypassing, one way or another, my whole life.

This time there was only entering the pain and being with the pain and then healing, but to be clear, I don't think healing means the pain ever goes away 100 percent. Even if it means it's just the memory of the pain. There's no bypass. Like activist Glennon Doyle says, "First the pain, then the waiting, then the rising." I wanted to throw my fucking crutches at the wall.

CHAPTER 26

What You Need

IN MY WORKSHOPS I say you only need two things: to listen and to tell the truth.

Once, when I was in Dallas to do a workshop, my friend and I stumbled upon a man giving free advice in the park near her house. He held a small homemade sign that said *Free Advice* and an American flag and another sign that said *Kindness Matters*. There were chairs set up in a circle for people to come and sit and listen to free advice, and a stuffed dog keeping guard.

The first day I walked by and saw him, I sat down. There was a boy there, about nineteen years old, who said his girlfriend had cheated on him with his best friend. He'd started to cry. Big fat teardrops fell onto his thick thighs and I remember feeling like a voyeur because he was in so much pain and there I was, a stranger. I hugged him before I walked away and told him to take care of his heart.

The next day when we went back (I couldn't get enough of Free-Advice Guy), a different group of people were there. Rod, that was Free-Advice's name, kept putting his hand on the leg of his partner. He was talking about love and beauty. He had his hand on her leg and said something like, "And if she ran away and married my best friend, it would be interesting to see what *in love* looked like under those circumstances, but I bet ya, on an old nickel" (he had a thing for old nickels and his grandmother) "that I wouldn't fall out of love."

I remember this clearly because it was astounding what he was suggesting. To love unconditionally. I wanted to hear more. I told him it was hard to accept that statement. He pointed to his partner or wife or whoever she was to him, and said, "She is more beautiful than betrayal."

He said that he didn't know if that was always true, for everybody, and I appreciated that honesty.

Then he said this, and I had to remember, because there I was, with a broken foot, always talking about *beauty hunting*. He said, "I'm not sure what love is. I know what beauty is. Beauty makes me love. It just happens. Like dominoes fall."

He went on to talk about what would happen if his lady betrayed him. "If she betrays me, I'm not capable of treating her any worse than crazy Eddie, the head of the youth gang that bushwhacked me one day. I am captured by beauty."

By this point, I had looked at my friend and whispered, "Where the fuck are we?"

He continued on, "If she stabbed me in the back, it would be at least as beautiful as a supernova. As a star exploding!"

He told us all sitting around on those plastic chairs that he didn't talk like that a lot. And this was the part that made me realize he wasn't totally full of shit—he said, "This, what I am talking about, would not be good advice for that nineteen-year-old kid last night."

He said, "I can't afford the risk of betrayal to cause me to take my eyes off beauty."

....

DURING MY BROKEN-FOOT period, my friend who had also once broken her foot and struggled with anorexia texted me right after I broke mine and said, *The inner torture of a break cannot be comprehended.*

I succumbed to being still. I was terrified of change more than anything in my life. *What was going to happen to my body? What would I be incapable of? Would I fall into the dark vortex of depression again since I could not run and that had been one of the things saving me when I went off my antidepressants?*

I did not know the answers and I hated that. I wanted to know things would stay the same. I wanted sameness, things to count on, consistency, things that would not break or leave.

I knew things could be worse. So I had to cancel Seattle and two sold-out workshops? So? I needed to be driven around for six weeks? So? I got that *so-ness.*

I was afraid of what I would discover when I had to get still.

I was forced to slow down and I was terrified of what that meant.

In Andrew Solomon's book *The Noonday Demon*, there's a quote by George Brown, a founder of Life Events Research at the University of London, that says, "Depression is a response to past loss, and anxiety is a response to future loss." I was terrified of future loss.

When I finally went to the orthopedist, the nurse asked me if I was being treated for any medical conditions. I said, "Not really. Just depression."

She said, "Join the club, sister."

I was afraid I would not be able to climb out of the depression hole on my own and that I would get stuck again, but I'd tricked myself into thinking I would be a failure if I went back on medication. It was like that old eating disorder mind-set: all or nothing. It was also that old IA telling me that I should be strong.

People said that I should write about it, and all I could think of was why would anyone want to hear about me trying to get into the shower to sit on a stepstool Robert had put in there for me to bathe? And because of the crutches, my carpel tunnel was acting up and my hands had become unusable and I felt damaged everywhere. I couldn't hear, I couldn't use my hands, my foot was broken, and I decided to give up on bathing.

There is beauty in surrender.

I thought about the drive up to Ojai to lead the retreat and how unimpressed I was with my legs. Even the morning I broke my foot, I had worked out, and I had been unfazed. I, in no way, stood in awe of my body. I didn't stand there going, "Oh my god, look at my legs moving. Look at this goddamned miracle of my body." Why did it take crawling backward up the stairs on my ass, or the doctor telling me that I cannot use my right foot, or becoming incapacitated to become deeply appreciative of my body all of a sudden? This body that had always been my enemy? As strange as that sounds, I was afraid for that to change, too.

CHAPTER 27

The Human Impulse

The "Pathetic" in You Has a Point

DURING MY RETREAT in Costa Rica in April, a month before my foot had broken, I'd signed up to take a writing workshop in Portland, Oregon, that May with Suzy Vitello and Lidia Yuknavitch. I was ready to be a student again, and I also wanted to finally develop a consistent writing practice. I loved Suzy's writing, and I had just read Lidia's *The Chronology of Water* during the retreat and it had shattered me. When I finished the book, I opened it again and started over and bawled the entire flight home from San José. That retreat was one of the four I led while I was off my antidepressants.

The night after the retreat had ended I wanted to be alone. My friend Melissa was going to meet me later in the evening in San José for dinner, but I wanted all day to myself, so I booked a boutique hotel where I knew no one else from my group would be. The night before I left, the last night of the retreat, I started to panic that I booked the wrong hotel.

If I could measure my life in moments of self-doubt it would look like yardstick after yardstick of questioning my choices. From what I order for dinner in a restaurant to whether or not I should have a baby. *There's no pool at the place I booked. It's a golf bed-and-breakfast? What was I thinking? I hate golf. Could I change it and stay somewhere else?* Even though it had nothing to do with the hotel, it was indicative of the way my mind works. Choose A. Obsess that I should have chosen B instead of A. *Why do I always choose the wrong thing?*

After I got off the tin can of a plane and got my bag, a little girl emerged from an SUV holding a torn piece of paper with my name on it. Choice A was eleven years old. See, it was the right choice. It almost always is, and if I could just learn to trust that, I would be happier. Or happy-ish. Luciana was her name. Choice A's name was Luciana.

Her grandfather was the driver. He spoke almost no English, so she translated back and forth. She was so mature that I had to lean forward toward the front seat to see her face up close, in case she was thirty and I just thought she was a kid. She pulled out this little ceramic animal from a brown paper bag to show me and then blew on it. It was the most beautiful whistle sound and she played it almost all the way home. I say *home* because that's really what it was. The grandfather driver and his wife, Cecilia, have lived in this home for twenty-seven years, but now, in their advanced age, they didn't feel the need to have such a big house, so they turned it into a hotel.

Luciana told stories from the front seat about some kind of music festival she'd gone to where she got the whistle/animal, but the news was on in Spanish, a low hum, and I really couldn't understand a lick of what she was saying because I couldn't really see her mouth to read her lips. Plus the radio, drowning her voice out, but it was worth it to watch her grandfather's face when she spoke. *This is love,* I thought. Watching them together shone a light on the big hole in my life of what was missing.

Cecilia, the wife of Grandpa (I couldn't hear his name), was one of the loveliest humans I had yet to cross paths with. She was tall with this big head of black hair and gigantic blue eyes. She told me to lie down and *did I want a cheese sandwich?* She said she'd bring me a typical Costa Rican refreshment, the *refresco.* She said this like a secret, so I felt like something major was passing between us. The drink was delicious, whatever it was. Some mix of coconut and pineapple and grapefruit (and probably sugar), over ice. We hadn't had ice all week at my retreat, so that felt like the real treat. I sat and drank it with her on a patio overlooking the golf course. A glorious breeze came through and I listened to her tell stories of how she raised her family in the house. "Look at this," she said, bending her head down, "I don't dye it." She was seventy years old. Not one gray hair. She told me she had just gone to California for her uncle's one hundredth surprise birthday party. All the photos she showed me (and she showed me hundreds) were of him with various family members (great-great-great-grandbabies) and sons and nieces in front of a huge picture of a train.

I finished my drink and thought about how the choices we often make lead us to dead ends in our lives, but they also lead us to moments like the one where you're talking to a woman so full of life that it oozes out of her and into you. So I woke up. As tired as I was of people and talking and having to listen and all the emotional heavy lifting of my job, I woke up and wanted to be in her presence, if not forever, then for at least a little while longer.

I texted Melissa, *They're so nice here. I cried.*

When she arrived, she walked into her room and I saw the tears in her eyes. She said she cried, too. She grew up with a father who had abandoned her, so to feel so taken care of by a man, and an older fatherly one, well, it can be overwhelming.

When we went to dinner that last night before our early morning flight the next day, they insisted on driving us (like we were teens and they were our parents) even though it was only three blocks away. Grandpa said to our waiter to call when we were done. (The waiter translated it for us.) I asked for the bill with two still-full glasses of red wine, but all of a sudden Grandpa appeared and we realized the waiter had called him when he dropped the check. We were both moved. He put his arms around us like a dad. We said we loved Costa Rica *and could we stay forever?*

The morning of the flight home, they put coffee outside of our door at four thirty a.m. since we had to leave at five for our seven a.m. flights. Cecilia, the night before, had asked, "What can I put outside your door? Coffee? Fruit? Juice? Can I make you a cheese sandwich?" and we had both been sort of stunned by her kindness and wanted to say yes to it all, yes please take care of us and yes can we stay here forever and yes cheese sandwiches and will you be our mom, but we just said *yes* and *coffee.*

Grandpa was waiting to take us to the airport at five a.m. and again we cried a little. Melissa asked me if she should tip him and I said he wouldn't take it but she did anyway. And he wouldn't take it. We stayed near the car like little magnets until we finally headed toward the building. Both a little teary, I said, "Look at us with our pathetic father shit," and we laughed and checked in for our flights.

I knew the pathetic in me had something to say about grief and the way we put it in our bodies and moved through the world and how we assimilated it and how it changed shapes. The pathetic in me wanted to talk about how losing a parent so young can break you and shape you in all sorts of ways and how there isn't a narrative for that, because once you're an adult, you're meant to *kind of, like, get the fuck over it.* I would never get over my father, but I was starting to grieve, finally, after years of fighting it. The pathetic in me wants to say that I am not pathetic at all, that I'm human, like you, and that we're in this together. The *human* in me, I should say. And the human impulse is always the right one.

So I knew I had to take the workshop with Suzy and Lidia.

I MESSAGED LIDIA twice on Facebook to tell her she had changed my life, but she didn't respond. I could see she read the message, so I made up a story that she hated me, or that I was a big idiot for reaching out, but I decided I didn't care, I needed to be in her presence. I needed to learn from her. I was determined to take the workshop and meet Lidia, broken foot or not, suicidal depression or not. I had been fully off my antidepressants since September. It was now May. I had suffered an ectopic pregnancy, a broken foot, the worst depression I could remember, and still, I was not going to cancel the trip. I also was not open to going back on meds, because I somehow convinced myself that they would make me weak. Bullshit story alert.

Sitting on the floor of an airport always made me think of all the other airport floors of my life.

And every time I've sat on an airport floor, I'd think of Steve Bridges and me, sitting there, before my Mexico retreat, leaning on the glass of an airport window as we waited for our flight to board to Mexico, and him saying, "I have a great life, Jen."

I've sat on the floors of airports in Alaska and also Houston, Toronto, and Taiwan on a layover. In Houston, I watched a boy take pictures of trash cans that looked like faces. He was a face hunter.

Sitting on the airport floor reminded me of that boy and also of the time I cried on the floor of LAX when I missed my flight to Santa Fe to see Ronan.

I sit on the floor a lot. It makes me feel safe, connected, close to what's constant.

I sat on the floor as I taught a yoga class at a rehab facility. I used to teach a weekly class in this poorly lit, artificially cooled office space for addicts. When the weather permitted, we went outside. On hot days, we stayed indoors and sat on the floor on stinky yoga mats. One person usually fell asleep. I did not take it personally.

I had the group write down their Personal Manifesto, one of the exercises I sometimes do in my workshops. One guy, a recovering heroin addict, had this on his list:

- Look for something that does not appear to be there
- Go outside at night
- Give something to somebody everyday
- Don't run away

The list made me think about being in Alaska at the airport on a layover to China and how I pressed my face into the glass, but still, it was too dark to see anything. There was snow on the ground. It looked blue. I wrote a postcard I never sent, which said, *Hello! I'm in Alaska! It's daytime but it's dark out!*

I thought about his list and how I got it wrong. Here's my list in comparison to his for proof of how wrong I got it:

I looked for something that didn't appear to be there. But then I got tired. I got tired of looking for things that weren't immediately knowable—things that had existed and disappeared. My father.

Feeling safe. The sun in Alaska. I gave up and wrote a postcard I never intended to send.

I gave nothing of myself. Not even a postcard. I retreated toward the idea that I was damaged and would forever be stuck in an invisible pain prison.

I ran. From everything. I left New York City and dropped out of school in my mind before the plane even landed back at JFK. I sat on an airport floor and knew I'd run. All my clothes and pillows and books in a big black plastic trash bag with a note that said: *I'll see you in two months.* I ran so quickly from those things that I should've known I would never come back.

With my broken foot in 2014, at the airport in Los Angeles, I waited in the car at the curb until my wheelchair arrived. I sat in the wheelchair with my backpack on my lap and my crutches in my left hand while the lady who was pushing me asked for the confirmation number for my flight. Her name tag said "Luz." She wrote my number on her hand, on her palm, next to another number. She parked me next to other wheelchairs and left me there while she went off to find the next person who would take over my wheeling duties. She noticed my tattoo on my left arm. It was a temporary tattoo that said *Breathe.*

"You got ink on your left arm?" Luz said.

"Yeah. You like it?" I said.

She nodded.

I reached into my overflowing and dirty backpack and got her a *Breathe* tattoo and she said, "Where you from?" as she looked at my boarding pass, my last name.

"You mean my name?"

Uh-huh.

Russia.

She grinned like I reached bad-assery status, and the next guy came over to wheel me to security. He looked at my tattoo and said, "That's the nicest one I've ever seen." I told him it was fake and he seemed impressed by that. "Well, it's nice. Breathe." He said *Breathe* as if it was a command to me.

Yes, sir, I said. What I didn't say: *I am trying to. But I went off my Cymbalta and Prozac and it's hard.*

CHAPTER 28

I Am a Body

Suzy and Lidia's workshop was being held at the McMenamins Kennedy School, where Lidia and I would later hold our "Writing and The Body" retreats. In Portland, at the elementary school turned hotel, I sat at the old wooden desk in my hotel room and stared out my window at the lush greenery. I had just ordered an overpriced veggie burger and some questionable triple-bean soup from room service. It was just about dusk, the sun was setting later and everything felt like it was hanging on something else. The trees drooped as if they were trying to get closer to themselves. I thought about how I used to be jealous of trees, how I used to write poems about my envy of their ability to be stick thin and not feel pain. The trees looked as if they were being pulled down toward the earth. Heavy with their own bodies. How I felt.

This writing workshop was for self-care. I had canceled all my other commitments. I felt lonely. If it had been dark, I think I might have felt less lonely, but when it is light out I have always felt as if I *should* be outside doing something, making myself useful. (The word *should* is an asshole.)

In the months since I had gone off my medication and lost the non-pregnancy pregnancy, when the morning came, I gasped. As if I'd forgotten where I was and only with daylight did I remember, *Oh I'm here. Here I am. This is my body. I am a body in a bed.*

Lidia said to the room, to this gorgeous group of writers: *What do you have to do to language? How can you stretch language?* and it made me think about breaking things open, about what we find inside. The inside of a bone. The inside of pain.

And we kept going deeper with the writing, with the work. She prompted us, *And what's underneath that?* She said for us to put our body through it.

So I unlaced my boot.

She asked us where were we the most present in our body and what would that part of our body say? I knew then that Lidia was my sister and it was as if she were speaking directly to me.

She said I will be okay, that it will be okay. I told her that those were my favorite words, then I said, *Isn't that corny?* She said our daily experience is that it's *not* going to be okay. And that we needed to be reminded. I knew I was in love with her. It was the first time I came to one of my favorite words: fall-in-loveable.

She did not think it was corny.

I was still intimidated by her, but I wanted to be in rooms with her for the rest of my life.

You're going to be okay. I wanted to plant her voice in my head.

And underneath that is? That was her next prompt. *Underneath that is?*

Everything. Water. Blood. Guts. Life. So much life. Once we break open, there's everything coming at us. At once. And that is what I have been so afraid of.

The last prompt she gave us was, *Put yourself in a difficult place and navigate yourself or the character out of that place.*

Here I am. This is my body. And I knew then that I would not survive if I did not go back on my medication. I was sliding onto the floor and I had no desire to get up. I seemed to always end up on the floor. I could hardly lift my pen to write, I felt so tired. I was in a difficult place. And in the words of Lidia's prompt, the navigation out began.

I was not a failure. I was proud to be making a choice, and that was not to die. I was changing my mind.

CHAPTER 29

How to Open

It Takes Time

IN JUNE 2014, a few weeks after I returned from that Portland trip, I was set to lead a retreat to Tuscany, despite my foot still being broken. The previous six weeks I had been stuck on my sofa trying to figure out if I wanted a baby, could I brush my teeth that day, did I want a family, did I want to be married, how was I going to lead a retreat, how was I going to walk again? I'd carried the Prozac around with me but never took them. I felt like going back on them would make me a failure and what if I did want to have a baby? And I had worked so hard to get off. So I kept carrying them around *just in case*.

On June 22, the day I was to fly to Paris with my mom for a preplanned holiday before my retreat, I woke up and knew that I would die if I did not do something. I was six weeks into the foot break, so just about done with it all, but I had fallen so deep into the pit of depression that it was almost too late. I did not care if I died.

I leaned over and reached into my bedside table, unscrewed the lid, and swallowed. My emergency pills.

Robert and I hadn't touched in weeks. We barely grunted at each other. I felt misunderstood and unhappy and scared, and he felt taken advantage of and trapped and frustrated with his work. But we didn't talk about anything, so this was all guessing on my end. I felt like I was being suffocated. I e-mailed my doctor and told him that after almost a year being off, that morning I went and took Prozac and how long would they take to have an effect? He said they would take a couple of weeks. I was scared. I was leading a retreat in a little over a week and I couldn't find myself anywhere.

Paris was a bust. I had taken the boot cast off the day before we flew, but for the sake of travel, I put it back on. I had to be pushed through the airport in a wheelchair again, my backpack on my lap, my mom at my side. I still had my boot on for the broken foot, which was unwieldy and had to be put in the overhead bin (but not before I dropped it on my mom's head). I couldn't get my seat to recline and I had a panic attack. I asked my mom how long she thought the Prozac would take to kick in and why had I waited so long to go back on medication? As if she knew the answers.

We got ripped off in the taxi headed to the apartment we had rented in Le Marais, which was so beautiful I wanted to weep. My mom had found it on Airbnb. She's always a detective like that. There were two big windows that overlooked Rue des Barres and a bedroom with a window that overlooked a different part of the neighborhood.

The second day we awoke in Paris, I felt less depressed. Part of that was probably that it was the first time in six weeks that I was walking, albeit miserably and with a lot of pain. My mom came into the bedroom and asked me if I wanted coffee, that she would make it. *We are off to a good start,* I thought.

She made me coffee with the little espresso pot you put on the stove (I don't know how to work that thing) and then got into the shower. I was in Paris and I had Parisian coffee in bed and my foot was not broken anymore. That I was noticing anything at all felt like progress.

I heard my mom yelling from the kitchen, so I wobbled out of bed and carefully walked in. It was like I was learning how to walk again, I had to move very slowly. *Did you put the hot coffeepot on the wooden counter?*

I did. Fuck.

Why didn't you put it back on the stove?

I don't know.

You have to think, Jennifer.

There was a burn mark on the antique wooden gorgeous countertop.

My mom's towel fell off so that she was standing naked in the kitchen vigorously rubbing the burn mark. I Googled: *How do you get burn marks out of wood?*

We tried everything. My mom had poured salt all over the counter (no idea what she was thinking, but she said later she was trying anything he had). White vinegar, toothpaste. It was not coming out.

I took a picture and decided I would e-mail the nice Italian who rented us his French apartment.

He replied:

No problem, Jen, I'll fix it, but be careful . . . please, it is my mother's apartment and there are other guests coming soon :-(

Great. It wasn't even *his* apartment.

He wrote back again: *But is it burned?*

Me: *Yes.*

Him: *I can't call right now, I'm in a meeting, but don't worry, just please be careful. The problem now is that if it is burned, I've to call a woodworker to recover it, I'll do that when you leave, don't think about it now and enjoy your holidays.*

She started scrubbing the burn wound again with salt and her arm knocked over one of the wineglasses from the night before that I had left on the counter and it shattered all over the floor and mixed in with the salt.

Goddamn it, now we have to replace a wineglass, too, she says.

I thought of his e-mail, the words *just be careful.*

Just be careful.

I crawled back into the bed and heard another crash.

I broke another glass! from the kitchen.

I was thinking, *There is no way that within twelve hours we have done so much damage to this nice Italian guy's mom's apartment with the same name as my friend. There is no way.* But we had.

Hours later, we went to the Rue des Rosiers, where there was a synagogue and men walking around with yarmulkes and the most delicious falafel I had ever spilled on myself. I put my splint on and tried to keep up. Mom carried the wineglass in her backpack. *Keep your eyes open,* she said. *For wineglasses.*

We didn't find the glasses. We were one for one. I ruined the counter; she broke the glasses. I started calling us Dumb and Dumber.

We are a bad pair together as travelers. She panics easily and I follow suit. When I was in middle school, she used to wake up in the middle of the night and shoot up off the sofa (where she preferred to sleep for some reason) and yell, "My pocketbook! Where's my pocketbook?" like someone was trying to break in and murder her. "It's okay, Mom, you're just having a bad dream. Go back to bed. Go sleep in your room."

I didn't last long walking around; I was in tears after an hour. I had no idea how I was going to be okay to lead a retreat in Tuscany in a few days. I had never experienced pain in my body like this. It was humbling and it felt like a betrayal.

I took a lot of Xanax on that trip to Paris and then in the retreat to Italy as my brain acclimated to being back on antidepressants. About two weeks after I took that first pill, I began to feel like myself again. In the meantime, the UK edition of *Grazia* published a piece on me, calling me a "Happiness Coach." I laughed at that label and my tooth cracked. Literally. I was chewing on a gummy that someone had given me that was supposed to "calm you down naturally" and it pulled my tooth out. I was in Tuscany at the time with a hole in my mouth and a brain that only felt half mine. But, hey, apparently I was a Happiness Coach.

Being Open

Lidia's writing had transformed me, and I wanted to be in touch with her. I thought she hated me, but it was not about me at all, as is usually the case. Lidia is painfully afraid of people. She would not leave her bed if she did not have to. Later, she would message me on Facebook and tell me that I was one of the most remarkable people she had ever met and she wanted to work with me. Isn't it amazing the stories we make up all the time? Here was a woman who is shy, a self-proclaimed misfit, a human so scared of others that it nearly kills her to be in front of them, and I made it about me. What an asshole.

It would take me going back on antidepressants to be able to finally get out of bed and fly to Seattle to do the makeup workshops I missed when I broke my foot. It was mid-July 2014, and there I was, sitting on the floor of the Seattle airport waiting for my flight, when I got the messages from Lidia and I was able to say *yes*.

A memory floated back to me: a dentist saying to me once when I was convinced my jaw was locked shut: *You just have to try and remember how to open.*

Being open meant I was always talking about my uterus with anyone and everyone. I was forty and married and had been pregnant once before, so whether I was going to have a baby was always a popular topic of discussion.

Are you going to have a baby? I know you have been trying all this time since you had that ectopic. You better hurry. Do you want a baby? You don't really know what love is, not really anyway, until you have a baby. Does Robert want a kid? Don't worry if you can't get pregnant, there are other ways to be a mother. It gets a lot harder, you know, after thirty-five. Are you going to try again? I am sorry you haven't been able to get pregnant again, Jen.

All those assumptions that I was trying to get pregnant since the ectopic were false. They rattled me and made me feel self-righteous. *You don't need to have a baby to have a fulfilling life! A child doesn't complete you. You can most certainly know love without having a baby. A child doesn't define you.* I had an answer for everyone, but mostly I didn't know what I wanted and I felt time was running out, which made me panic and want to punch the people in the face who kept asking me, *Well, what are you going to do?*

The last time I saw Wayne Dyer speak, I went backstage with his daughter to say hello and give him a hug. He asked me if I had kids, said he couldn't remember. I said, "I had an ectopic. I don't think I am going to have any, though."

He whispered, "Well, it's not up to you, anyway."

I rolled my eyes a little because it felt a little too woo-woo for me, but I hugged him and we took some selfies and I thought, *Yeah, right, it is up to me.*

In September, Robert was getting ready to leave to spend a month in Iran with his father, as he hadn't been back there in over twenty-five years since his family had escaped during the Revolution. I was getting ready to do workshops in New York and then do another retreat in Tuscany, followed by workshops in London. (You see? How could I have a baby? I was too busy! *Bullshit story.*)

I knew Robert wanted a child. He had this attitude like, "When we have a kid," to which I scoffed because of the word *when*.

"When?" I would ask. "We live in a one-bedroom, I travel for a living, and we are not spring chickens."

I knew he wanted a child and I knew I mostly didn't. I sat him down on the couch the night before he left for Tehran and said, "Babe, we need to decide. If we are going to try, we need to do this. I don't think I want to, though."

I again thought about myself on my deathbed with all my Jewish regrets and I imagined that I would appease myself for not having a child by the fact that I at least didn't try to *not* have one.

"I don't think we should, but maybe we should just let it be?"

So that night, before he left for the Middle East, we had sex and once again, only the second time I have ever said to him *don't pull out,* he didn't. Then he left.

When I arrived in Italy, everyone was once again asking if I wanted a baby. I joked that *No, I hadn't but I could be pregnant right now.* I must have said that twenty times at that retreat.

After I left Tuscany and arrived in London, my period was late. I knew but I pretended I didn't. Robert was still in Iran and I didn't want to take a pregnancy test until I got back to Los Angeles because aside from Jewish guilt, denial is one of my inherited traits.

I went out for tapas with my friend Nathan from Snow Patrol, once a private yoga student, by then a soul brother and best friend. I told him I thought I might be pregnant, but we shared a bottle of wine and some spicy potatoes and octopus and I said I would deal with it in L.A. It was raining in London and I didn't want to think about being pregnant. So I didn't.

I decided that, by forty, my guilt and denial were becoming old hat and boring, so my body walked itself into Waitrose and bought two pregnancy tests before I went next door to Costa and got a soy latte.

I peed on the sticks and then hid them both in the trash out front because I was staying at my mother-in-law's house. My husband was still in Iran.

I didn't cry, like I had two years prior. I didn't write notes to myself that only I could understand: IDWTBPIHM (I Don't Want To Be Pregnant I Hate Myself). I just sat down and texted some people.

I knew it. I was right. I am.

Again, electronic words changing lives.

I was glad I had that bottle of wine with Nathan the night before when I still wasn't positive because now I couldn't, in good conscience, toss a few back. That was really a thought I had. *Glad I had that wine last night.* I texted Nathan and told him my suspicions were correct, and when he asked if I was all right, I said that I didn't know.

I told Robert in a cab in London and we flew back to Los Angeles together. I still didn't know how I felt. Could that be possible? To be that disconnected from your own body that you feel nothing? I didn't believe I had a baby inside of me because surely I would feel something. Joy? Excitement? Fear? Love?

Once we found out it wasn't a black dot again and once we heard the heartbeat, I started to shift a little. I found myself leaving the corner of Denial and Guilt and heading toward Acceptance.

The baby could possibly have a genetic disorder. We were clear that we would terminate if that was the case. I saw what my sister's life was like with Blaise, what Emily went through with Ronan. I knew I couldn't do it. A needle went in through my belly and then I had to wait two weeks.

Lidia sent me a message, *I love you inside the waiting. I love you on the other side, already.*

She's a warrior of words and water and women and she says the right things. She makes me feel like it is going to be okay, so I had to ask her the old standby, *It's going to be okay, right? Right?* because she made me feel right in the world, in a place where otherwise I didn't know where to put anything. I texted her back, *Thank you. I love you, too.*

After years of not feeling, when we got the results of the genetic test, my grief registered as grief, melancholy as melancholy, joy as joy.

The baby was okay. We would not terminate. I was going to stay on antidepressants. And I was going to be a mother.

CHAPTER 30

Little Beauties Everywhere

MY CHILDHOOD BABYSITTER who lost her son in a car crash let Robert and me use her house in Carmel, California, for a little getaway. She has pictures of her late son, Keenan, all over and a little shrine of him by her bed on this old wooden dresser. She keeps a book by her pillow called *Understanding Your Grief.* You can feel her son there.

The small boy of him, the football player—all the stages of his life on various pieces of furniture, bookshelves, the refrigerator. How everything leads to something else, and if you look for it, traces of people we love, of people long gone, of beauty, are all around us, all the time. Even when we are about to turn onto a freeway in San Francisco and we see two lone shopping carts and those carts by the freeway might mean something before you go on your way and so it makes sense that the dead son of your childhood babysitter is everywhere in her apartment.

It's unfair to anyone who's never met my father. *You've had to have met him! He'd moon people at parties and people loved it! You didn't know my father? That's impossible! Everyone knows my father.*

Things permeate us. Like smoke, they billow up until we finally notice and swat them away. Only, no matter how hard we think we're swatting, nothing's really going anywhere. It's all right here. That is what I am working on sharing in my workshops: how our stories are within us and they deserve to be let out, they deserve to be heard.

Recently, when I was at the bank in L.A., an old woman at the teller next to me was talking loudly, and she sort of leaned in toward my direction as if she was talking to the air, to anybody really, but would be happy if someone picked up on the hint that she needed someone to connect to. So I did.

I smiled at her. *Pardon?*

She showed me a check in her hand. And she was shaking, Parkinson's maybe, and she had tears in her eyes and they fell as she told me, "Someone I know from elementary school sends me money every month, every single month, seven hundred and fifty dollars, to help with my medical bills. There are so many good people out there. We just have to see them."

It was funny because she said that while I was in the middle of this game with myself that went: Smile at every single person and be as nice as you can be and watch what happens. So, at the DMV, where I'd gone the day before my license expired to renew it, I'd found that everyone I interacted with had a sense of humor. Everyone I made eye contact with smiled back. *My game is working!* I left and went to the bank, where I continued my *I'm going to be nice, nice, nice, nice.* The old lady was like a magnet toward me, her cane pulling her closer, and it's ironic because often I've thought of myself as a pain magnet, but this eighty-five-year-old woman shimmied her way toward me in a bank to tell me of the kindnesses in the world.

There are little beauties everywhere. We just have to look for them. And then when we find them, we have to keep them close, even when they die or drift off to sea, and that isn't hard, really, when you think about it, because everything always leads to something else and when you feel sad and empty and like it all means nothing, you might look out and see two shopping carts and you might remember: I just have to look, listen, and tell the truth and the beauty will be there. That's what beauty hunting is.

I RECENTLY FOUND something I wrote when my son, Charlie Mel, was almost a year old. *I am not dead (but I am really fucking tired). It has not destroyed me (although sometimes I feel as if my son is trying to with his constant nursing and my lack of sleep).*

HE CAME TWO and a half weeks early and in true form of a neurotic Jew who's also a little woo-woo, I had an epidural and I also had my friend Fawntice come and put Tibetan singing bowls all over my body as I was in labor. My son came out on a laugh. There was a nurse in the room who was so funny that I asked her if she was a comedian while I was pushing and if I could have her information on social media. She made a joke, I laughed, and out he came at six pounds, five ounces. I was scared of the slime and I asked, "Do they always look like this? Is something wrong with him?" They put him on my chest and I don't know what I felt. That's not a lie. I didn't feel that "love at first thing" women speak of. I know I felt scared and numb from the waist down and I had bronchitis, so I felt exhausted on top of just having delivered a human, but I didn't feel a surge of bliss or love.

Now, almost eleven months later, I love him so much I want to eat him. I want to take his feet and put them in my mouth (sometimes I do) and swallow him whole. He is the most delicious pain in my ass I could have ever asked for. Something opened up in me over these last many months that has been closed since my father died and it has not killed me.

I was still struggling with allowing myself to feel things (don't we all to some degree?), but by then I was leading workshops with Lidia called "Writing and The Body." I listened to the stories that the participats shared, and I let them enter me. I practiced rooting myself to the earth so I would not fly away anymore.

I don't believe that everything happens for a reason, or any of those platitudes people shuck out to squash grief. (A great book to combat those words is *There Is No Good Card for This: What to Say and Do When Life Is Scary, Awful, and Unfair to People You Love*, by Kelsey Crowe and Emily McDowell.) I don't know why my friend's baby died or why my dad died so young or why my nephew has the most cruel disorder I can think of or why I can't hear. There is no why. Why is a nonanswer. I don't believe God "only gives you what you can handle." I believe the only way I would have ever had this child is if I let go of trying to know. If I would have had to go through fertility treatments or IVF, I wouldn't have done it. The only way I could have had him is if it was as easy as it was, and you can call me an asshole for that, for I surely am at times, but it is the truth.

I am terrified every day. I am scared to make a decision because what if it is the wrong one? I am scared I will ruin things again or kill someone or they will leave me or I won't be able to hear for good. I am scared of so much. The only way my son was able to be here, besides the fact that my husband and I had sex while I was ovulating, was if I listened to what Wayne Dyer repeatedly said and let go of what I thought I knew for certain. *It ain't what you don't know that gets you into trouble. It's what you know for sure that just ain't so.* And what I thought I knew for certain was that loving someone so fully would kill me. That I wouldn't be able to contain it in my body and I would cause myself or the person to die. Like I had my father. I would rupture.

I had to let that certainty go because it was a bullshit story.

CHAPTER 31

I Got You

Let the Snot Fly

In 2017, I finally convinced my in-laws to come to my June Italy retreat, after years of trying. They lived in London and it seemed so much easier to schlep (though does one ever *schlep* to Italy?) to Tuscany than to Los Angeles. My mother-in-law flew out often to visit us in L.A., but my father-in-law could not deal with the long flight and the hassle of security, so he never came (except when our son was born). So I convinced them and I felt really good about myself because I knew, in the end, it would be one of those things that we would be grateful for until the end of our lives. My Iranian father-in-law, Ali, was a Rumi scholar and poet and brilliant man, who had offered to give a lecture on Rumi at my retreat. I was thrilled. I had never heard one of his lectures and I loved Rumi, although I only knew a few of his poems and quotes.

As usual, my father-in-law got dressed up for the flight, despite it being nearly 100 degrees. He had on his seersucker jacket and fancy trousers and he looked sharp. That was his way, old-fashioned and formal.

Robert was closer to his parents than anyone I have ever met.

He Skyped with them every day. My son knows them because of this, despite the fact that they lived in England. My mother-in-law sang him nursery rhymes with her sweet English accent and my father-in-law called him *Shazdeh*, which means "little prince" in Farsi. I sometimes hated how overconnected (read: disconnected) we all are, but this connection genuinely touched me and I wish I had experienced this closeness as a child. Keeping in touch with my friends and family who lived across the country after we'd moved so far away. Getting to see their faces on FaceTime or Skype. All we had were letters in the mail and landline phone calls. I do miss actual letters, though.

I was ecstatic they'd made the journey from London. Charlie had just turned one the month before. He'd started walking about a week before his first birthday and was waddling and falling all over the place. My sister was also there and I was excited to have so much of my family all in one place, as well as so many hands to help with this tiny person who had just discovered running and who was still obsessed with my boobs.

My in-laws were impressed by the place from the minute they stepped down from the van that had brought them from the airport, paninis in hand. I had been wondering what was taking so long for the van to arrive from Florence and it turns out they had stopped for a pee break, lunch, and Chianti.

"*Shazdeh!*" my father-in-law exclaimed when he saw Charlie in my arms. I handed the heavy sack of potatoes that is my son over to my father-in-law.

The villa itself is impressive. Locanda Cugnanello is an eight-hundred-year-old house, nestled among olive groves and lavender fields, completely refurbished, so it feels more like a five-star hotel (at least to my tiny-apartment-living ass). There's a gorgeous wine cellar where we have wine tastings and eat our pizza that we make in the pizza-making party (the Romanian employees there, who have become like my family, lovingly call it The Pizza Extravaganza Night), and where I go to write or get quiet. There's even a gym, although I have never set foot in it, as well as a beautiful pool and a hammock and so many nooks and crannies to go *Oh My God, I am in fucking Tuscany* in as you read or just stare up at the Tuscan sun like Diane Lane.

Ali would give his talk in the wine cellar one evening before dinner. There was a long wooden table on one end of the room that could seat thirty people and he could sit in the center.

Ali had written many books, but he brought two specifically to sell at my retreat (I would use the money toward giving someone a scholarship). One was his book of poems, *Dawn*, and the other, *Memoirs of a Persian Childhood*, his memoir.

One of the women at the retreat was there on a scholarship, which, by this time, was called "The Aleksander Fund," named after one of my readers, Julia Anderson's baby boy, who passed away when she was forty-one weeks pregnant. She attended my retreat through generous donations from my social media followers and we came up with the idea to keep the scholarship going and to name it after her boy one night while we were talking in the kitchen.

Tara, one of the women at the June retreat, had given birth to a stillborn baby who'd had Down syndrome. She'd written me: *I found your trip through a post that Julia Anderson made on a private site we both follow for grieving parents. I read her story and it resonated with me so much. Having also lost a son to stillbirth in my third trimester, I know her pain. It's excruciating. Through writing and yoga, I've been able to come to a place now where I can find joy and peace when I seek it out, but this journey of grief continues day in and day out and it will for the rest of my life.*

It is an honor to have people attend who have experienced such profound loss and to try and give them a week of uninhibited joy (which often included a lot of tears). I was grateful that Ali would share the wonders of Rumi with us, and especially with anyone who had experienced such heartbreak, like Tara.

The week was magic. We made pizza. We went to the Mediterranean Sea and had a picnic. Some of us went skinny-dipping under the stars. We danced and sang. We ate our faces off. We made our own pasta. We wrote and shared. We swam. We meditated, and my beloved assistant Elizabeth Conway, now more of a co-leader at my retreats, who leads meditation and yoga every morning, gave us a healing concert with Tibetan singing bowls. We did yoga. We cried. We bore witness to grief and joy. We saw someone fall in love. We watched people crack open. We got carsick. We drank wine. We had dance parties. We ate so much gelato. We celebrated ourselves and everyone at the retreat. We wrote everybody a note that listed the five most beautiful things about each person so no one left empty-handed. Each attendant left with their own personal satchel of love notes, something I do at all my weeklong retreats to help us be beauty hunters instead of fault finders. We listened fiercely, like our lives depended on it.

Having Ali there to talk to us for hours about Rumi and to share with us his gifts, felt like a privilege to every one of us. I only knew him as my husband's father, but to hear him recite all those poems from memory and talk about Rumi's history and the circle of life, I was blown away. We all sat around filming him and taking notes as we drank our Chianti and he spoke to us in his thick Iranian accent about his mother.

As I had at that poetry reading at NYU, and as I had felt as people shared their words with me in my workshops, I felt so grateful to know this man, to hear his words, his voice, and to know that everyone gathered there was doing their best to be the best they could be. They all were: being human.

CHAPTER 32

The Inner Asshole: Acceptance and Resistance

I Am Worthy to Receive

It wasn't until I finally had the courage to openly talk about something that caused me undue shame, my hearing loss, that a new world opened up. I had blogged about how much shame was wrapped up in my deafness and how I used to be mortified at the idea of wearing hearing aids but *now, if I could only afford them, I would wear them in a heartbeat.* A kind woman who took my yoga classes in West Hollywood read it and e-mailed me immediately that she had some connections and a pair of hearing aids were waiting for me at an audiologist's office in Beverly Hills.

Those were my first hearing aids, in 2009, for which I am eternally grateful. They had belonged to an older man who'd died and never worn them, so his wife donated them to the audiologist he'd bought them from. The woman who took my yoga classes put in a call, she was some kind of high-powered lawyer, and just like that, I had a dead man's hearing aids in my own ears.

They didn't work very well and were fairly old, but they were better than what I'd had before, which was nothing. Once they were in my ears you couldn't see them at all. I wondered why there was such a stigma (in my mind) about hearing aids and hearing loss. I thought about those huge hearing aids from when I was a kid. My fat ego was always like, *Hell no, I would rather be deaf.*

Once my hearing got bad enough, I didn't care, and by then, hearing aids were microscopic. I would have worn them no matter what they looked like by the time I faced the truth that I couldn't hear. I wish, sometimes, that I had thrown vanity out the window and just gotten the hearing aids earlier, but then the cycle starts: *I've done it wrong; I don't know myself; I've made it worse,* and I have to shut it down. I didn't accept my deafness, that was a fact. But now I do: also a fact. We can only be where we are.

I lost those donated hearing aids during one of my retreats and posted about it on Facebook. Hearing aids cost thousands of dollars and are not covered by health insurance, for the most part. Someone read my post and immediately started a crowdfunding campaign. Money poured in almost immediately. People all over the world. People who said how much I had helped them and what an honor it was for them to be able to return the favor. People I had met. People I had not met. People who had read my essays and blogs and followed me on social media.

I was scared to look as the money kept pouring in. Scared to look at the names of the people who were donating. I thought because I was "successful" that I should have money and to accept this generosity was some sort of admittance that I was a sham. I also felt unworthy, like, *Who was I to be so loved?* (Granted, there are people who hate me, so calm down if you are one of them, but when you see how quickly people will go to bat for you, it is bring-you-to-your-knees humbling.) Your mantra of *I am not worthy* or *I am garbage* doesn't have any weight. Your IA whimpers and hides in the corner. I didn't want to look at the list of names, because it would make them real, and also, I would have to practice what I preach.

Which is to say that I would have to be able to ask for help, to receive, to show people that even though my IA says I am not worthy, I can quiet that mofo down and accept this love and say, *Yes, I am worthy,* even if my bullshit story tells me otherwise.

That crowdfunding for my hearing aids reminded me of when my dad died. Or when Frank died. I wanted to run or hide or do something so I could float away, so I didn't have to look at the beauty surrounding me. At how all these people were not going to let me suffer. How my mom was doing the best she could back then. Eventually I had to look and take the money and say *thank you* even though my IA was telling me I did not deserve this, that there were people worse off, that I was used to not being able to hear and it was my punishment for being a bad person. That old bullshit story. I had to go get new hearing aids and face the world and turn those puppies up to drown out my IA, which had grown so loud over the years.

My whole career had become about listening. Even though I had either had no hearing aids or crappy ones, people were saying that I was the best listener they had ever experienced. I had taught myself to listen without my ears. But now that I was able to afford a pair of hearing aids that could help me, I was going to get me a pair that worked. I got the top-of-the-line pair that I could adjust with my iPhone! They were Bluetooth operated and the sound went right into my head, so you never knew if I was watching a show or listening to music or on the phone. It was like some *Black Mirror* shit.

The way my life opened up after I got those hearing aids was indescribable. I had to come to terms with how much I had been missing. I had been walking around hearing only about 15 percent (if that). I had gotten so used to it that when I got the fancy hearing aids, I felt embarrassed at how I had been functioning before. Had I been saying stupid things all the time because I certainly was mishearing almost everything? What had I been responding to? All the stories that had been shared in my workshop, despite the fact that I got down on my butt and scooted around the room to lip-read and almost sat in the speaker's lap, I still had missed most of the details. Once I was able to hear better, I realized what I had gotten accustomed to living with and I felt an incredible sadness for the IA that lives in all of us. My IA didn't think I deserved to hear. My IA told me I could handle anything, any kind of loss, including my hearing.

What a miserable existence, the IA. The effort I put into trying to make out what is being said feels like running a marathon (not that I ever have or will run a marathon) and screw you, Inner Asshole, for making me feel like I was tough enough to withstand anything.

I wait until I am nearly dying from pain or discomfort before I do anything about it. And I never went for years, until it got so bad that I couldn't avoid it anymore. Then I finally went to the audiologist and said, "Okay, test my ears." And I wept when I saw the results, which was nothing I didn't know in my body already, but now I had substantial proof. A chart. A graph. Facts. And I couldn't afford hearing aids. My IA had laughed at me.

At one of my most recent retreats, the group learned sign language for me. I walked into our closing circle ceremony and found the group signing something to me that I could not understand. I asked my friend Ceri, who leads yoga and meditation at all my retreats now, how they pulled it off. How had they learned the signs without my knowing about it?

She told me that at one point she saw one of our attendees, Dee Anne, signing. Elizabeth said it took her breath away; it was so beautiful, and it was such a language of connection that came from the heart and lived in the body. Dee Anne is a speech and language pathologist. And Elizabeth said, "I wanted you to hear us in a language, something that was clear, with two phrases you say often that are powerful reassurances. I floated the idea to Dee Anne of teaching us all and she said 'I got you' and 'I have done love' would be easy and they were her favorites."

Dee Anne taught four attendees and they took others aside and taught four more and everyone practiced in their rooms and they were all signing to each other these phrases in the van, in the Duomo in Siena, in gelato shops in San Gimignano, and it was a beautiful secret I had no idea about. People apparently stressed about getting it wrong; that they might say *the cow jumped over the moon* or something, but Dee Anne kept them all together, teaching the exact way to do the gestures. And they waited for closing circle and stood like a choir and silently signed to me as I walked in. They all just kept signing over and over *We got you* and *We have done love*. And it inspired me to finally learn sign language after all these years.

Embodied language. A full-body expression of *It's going to be okay*.

Receiving love and care is just as important as giving it, and yet it's harder for most of us. To remember the mantra I try (and sometimes fail) to live by: *I am worthy to receive*.

The second time a crowdfunding campaign was created for me was just as hard to accept in some ways. I was further along in my career, making more money, but still, when we found out my father-in-law was dying from pancreatic cancer and would most likely be gone by the weekend, well, who has that kind of cash lying around? To buy three tickets leaving the next day to London? To rent an apartment to be next to that dying father?

"Who has that kind of cash?" I asked Lidia.

"Rich people," she replied.

We laughed.

I thought I should be a rich person, and people probably thought

I was, but then I remembered that *should is an asshole* and that I was being given another opportunity to truly practice what I teach. To bring it to life. Within a day, enough money was raised to send me, my husband, and my son to London. Just a few months earlier, at my retreat in Italy, there was no way we could have known that he would be dead by February. Or when we saw him again in September and he pushed our suitcases down Upper Richmond Road in Putney like a teen boy, laughing and speaking in Farsi.

One person texted me that I shouldn't allow someone to create a crowdfunding campaign for me because it might be bad for my image. As if it would let people know I was not as successful as they thought I was because I was receiving help financially. This is a ridiculous comment, because most people receive some kind of support financially, at some point, and it doesn't diminish the power of their accomplishments. Still, I felt shamed. I almost believed her and almost shut it down. But then I decided, *What image?* My image is real motherfucking life. My workshop is called On Being Human. What image have I ever tried to create besides being utterly myself? I decided not to listen to the one out of the one hundred. Sometimes that one is your own IA, sometimes it's someone else. There will always be the one who doesn't like you, the one who says, *No, you should not do this, Yes, you suck.* And we always always have two choices: keep going or shut down.

CHAPTER 33

Keeping of the Going

WHAT I ALWAYS say in my workshops is that I am concerned with the keeping of the going. It's easy to make plans in a group of supportive, open people, but what do you do when life enters in once again?

Therefore I decided to keep going. I went to London with Robert and twenty-month-old Charlie Mel and it was the worst flight in the history of flying and I vowed to never again fly with my son (besides the obvious flying back home from London), but we kept going and got there to say good-bye to Charlie's *Agha June*. We kept going all the way until we got to the apartment I rented with the huge windows (and the TV and the table and the chairs and the walls) that Charlie proceeded to get his handprints all over. We kept going until we got to my in-laws' apartment next door and it was only when I saw my father-in-law, *Agha June,* lying in a ball in his bed, curled up like a baby, half the size from the last time I saw him, did we stop the keeping of the going. He had on flannel pajamas and I gasped because as much loss as I have had, I had never seen a dying person. A dying father.

My own father had gone so quickly, without warning, good-bye-less, and I wondered if I had made the right choice accepting the money from the people all over the world because had I not accepted it, I wouldn't have gone and if I hadn't gone, I wouldn't have to face this decay. It made me want to hold on to my mom forever. I knew parents died. Hell, I lost my dad so long ago, I had known that fact for as long as I could remember: parents died. But as time went on, I lost my *I am strong* mantra and started replacing it with *I can't handle anything* and the thought of losing my mom made me feel like I would die. *I can't handle anything.* I had used up all my strength—the pushing kind, the powering-through kind, the nobody-can-touch-or-hurt-or-see-me kind in my younger years. The reserve I had was long gone, and when this happened, I was forced to confront my softness, and I relaxed into it, and that's when my career took shape and took off. When I wasn't pushing so hard.

I can't handle anything. I want to shut down.

But I kept going.

I leaned in and kissed his face.

"Jen, Jen, thank you so much for coming," he whispered. His voice had always been loud. I used to always ask Robert why his dad yelled all the time. *That's just his voice,* he would say. It was faint now. "Jen, thank you for coming. It means so much to me. And for bringing Charlie."

"Of course. There was no option," I said.

His sister Pari, Robert's beloved aunt, had flown in from Tehran the month before when we found out he was sick and had not left his side. She was eighty-seven. She had a chair set up next to his bed and would pat his mouth and wipe away the ice cream dribble. He could only eat a few bites of ice cream and a few sips of Ensure, some kind of drink that provided nutrients, since he wasn't able to eat. Pari touched his foot and tenderly wiped his mouth and I wanted to look away because I was never able to be that vulnerable with my family.

With people in my workshops? Yes. With strangers? Yes. Friends? Yes. My closest people? No. I have never held my sister's hand. I am afraid, to this day, of showing them I am soft. I have spent so long chanting *I am strong* that it's like a physiological response. I shut down around my family as if it will protect me, as if it will make them not leave, or, if they do, I will not be affected. I would feel so embarrassed if I showed my fall-in-loveable side of me to my family. It felt not only emotionally, but physically impossible.

But maybe that's a bullshit story and I can rewrite it?

He hugged me. "I am so proud of you, Jen. So proud of you. So proud of you." He said it three times.

Besides my fantasy words of *it's going to be okay*, my other one is my dad telling me that he is proud of me.

My father-in-law kissed me. "You are the daughter I always wished I had."

Charlie ran in the room and started climbing up on the bed and I wanted to look away. But I didn't. I wouldn't look away. After all, it is exactly what I ask of people in my workshop. *Please, do not look away.*

I wanted to hug every person who sent in money so we could get there. I looked around at my in-laws' cluttered bedroom and counted the five most beautiful things I saw:

1. My dying father-in-law hugging my baby
2. My husband's aunt sitting in an uncomfortable chair, keeping vigil over her brother

3. My father-in-law's books he had written on the bedside table
4. A porcelain bird that I would have normally thought was hideous
5. My husband, softened by grief, looking down at his father and his son, tears in his eyes. The first tears I had ever seen in twelve years.

Beauty hunting. The key to surviving death. The key to surviving life. The key to being human. The key to climbing out of the catacombs.

I HAD GOTTEN angry at my father-in-law a few years back when he sat me down at a pub in London and said, "Come on, Jen! Have a baby."

It sounded like a command and I was pissed off. I was in town doing a workshop and had come alone without Robert.

"Excuse me?" I said, dipping my chip in mayo.

"Time is not on your side," he said.

"Time is not on anyone's side," I replied immediately.

I said, "And besides, do you think the only way to have a fulfilling life is by having a child?"

"Yes," he said. "Absolutely."

I scoffed. I was angry. I didn't think I was going to have a kid and who was this guy to tell me what to do? I was a feminist and, excuse me, I said, "But this is a conversation between your son and me. No one else."

I went on to make a *don't be an asshole* video about assuming that all women want to, or are able to, have children. I became a spokesperson for not having kids. My best friend, Annie Sertich, and I talked about it endlessly over coffee. I was livid.

He apologized and seemed to respect me even more after I stood up to him. I was not going to tolerate that old-school machismo patriarchal nonsense. I was the *don't be an asshole* lady and I could do what I wanted and if I didn't want to have kids, I wouldn't. Annie and I had started the *don't be an asshole* campaign one day over coffee when we realized how much of our lives we spent being assholes. No siree Bob, as my dad would have said.

As he lay on his bed, dying, Robert kept saying. "Well, at least we have Charlie because of him."

"Babe, Charlie is not because of your dad. Um, hello? Your dad did not have sex with me."

"But he encouraged us," he said.

"Okay, if you want to call it that."

But then I let him have it. "Okay, we have Charlie because of your dad," and I wondered if part of it wasn't true, because that small part of me that didn't want to have a baby, that was so terrified, kept hearing his voice in my head and although his voice did not make my husband's sperm fertilize my egg, it made me stop and ask myself what I wanted and what I was so afraid of. The answer was, *I don't know.*

I embraced the *I don't know* and I got pregnant. *I don't know* is what allowed me to open myself up to possibility, which in turn allowed me to see myself as a mother. The *I don't know* made me accept that maybe I didn't know that bad things would always happen to me, that maybe I didn't have to be strong and be responsible for everyone. That maybe I could allow for tenderness.

My go-to mantra when my own dad died was *I don't care,* but when I changed it to *I don't know,* everything shifted. I don't know that I will be a terrible mother. I don't know that I will die young. And if Charlie could communicate better, if he had more words, he would say, "That's right, asshole, you don't know, you're a great mom, but don't make me brush my teeth." But now, he just looks at me and pulls my face into his and kisses me and rests his head on my shoulder.

CHAPTER 34

Fathers Everywhere

I REMEMBERED GOING to a friend's baby shower, a woman who had come on a couple retreats. I was pretty sure I did not want a child, but I remember being sad after the shower and writing in a half-used journal on my desk:

It comes down to this: there are fathers everywhere.

Look. There's one. And another. You just missed one! Right there, there's one. And here. They're everywhere really, the fathers.

And they always will be everywhere.

Here's one, proudly thanking everyone for coming to his daughter's baby shower, first grandchild, so proud. One's holding the hand of his little boy, *Watch out, it's crowded here, hold tight.* Herds of them driving down the highway in the rain, never coming back, not while it still matters, anyway. And it'll always be that way. The everywhereness of them all.

You will look up and the world will be a sky of fathers, men puffing cigars will fill the air, men in droves, men with daughters. Everyone will be a father pulling out a picture of his first grandchild to show the world: *Would you look at that? Would you just look at that?*

You will look up and notice, and you may be the only one who notices, that the sky has been replaced with these fathers, and also the banks and the streets.

There will be nothing else, and at times it will be all you see.

It comes down to this: whatever you are missing will suddenly appear to be back in the world, its own cardiovascular system of pain, forgotten until you realize that as much as it's back in the world, it will always be just beyond your reach.

You will notice it everywhere, like when you start to notice pregnant women everywhere or how many blue cars are on the road. (*They are everywhere! Would you look at that? Would you look at that?*) Your heart, once again a closed fist. A hand open, flat and rough, its lines suggesting "long life and contentment with love life." But the heart line is missing.

It comes down to this: your pain comes in waves, it turns, leaches into things. Years of your life, for example. Your pain wraps itself around whole years like a tentacle and won't let go until you understand that it is the organ of touch, so you reach out and touch it and then, only then, it slithers off, as if all it needed was to be noticed.

The woman's father stood up at the shower to make a speech and looked over at her big belly with a swell of the chest, *Look at my little girl. Look at us.*

I was thrilled for her and yet tears (where are these coming from?). Tears in my egg whites and arugula with the chicken picked out of it.

The pain comes in waves. The initial shock of loss. The teenage-years angst. The reduction of it all to poetry.

Then, the loss of what is yet to come. The mourning of something that hasn't even occurred yet.

It comes down to this: we recognize when possibility has been eliminated.

When there is never a chance of this or that, we know it, and our hearts mourn something that doesn't even have a name yet. I'll never have that and yet I am sad. I am devastated. I can't go on.

Sometimes, when you least expect it (and I hope for all of our sakes that we aren't always expecting the worst), we will crumble at the site of a seesaw, a beard, a Pepsi. I wish it wasn't a fact. I wish that you and I could go on and pour salt on our eggs and clap with the rest of the people and that we wouldn't feel a thing. Not even a twang.

But that would be a lie. The things that shape us are where the beauty resides. And if you let your grief metabolize, you can turn it into art, or creativity, or simply an offering of compassion for another. I was finally feeling what I didn't allow myself to feel for my father, decades earlier.

IN LONDON, CHARLIE and I stayed in the apartment all week. It rained and it was cold and ugly outside, and *Agha June* went back into the hospital, so we couldn't walk over to the apartment next door to see him anymore. We watched *Shrek* seventeen times. I watched anything I could find on Netflix, my reliable best friend besides Annie. I watched *The Sinner* with Jessica Biel and Holt's show *Mindhunter* and sat awake thinking of serial killers and wondering why I was watching such dark shit in such a dark time but I couldn't stop and plus, I knew him! He was my pal! He had helped me become a yoga teacher, which, in turn, helped me become whatever the hell one called who I was now. The thrill of watching my friends on TV or reading their books never goes away for me. I ate cold pizza in bed while Charlie slept and I watched with subtitles until five a.m.

We got to see *Agha June* one last time. I rode with Charlie in a cab and we went to the hospital. Charlie sensed something immediately and morphed into a silent angel child. I think an alien kidnapped him for an hour and put someone in his body, but he was a cute alien and I have no complaints.

My father-in-law again told me how proud he was of me. "Keep writing, Jen. You are a writer. Write your book," he whispered. There was a bag of chips on the windowsill and a bottle of Ensure, a wilted flower, and one of his memoirs.

"I will write it. I am writing it," I said.

I wished I could cry. My antidepressants make it nearly impossible, so I often feel like I am constipated in the tear ducts. Between my eyes tenses up, but there is never a release.

I left with Charlie and ate pizza for the gazillionth night and Robert slept in a chair next to his dad's bed in the hospital and I watched serial killers again on Netflix and once, my body gave a little heave, my chest, as if it had been holding on for a lifetime, let go of something akin to an elephant, so I looked around the room expecting to see some kind of animal sitting on the floor next to my dirty jeans, but that animal was just grief, a beast with sad eyes, so I hugged my son and slept all night with him, curled into him until his little heaves soothed me and serial killers and dying dads were gone.

When I go and visit my sister and her two sons, I marvel at the fact that once upon a time we beat the shit out of each other. My mom (Mom Mom) plays with my son, gives him a bath, takes him on long walks in his stroller so he can look at cars, rubs his back so he can sleep, and I try to remember if we had these moments when I was a kid.

As Lidia taught me, there is always a story under the story. The story under this one? I've learned how to ignore pain, and as much as I used to think it meant I wasn't feeling it, it doesn't. It means I am good at looking away, at escaping.

I try to not look away anymore. To stay. To let things in, to let people in. My mother, my sister. We are so close now. Every time I feel the urge to escape I whisper, *Come back*, and sometimes people will stare because often I am talking to myself but I don't care. I'd rather be a person who talks to herself than a walking corpse.

My mom travels with me to all my international retreats and sometimes we almost kill each other, but mostly we laugh and eat and take naps and talk about our past and my dad, even though her version and my version are always different. She has no memory of me being upset when she yanked us from California and brought us back to Jersey. I scoff and at first get angry until I just breathe. *JB.* Memory is malleable, yes. Also, fallible.

My mom constantly apologizes and says, "I did the best I could, Jen. I know you wish you had a different mom."

This isn't true and I tell her I love her. I'm working on softening. For the rest of my life I will be working on this.

Things aren't perfect now, but show me a family that is. We usually just eat gnocchi and I spill it on myself and we laugh at how badly we travel together. I hug all my retreat attendees and my friends and I am a big toucher, but when it comes to my mom and sister, as close as we are, being physically affectionate with them does not come easily to me. Years of armor and rigidity can take a lifetime to come off. Little bits of metal remain sometimes, even when you think it's all gone. Shards in your heart, splinters in your skin, you might spend your whole life picking out the remaining hardness. And that's okay.

CHAPTER 35

Give Yourself a Fucking Medal

(No One Will Do It for You)

RECENTLY, I GOT an e-mail after I posted something on Facebook about how bad I suck at organizing and planning and that I couldn't even commit to the following weekend but now I had to plan at least a year out. The e-mail said:

> How in the world did you go from being a waitress to what you do now, with thousands of followers? I realize it was a journey, but how did you make that transition? I'm very interested in how people reinvent themselves, since I'm in the process of doing it myself. Well, when we're past our twenties, our paths become more circuitous. There are always things that come up in my life that seem out of left field to other people, but to me it's like, "What do you mean? I've been doing this all my life. It's just not what I was officially doing for a living, etc." I see that type of thing all the time. An actress or a writer "bursts" on the scene, after twenty years of hard work and toiling in obscurity, etc.
>
> I know there is much more nuance to your story and that is why I'm interested in reading it—not as simple as "waitress

becomes inspirational coach and teaches workshops around
the world overnight."

I stood in my kitchen with the fridge open, hanging on the door,
and thought about her questions. How did I get here? I always hear
that Talking Heads song, "Once in a Lifetime," when I am asked
that: *"And you may ask yourself . . . Well? How did I get here?"* I sometimes take for granted that things didn't just happen, that I didn't
just wake up one day and not have to go to The Newsroom to serve
chicken potpies and turkey meat loaves, that I had been doing retreats around the world forever, that people always cared what I
said. Not sure they do now, either, but hey, the things we tell ourselves to get out of bed, right? Not that many years ago I was still
waitressing. I hated myself. But now, I am in my kitchen and wondering how to answer someone when they ask, "Well, how did you
get here? How did you go from there to here?" From feeling stuck
to leading retreats around the world that teach people, essentially,
to get unstuck.

I'm fascinated with the idea of memory. The memory of pain.
Paul Auster says, in *The Invention of Solitude*, that "In the space of
memory, everything is both itself and something else."

He also says, in the same book, "Memory: the space in which a
thing happens for the second time."

For example, I was getting this really incredible ashiatsu massage last time I was at Canyon Ranch. A woman named Sasha hangs
from the ceiling and steps on your back. At one point it was so deli-
ciously painful that I wanted to slam my arms on the side of the
table to get her to stop. And that made me remember being in Italy
at one of the farmhouse retreats. There was an Italian guy there, a
healer who now lives in Saint Louis but comes back to Siena for the

summers. He did these wacky healings he called "mouth yoga." I had a cold as I arrived and knew I had to be "on" for the weeklong retreat, so when my friend said, "The mouth yoga will really help you, Jen," I believed her.

Anahabra, whose nickname was Anaconda, led me into a bathroom with a lone lightbulb and sat me down at a sink (like maybe he was going to cut my hair or show me how the drain was stopped up). He put on white gloves and I was thinking, *Oh my god, what the fuck have I gotten myself into?* I could barely hear as it was and he had the thickest Italian accent and I was scared, so I tuned out even more until he said he was going to stick his fingers in my mouth and get rid of any mucus. He told me he had cured his mom of cancer with this method, so I was like, *Okay, my cold has a fifty-fifty shot of surviving.* He basically made me vomit, which, since I'm a former anorexic, is like playing with fire. Bringing out old demons. He told me to bang the side of the sink if I needed him to stop, like some kind of safe word that wasn't a word at all. "If it gets too much, bang sink hard!"

It was so weird and surreal (and my cold turned into pneumonia) that I have sort of blocked it out, although Anahabra/Anaconda is a lovely lovely man and I'll probably see him at my next Italy retreat. As I wanted to slam my arms into her massage table in the Berkshires to beg the masseuse to stop, it reminded me of "mouth yoga" and I thought how interesting it is, where the mind goes when it's confronted with pain. One pain becomes all pain. And that pain builds upon all the other pain and all of it becomes the same memory, revisited in the body, over and over again.

The ashiatsu massage pain ended and was replaced with sheer bliss. (I highly recommend this treatment.) Sasha says she loves it because she feels like she is dancing on the person.

En route to Canyon Ranch I had stopped in New York to do a workshop. When I landed at JFK it was late and very cold out (high of twenty-seven) and I was schlepping all my stuff, so I wanted to find a taxi as quickly as possible. I debated asking someone to split a cab, but everyone was busy looking down at their various devices and iPhones or just looking generally annoyed, so I opted against it. I stared at the woman's back in front of me for a while and then decided *why not.*

"Where are you headed?" I asked her.

She looked at me like I had two heads for a moment, then decided to tell me, before she begrudgingly shared her cab with me. She slid way over to the other side of the taxi and obviously had no intention of talking, which was actually fine with me. But inevitably, she turned and asked me why I was in New York and did I live there and it turned out she also lived in L.A. and then she was asking about my workshops and seemed generally fascinated by the weird hybrid of what I did. And we talked and talked and she told me her mother was a writer and that when they were kids, the mom used to take them to a restaurant and as soon as they sat down she'd say, "Shhhhh."

And they'd hush.

And she'd tell them to eavesdrop on the tables around them. Each kid had to pick a table. The rest of the meal was spent making up stories about the people around them.

I loved this idea. It's like beauty hunting, isn't it? What a way to harbor creativity, to create interesting conversation, to train the imagination, and to instill the art of storytelling. She said that instead of whining about how long the food would take or *why are we here at the stupid restaurant, Mom?* Or, *so and so pulled my hair,* they'd sit around telling stories.

If I tried to save face and hadn't asked her to split a cab, I would never have heard this story.

As a writer, I try to do this sort of eavesdropping anyway, except since I am profoundly hard of hearing, my eavesdropping is much more reliant on my vision and imagination than on my ears.

We all do it anyway, don't we? Make up stories about people.

Come on, you must do it, too.

Once, this girl came to my workshop in NYC wearing jeans. (It's hard to do yoga in jeans.) She wouldn't dance or sing and she wouldn't share out loud at all. It was if she stumbled into the wrong room. So I made up all these stories about her. But at one point, when she had dropped into a child's pose, I put my hands on her back in hopes she would let out a deep sigh or at least some sort of movement that suggested she was relaxing a bit. (She didn't.) She was stiff and awkward. She left before I could chat with her.

My mind filled with stories.

The thing is: We can't save anyone, and we can't connect with everyone. I forget this.

We can't get everyone to love us, we can't "get through" to everyone, and mostly, one of the truest trues there is, I actually have no fucking clue if she did or did not get anything out of the workshop. Maybe she cracked open a little inside and as she was walking home she turned down a different street and stopped in a bar to have a cocktail and chatted up a guy and went home with him and fucked his brains out, which is wild because she'd never done anything like that in her life. But again, that's a story I made up. I have no idea who she is or was or what she's ever done or might do, but my point is, life is pretty filled up with all of us walking around telling stories about each other and to each other and about ourselves.

I recently found an old journal someone had left at The News-room. I had saved it all this time in a drawer. It's been ten years since I peeked into it. There are all these weird drawings of a woman on a bike and the words "I love you. . . . But I'm shy."

One of the bicycle drawings was a head with no body. So the world without stories would be like a world of bodiless heads. Be-cause most stories—the good ones at least—come from the heart and not the head. They come from the body. Which is why I love Lidia's work so much and specifically our work together, the Writ-ing and The Body workshop.

One pain becomes all pain. A little refrain I keep hearing in my head.

I met with one of my oldest friends the other day in New York. She has a big important job and has a family of her own, but some-times, when we're together, it's like we're ten years old again. It wasn't always that way. For years I felt disconnected from her for various reasons, but lately, we're much more open. She sat in front of me and started to cry over lattes.

There are not many relationships I have like this (almost thirty years). I assume it's a rarity for most people. It's hard to maintain something beyond having a "shared history" once you grow up and start your own lives. And we're all so busy, busy, busy all the time.

What I know most about her is that she is a writer, but she doesn't write much anymore. She is fiercely private and mentioned some-thing about that at breakfast: "You know, I can be really private."

"Realllllly?" I said sarcastically.

She laughed.

"But," she said, "I have all these observations and tell all these stories all the time. But to myself." And she cried again and reached for my hand.

Stories and words need to be sent out into the world. What good do they do if we keep them all to ourselves? That is why I am telling you my story, I hope you'll tell me yours.

Write It Down

Last year, after she'd become an avid fan of The Manifest-Station, the poet Naomi Shihab Nye invited me to come as her guest to a reading she was doing in L.A., followed by a dinner. She said that one of the exercises she gives to the kids she teaches is to write down two things a day they'd have forgotten if they hadn't written them down. (I went into a kind of panic because I never write things down and I feel like years of my life have evaporated. My father? *He existed?* My twenties? *Didn't happen.*) Since then I've been writing down the forget-me-nots, so I'll share some with you. She also said that writing (as well as life) needs more playfulness. In other words: don't be an asshole.

Things to not forget:

If I didn't write down a note about the two bald men, both sitting aisles apart on the airplane, eating red licorice, I wouldn't remember. Imagine: two grown men in the air, wrestling with licorice in their mouths like dogs. I don't think they knew each other. It made me laugh. Red Vines. They were in their sixties and seemed to be flying solo. The seriousness on their faces. The toughness of the licorice and how each went at it like it was a thing to be conquered.

Recently in a workshop when I asked the class to make their "Fuck It List" (my friend Kathleen Cunningham made that phrase up, instead of "Bucket List," when her cancer came back again), this very old woman said, "My face is so red, look at me, I'm shaking, I don't think I can do this."

"Yes, you can," I said.

And with the thickest Jersey accent ever, she said, "If I wasn't afraid, I'd take classes. At Harvard [but she said it like Hah-vad] I would sing every day." And then she couldn't go on, because her mouth was shaking so bad and it was just about one of the most moving experiences of my life. She was so brave and kept saying, "If I was brave . . ." And I thought how "brave" can look like so many different things. Like you reading this. I'm sure you've been brave in your life and I'm sure it looks different from my brave.

Versions of Brave

Brave is: red, blue, whatever the fuck color you say it is, a widower saying, "I want to cope," when I ask him what he wants. It's an old woman showing up to a weird kind of yoga class and speaking out loud even though she is terrified, it's me writing about my life even though I feel totally inadequate. It's my nephew who has special needs and yells, "Stop man!" to passing cars, it's my friend who had another baby after her first baby died last year, it's telling the truth, it's being present, it's writing, it's fighting, it's knowing when to not fight, it's keeping on, it's getting out of bed, it's saying *yes*, it's saying *no*.

Here are a few more things that if I didn't write down I would forget.

A woman at Canyon Ranch came up to me and said she had been so touched by my workshop that she wanted to give me something. She handed me a long pair of sparkly black socks and said, "I only wore them once. Today." And I put them on. Right then and there.

A friend once told me that he thought the most profound lessons in life were unexpected.

It's true, isn't it? I mean, I wasn't expecting to witness a beautiful old lady's lips quiver as she told me she'd sing every day if she wasn't afraid and I surely wasn't expecting to think of Bubbe or Yiddish, but all these things, they're all around us and, my god, do we ever have to pay attention or we miss them.

Auster also said, in *The Book of Memory* (when he was speaking about the writer Francis Ponge), that "there was no division between the work of writing and the work of seeing." Maybe we all just need to make sure we are seeing. *It's very beautiful here and I like it.*

Maybe it's all beautiful. Even when it's not.

I hope you'll write down some stuff you think you might not remember otherwise. And send it out into the world. And that someone will save it in a drawer for a long, long time. Or carry it in their wallet, or heart, or wherever it is we carry things we cherish. I have them stuck all over my bedroom wall, as well as bags of notes from when people on my retreats wrote down what they found while beauty hunting.

WHILE I WAS still waitressing, I went to see Wayne Dyer speak and he asked the question I've tried to live by: "Who would you be if nobody told you who you were?"

Once, there was a woman at my retreat who did not and would not soften. I have had people show up with so much armor on, arms crossed, already having decided that they don't need what I am serving, but by the time they start listening to the other people in the room, they begin to allow themselves to be fall-in-loveable. They allow themselves to be seen. Usually, if someone shows up who is all *nah*, when they start fiercely listening to people sharing their stories, the snot starts flying and they forget they were a *no* and succumb to the *yes* that community can be. We all carry so much.

I am of the belief that it is one of the greatest privileges of our lives, this bearing witness to others, and when we wake up to that, we usually forget that we came in the room with armor on, we are too busy nodding *me too* at the person across from us. We are too consumed with listening that we forget about our own judgments or predeterminations. Usually. Not her.

The retreat was four days long. I had noticed, of course, that she was tough. And of course I was drawn to wanting to please her, feeling that she didn't like me. Do you do this? I once wrote a quote that Emily McDowell turned into one of her greeting cards that said *Instead of getting caught up in who doesn't like you, get caught up in who does. It's much more interesting.*

I was caught up in this woman. The old 1 and the 100 again.

Three days in of the total four days, someone came up to me after lunch and told me that the tough woman was leaving. She was beautiful and wore these big hats so her perfect skin would never see the sun. I couldn't believe it, despite the fact that I sensed her not being into it. You had to be really not paying attention not to sense it. And I was paying attention. Especially to her. Because 1 and the 100. How could she not be moved by the stories of others? Even if she hated yoga, hated me, hated the house, hated all of it, it is (and I know this from experience of working with thousands of people) almost impossible to walk away from someone baring their heart and soul and snot. One stays because it's an honor and it's just so damn beautiful to see (or at the very least out of basic human decency). Even if you don't want to share your own story, even if you simply spend the whole time listening, you will be changed. Of course this means that you must be listening or paying attention or beauty hunting or whatever you want to call it.

I ran out in the circular driveway where she was pulling away. She kept driving, slowly, so I jumped in front of the car, waving madly. She almost ran me over.

"Wait," I yelled as she slowed down. I motioned for her to roll down the window.

"I've got to go," she said.

"Okay," I said, feeling stupid.

"I need *yoga*. This is Feelings 101. I have to go."

"Okay. But you were just going to leave and not even tell me? I would've thought you were just napping or something. Why wouldn't you say anything to me?" I asked her, feeling myself shutting down. Always two options: keep going or shut down. I was getting smaller as she spoke. My shoulders began to hunch toward her Audi.

"I wasn't going to tell you because you just gave that whole speech about the one and the one hundred and I am being the one."

Boom. There it was. It was like I was punched in the nose. The gut. My spinach pie began to come up.

"How did you end up at my retreat?" I asked her.

"I take your yoga classes in L.A. and they are really great, but this is nothing like them. To be fair, you and your mom told me what it would be like but I have to go. I need yoga." And with that, she rolled up her window, put her big sunglasses on, and drove away. She didn't have to put her armor back on because it had stayed on. I, however, felt mine forming around me.

Everyone hates me. (Forget the forty-six people inside the house who were loving it.) *See? I suck. I should just teach yoga. Why am I doing this?* My IA on the inside, armor on the outside, I walked back in the house and announced that our second session of the day would be just yoga.

"We're just going to do yoga, you guys. Don't bring your journals," I said to the group. I was trying to please the one. The one who wasn't even there. The one who wasn't even there was ruling me. My IA was ruling me.

I taught the "just-a" yoga class and it was fine. Headstands or something, who knows. It was fine. I am a good teacher. I can move people's bodies into poses and keep them there, make them sweat. But it's not what I wanted to do. I was shutting down, which I was well aware of, and yet I could not stop. Being self-aware is the worst sometimes. *Oh yeah, I know I do this thing. Now what?* If you're self-aware and you can't or won't do anything about it, then you just hate yourself even more and the IA takes over. I would rather be ignorant of my bullshit. *Oh, this is my bullshit story? I know. I'm going to stick with it. That's my (bullshit) story and I'm sticking to it.*

I was shutting down because some finance lady with good skin and a big hat didn't like what I was doing. She wanted power yoga and so I decided I should stop what I was doing in the world because she was right and who did I think I was anyway? The *one* became *every* one.

Later that night, in the kitchen, as I was chatting with some women at the retreat, I mentioned the woman leaving, even though I had promised myself I would not talk about it or feed it to give it energy. My IA was like, *Girl, you know you wanna gossip.*

So I stood there with my wine and said things like, "I mean, look what I've accomplished being a college dropout, having waited tables at the same place for almost fourteen years, being deaf. I've overcome so much and I guess there is always going to be that person."

I said a lot of other things, but what I remember is one woman wouldn't give me what I was looking for. A pat on the back. I wanted to be told it was going to be okay, that I didn't suck. I wanted someone to appease my IA. The woman just listened.

In that moment, an epiphany struck me and I said, "Excuse me," so I could call Elise Ballard, my friend who wrote a book called *Epiphany*, who is always asking me about my greatest epiphany in life.

"Elise," I said excitedly into the phone. "I had my epiphany."

"What is it, Jenny P?" I heard her slight Texas drawl.

"No one is going to give me a fucking medal," I yelled into the phone as if she were the deaf one. "I have to give myself one." There it was. My whole life I had been waiting for permission, waiting to be discovered, waiting to be acknowledged, chosen, given permission to take up space. All my life I had been waiting for someone to tell me I was enough.

The lady who left my retreat gave me a gift. She gifted me with the revelation that you have to do all the hard work of loving yourself *yourself*. In that moment in the kitchen with those ladies and the wine and the chocolate ganache, I finally realized that no one was ever going to save me. No one was ever going to give me permission to be me. I had to do it.

A few months later, I began to do my "Give Yourself a Fucking Medal" exercise, which is now a signature.

I would tell the story, which by then was just an anecdote and didn't sting anymore. Isn't that the best? I thank the big-hat-good-skin-lady. Think of all the things that you thought would kill you from shame or pain that didn't. The things you wept over that now you can talk about, if not laughing, with some kind of remove. I would ask everyone to give themselves a fucking medal.

"I want you to dork it out," I'd say, because I knew that the sillier they'd allow themselves to be, the freer they'd be and the truer it would be. If we don't do that, so many times the IA will take over and say, *Oh, I couldn't possibly say that. I couldn't ever admit that because it'd be like bragging.*

"Brag," I'd tell them.

"Give yourself a fucking medal for anything and everything. For all the things you wish you were acknowledged for. For all the things you never will be. Maybe you struggle with crippling anxiety and it took everything to get out of bed today. Give yourself a medal for brushing your teeth. If you don't curse, leave the F bomb out. Start the whole thing with your full name, like *I, Jennifer Lynne Pastiloff, give myself a fucking medal for . . .* , and go big. Have fun."

I usually play some fun music like Snow Patrol's "Just Say Yes." At first, the people in the room look serious, like they are doing math or something equally as horrible. Then they begin to lose themselves in the exercise and their IA takes a hike and the room feels joyful.

Sometimes when I ask people to share their medals, I have them sing. Especially if they sing badly. Or I ask them to turn it into an opera or a rap. The room hollers and whistles and laughs and claps and the person standing (they must stand because it's an award ceremony) is laughing and crying at the same time and it just feels like life. My favorite is when someone is crying and they start to laugh. People usually stomp their feet and the person giving themselves a medal feels a rush of *yes* and also really, really good. They usually stand there and look around, and after a moment of feeling awkward, they are able to take in the pure joy. They feel fall-in-loveable.

I realized that no one in real life will give us a medal for most of the things we feel, do, say, achieve, are. Sure, sometimes. But in the real world, it's a bunch of assholes (our own IAs) and we're all too busy thinking of ourselves. If we spend our time waiting for someone to say *Go*, we are never going to go and then we wake up and thirteen and a half years have passed and we're still wearing platforms and stealing muffins and wishing we'd graduated college. No one is coming for us. We have to give ourselves the medal for all of it.

I ask people to do it as often as they can. To do it with their children even.

Right now: What will you give yourself a fucking medal for?

If the woman who left my retreat that time is reading this book, I want to say: *If you come back, I hope you'll stay. I am working on staying, too. It's hard for me to stay in my body. Staying is hard. Not looking away is hard. And if you don't come back, I won't make it mean anything about me. I'll try not to. I might because I'm human.*

And because I am human, I still struggle and I still wonder if there would be a better time for the things I want to do. I remember so vividly how it was absolutely always the wrong time to have a baby, and yet, here I am deep in potty training.

I suppose we are never ready. To have kids or not. To enter a relationship. To lead a retreat. To stop waiting tables. To break a bone. To be sick. To die. Or maybe we are. Maybe we just need to say, *Fuck it. I'm scared and I am doing it anyway.*

When I was losing sleep over my decision to not have a baby, my friend said to me, *If there is any part of you that thinks you might want to have a kid, you should do it.*

I wanted to go back and look through boxes of hair or pictures of my father from the army. I wanted to hold the weird woo-woo necklace made from volcano ash that Steve Bridges's sister gave me after he died as I stood on his *Gone Surfing!* doormat and wept. And I wanted them all to speak to me. I wanted them to tell me, in their gravelly just-woken-up voices, how it is. And for my father, I want his picture to say, *I'll come back.*

What the dead leave behind: everything.

This is true, yes. They can't take shit with them. But here we are with the recipes and wallets and memories and all the things they left behind. And here we are, our bellies pressing into our waistbands, and here we are, our hair turning gray, and here we are hugging our kids or wondering if we should even have them and here we are here we are here we are. We are not dead.

The Art of Knowing and Unknowing

I USED TO get upset because of my bullshit story that said, *I have forgotten everything*. Until I stopped listening to that story.

Deep inside, below the gristle and bones, lies the memory of a memory.

Before I was born, I was a memory.

Sleeping like a lazy cat somewhere in the part of you that has forgotten its own name but remembers the sound.

July 15, 1983, was hot and muggy and humid.

I actually do not remember this at all, but I must assume that somewhere it was this way.

I was in South New Jersey, and my father was dying, and I am quite sure it was hot and muggy and humid because how else could it have been?

Every year I forget until I remember.

There is a sense of urgency in the weight of my footsteps, as if they are trying to get somewhere without me. I hear my voice and realize there is something behind the words, but I am not sure what it is until I hear the date spoken aloud.

Ah! The date my father died. A voice that either belongs to me or doesn't speaks inside my mind.

This is why I love yoga: it unburies the sound of things you have buried in your body.

It's the body that remembers. Always.

It's the mind that cannot be trusted. The mind will tell you it has forgotten.

The body cradles the memory within it and will show it to you in a flash as you buy milk at the store or fold forward in a yoga pose. The body will remind you that today is the day your father died all those years ago.

If the body forgot, there would be no more memories and today might just be another day on the calendar, like any other with its weather and dust and cups of coffee and love and disappointments.

July 15 is the day my father died in the middle of the night before his heart could be pumped back in time. And although I do not mark it down anywhere on any calendar, and although I sometimes do try and forget, my body remembers, and there comes a moment on July 15, no matter what year, when I bow my head and shake my fist at the sky.

Forgive your muscles and your joints for not forgetting, for keeping that imprint alive.

So let your mind be open and go ahead and buy milk at the store, and every once in a while when you feel a pang in your heart or a splurge of *oh my god* in your bones, please understand it is your life, trying to be remembered.

I remembered Free-Advice Guy's words in Dallas and I thought about all that I had mistakenly thought was wrong with me, all the ways my body, including my heart, had failed me. He said, *I am more beautiful than this betrayal of my body.* Because it's not your body that betrays you, this I've learned. Your body guides you if you listen to it, in whatever way you can: with your thoughts, with touch, with your hearing aids. It doesn't matter. Your body is always always talking to you, sending the messages you most need to hear.

Now What?

Once you really start listening, you might ask yourself how we get to the end of our lives, or hell, the end of our day, and feel like we truly lived, that we were fully participating.

I do not know the answer. What I do know is that when I get to the end of my life, I want to know I told the truth, I want to know I did love. In order for that to happen, I have to quiet my Inner Asshole. And in order to quiet my Inner Asshole, I have to buy my fear a cup of coffee and show it how it's done. But in order for that to happen, I absolutely have to ask myself, as you do, *Now what?*

No one has the answer, but we must keep asking it every single day and we must keep listening. The *now whats* might be the tiniest, most terrifying things. Or they might be beautiful and big and full of life. Every moment creates a life, and you create the life you make.

Asking the questions is a good thing and I wish for you, and for me, and for all of us that we never stop asking the questions. *How did I get here? What have I done?* And then look closely, with a magnifying glass. Then ask more questions. Then get a really good microscope and go deeper.

Here it is. Thirty-five years after I said the final words of *I hate you* to my father and then asked my first *What have I done?* Here it is. The answer: At the end of my life when I ask *What have I done?* one final time, I want to answer: *I have done love.*

So, I ask you, now what?

Acknowledgments

MAY I BE a Human Thank-You and not an asshole, although I am sure I will be an asshole and forget to name someone as I used to forget to bring ketchup to a table and only remember in the middle of the night. I will remember in the middle of the night, long after the book has gone to print, and cry your name into the void like I did with that ketchup for Table 31. I love you all. Nothing I have done, namely this book, was done alone. I believe in the power of lifting each other up—I live my life that way—and that principle came back to me tenfold. I was lifted by everyone around me, and because of that, you are holding this book.

My mom is first. I did not dedicate the book to her but I want it in writing for the world to see that I literally couldn't function a day without my mommy. Mom, thank you for running my business, and for helping me be an adult (it's so hard!). Although I don't understand your endless fascination with the Investigation Discovery channel and all things cold case murder, especially to fall asleep to, I still love you. Thank you for being a mother and a father.

Thank you to my superhero agent, Adriann Ranta Zurhellen, who believed in me from across the interwebs and co-created a dream with me. She waited, ever so patiently, while I made every excuse not to write the damn thing, and while I went and had a baby. To my soul sister who I am lucky enough to have as an editor, Maya Ziv, smart as a whip, tough, loving, and the exact person I needed in my life. (I think my father sent her. Is that too *woo-woo*?) To everyone at Dutton—Maddy Newquist, Rebecca Odell, Elina Vaysbeyn, and everyone else on my team—thank you for being the greatest group on the planet and putting up with me. You have no idea what your support did for me. The space it allowed me to go and write and create and do what I needed to. I will always be grateful. I know it's not every professional relationship that feels like a family and I do not take that for granted.

To my wifey, Lidia Yuknavitch, for coming into my life like a meteor and always being with me, no matter how many miles apart we are. You taught me that linear time is not real and that I can be whoever I want to be.

To Angela Giles, for always living the words *I got you* and helping me run The Manifest-Station. I could not survive without you. To Emily Rapp Black, for being my friend, first and foremost, but for also using your genius superpowers to help me with my writing.

To my dear friends, who, without you, I would absolutely still be at The Newsroom (it's closed, but I would be forgetting ketchup for tables somewhere else without my friends who urged me to write, and who believed in me). In no particular order: Karina Wolf, Melissa Shattuck, Christa Parravani, Amanda Kelly, Nana-Ama Danquah, Lori Leibovich, Caroline Leavitt, Elizabeth Crane, Cheryl Strayed, Gina Frangello, Sam Irby, Elizabeth Conway, Suzy Vitello, Megan Stielstra, Michele Filgate, Chris Avila Hubschmann, Janice Anderson, Amy Esacove, Shana Feste, Jen Besser, Loren Cagle, Nami Erskine, Holt McCallany, Laura Donnelly, Alicia Easter, Gayle Brandeis,

Jeremy Sunkett, Rachel Brathen, Elise Ballard, Lara Heinman, Shanna "Boof" Mahin, Charlotte Dekanter Chung, Emily McDowell, Alice Anderson, Liz Arch, Rebecca Soffer, Rene Denfeld, Lizzy Land Quant and Signe. Dee Anne Barker, Marissa Korbel, T. Chick McClure, Kelly Thompson, Sarah Sarandos, Frank Gjata, Valeria Gladunchik, and everyone at Corporeal Writing in Portland and the Kimpton Hotel Monaco in Portland, where I locked myself in a room to write, often. The whole Bumpus clan, Christy Turlington Burns, all my Newsroom coworkers (Hi, Quinn, Jordan, Tremell, Laura).

Also: Stephonik Youth, my soul brother Nathan Connolly (you are the brother I always wished for).

Thank you, Patton Oswalt. Truly.

Thank you, Alecia Beth Moore, otherwise known as P!nk, for being a champion of mine. I love you.

Thank you to my teachers: George Saunders, even though I never actually got to study with you, your teaching and friendship over the years helped me with this book more than you know; Dr. Wayne Dyer, my nephew Blaise, Glennon Doyle, Rachel Cargle, Simone Gordon, all my teachers from NYU, and a special shout-out to Stephen Policoff and Tim Tomlinson, and to Steve Curry, who was my dean, my boss, and an early believer in me. To Donna Masini, who introduced me to poetry. I blame her. Thank you to my dear friend, the poet Naomi Shihab Nye. You inspire me every day to look at the world with more wonder.

To all the humans who have attended my retreats and workshops: you have changed me. To the women who attended through The Aleksander Fund. Thank you for sharing your grief and letting us hold you. To baby Aleksander, who never got a chance to see the world. I love you. Thank you to Ronan, Emily Rapp Black's son, who taught me so much about what it means to love during his short time on earth.

To my hearing aids: thank you. Tiny miracles, you are. Thank you to all the people who helped me get them when I did not have enough money. I can now hear my son laughing. I bow to you.

To Nikki Terry of Orange Custard Studio for being my favorite web-designer/friend/brand manager/straight shooter.

My family: blood and chosen. Annie Sertich, Ana Margoth Guardado, Allan Peach. You have keys. Let yourself in. Put the coffee on.

The Napolis: your name obviously remained the same in the book. You mean the world to me. You are my connection to my dad.

Jack: my Pops. you are my father too. I love you so much. Thank you for being my dad and loving my sister and me (and our boys) the way you do. Well, and our mother.

Rachel, my sister: you are my best friend and every day I am humbled by your strength. That may sound corny but it's true. You are the strongest and smartest person I know. I am in awe. I am sorry we kicked the shit out of each other as kids sometimes. It's funny now, though, in hindsight.

My nephews, thank you for showing me love. I never thought I would have kids and I was just fine being Aunt Jenny! I love you.

My father-in-law and mother-in-law: Ali, your passing came during the writing of this book and you whispered to me "Keep going." It was the sign I needed. Susan, you are the rock of our family. I wish London wasn't so far!

My husband and son, Robert and Charlie Mel. You are building with blocks in the next room and I can barely hear you laughing but I can hear you just enough to know I am safe in the world. I have done love. Every night when I get to go to bed and ask one final *What have I done?*, let my answer be, "I have done love." Because of you, I fly. Because of you, I am. Because of you, this book is a thing in the world.

About the Author

Jennifer Pastiloff travels the world with her unique workshop On Being Human, a hybrid of yoga-related movement, writing, sharing aloud, letting the snot fly, and the occasional dance party. She has been featured on *Good Morning America,* CBS News, in *New York* magazine, *Health* magazine, and other media outlets for her unique style of teaching, which she has taught to thousands of women in sold-out workshops all over the world. Jen is also the guest speaker at Canyon Ranch and Miraval Resorts, and she leads Writing and the Body workshops with author Lidia Yuknavitch, as well as retreats with Emily Rapp Black. Founder of the online magazine *The Manifest-Station*, Jen is based in Los Angeles with her husband and son and a cup of coffee when she is not traveling, but her heart is still in Philadelphia, where she was born.